John Seymour Ellis

**Our Country**

It's History and Early Settlement by Townships

John Seymour Ellis

**Our Country**
*It's History and Early Settlement by Townships*

ISBN/EAN: 9783742809827

Manufactured in Europe, USA, Canada, Australia, Japa

Cover: Foto ©ninafisch / pixelio.de

Manufactured and distributed by brebook publishing software (www.brebook.com)

John Seymour Ellis

**Our Country**

# OUR COUNTY

## Its History and Early Settlement By Townships.

### ENTRY OF PUBLIC LANDS,

PRESENT OWNERS,

Reminiscences of Pioneer Life, Etc.

WITH ORIGINAL POEMS.

By JOHN S. ELLIS.

# NOTE.

I have no apologies to offer for what follows, but offer the following note of Dr. Green as one of my reasons for presenting this book to the public.—THE AUTHOR.

---

MUNCIE, Ind., July 19, 1898.

Dear Friend, Ellis:

I am glad you are writing the early history of Delaware county. We have had two previous attempts to write it. Both have been failures, neither being accurate or truthful.

Having been reared in the county your knowledge is so superior and so far your history has been good. Every teacher should file away the News for future school use as no such facilities for teaching local history and geography have been offered them. I hope you will later find it possible for you to place your history in book form so that it may be the better preserved. Many of the incidents I know personally and many more I have heard from my father who, you will know, was one of the early settlers and pioneer teachers of the county. Truly,

GEORGE R. GREEN.

## When Delaware Lodge Was Born.

The following poem was read before Delaware Lodge F. & A. M., on the occasion of its fifty-third anniversary, March 19, 1896, by the author, J. S. Ellis, a copy of which was ordered printed on white satin, framed, and is kept in the lodge room:

Turn back if you please just fifty-three years,
To the time when our fathers, the old pioneers,
Threshed grain with a flail and plowed with their steers
When the ring of the axe and the thud of the maul
Was heard in the woods from spring until fall,
When the woodman was cheered by the old dinner horn,
That is when Delaware lodge was born.

When the woods were lit up by great burning logs,
And acorns rained down to fatten the hogs,
When log-rollings, raisings and quiltings were rife,
Where many a Jehu courted his wife.
When "folks went to meeting" in a wagon or cart,
And log school houses were miles apart;
When boys went to mill on the old gray mare
And waited for hours for their "grinding" there;
Their saddle a sheep skin and a big sack of corn,
That is when Delaware lodge was born.

When dense forests covered the face of the land,
When roads had no gravel, but settlers had sand,
When teachers boarded 'round with scholars, and when
Preachers "rode circuits" on horseback like men.
When coon skins were traded for sugar and tea,
When a dance was a "frolic" and a drunk was a "spree."
When women wove home-spun their forms to adorn,
That is when Delaware lodge was born.

*In a large frame house—it stands there yet—
A room was prepared, and Delaware met;
No painted emblems bright and fair
Adorned the walls of the lodge room there.
No jets of gas in glittering glare,
Emblazoned the G o'er the Master's chair.
No carpet covered the old oaken floor
When the Tyler first stood at Delaware's door.

What changes have come all over the land!
Where cabins once stood, great mansions now stand;
Where the crack of the ox whip was heard, is where
The locomotive whistle rings out on the air;
And thus, great changes, all over the earth,
Have been brought about since Delaware's birth.

But the same old landmarks, the same old rules,
The same old emblems, Masonic tools.
The same old words, in language sublime,
The same old steps for the craftsmen to climb.
Each brother must travel the same old line,
Give the same old grip and the same old sign;
The same old Bible our alters adorn
That was used when Delaware lodge was born.

But where are the brethren who met in that hall
And took their seats at the gavel's fall?
Gone! gone to the lodge on the other shore,
Where they meet on the level, but part no more.

---

*The building referred to is No. 116 South High street, the former residence of Dr. Samuel P. Anthony, an upper room of which was used as a lodge room when Delaware lodge was organized in March, 1813.

# Perry Township.

Webster defines History as a "Written statement of what is known." Therefore in writing the history of Delaware county we must confine ourselves to facts already known to some one. We have been able to gather information from many different sources, and by compiling them, to interest and benefit our readers without going into detail regarding the first surveys of public lands which was made by the government in 1822 when the congressional townships were laid out, a township being six miles square. These are all numbered, beginning at a base line running east and west through the south part of the state, and as the south part of Delaware county is in section 19 it must be nineteen times six miles or one hundred and fourteen miles north of the base line. However our townships as they are named and generally known, are civil townships, laid out in 1827 when the county was organized.

In the organization of these there seems to have been but little attention paid to the congressional lines, as we find them running into each other in every case. Our congressional townships therefore are not used except in the description of lands. Hence in these articles we will have reference always to the civil, and not the congressional, townships, in speaking of them.

Perry township occupies the southeast corner of Delaware county, being bounded by Liberty township on the north, Randolph county on the east, Henry county on the south, and Monroe township on the west. Its dimensions are five tiers of sections (or five miles) north and south, and six sections (or miles) east and west, thus containing thirty sections or square miles. Counting 640 acres to the section gives us 19,200 acres in round numbers.

The sections are numbered from 1 to 24 and 31 to 36 inclusive.

The surface of the township is undulating, (or what, in this generally level country, might be termed hilly,) However, the hills of Perry can be easily cultivated, and add beauty to the prospect and benefit in the manner of drainage.

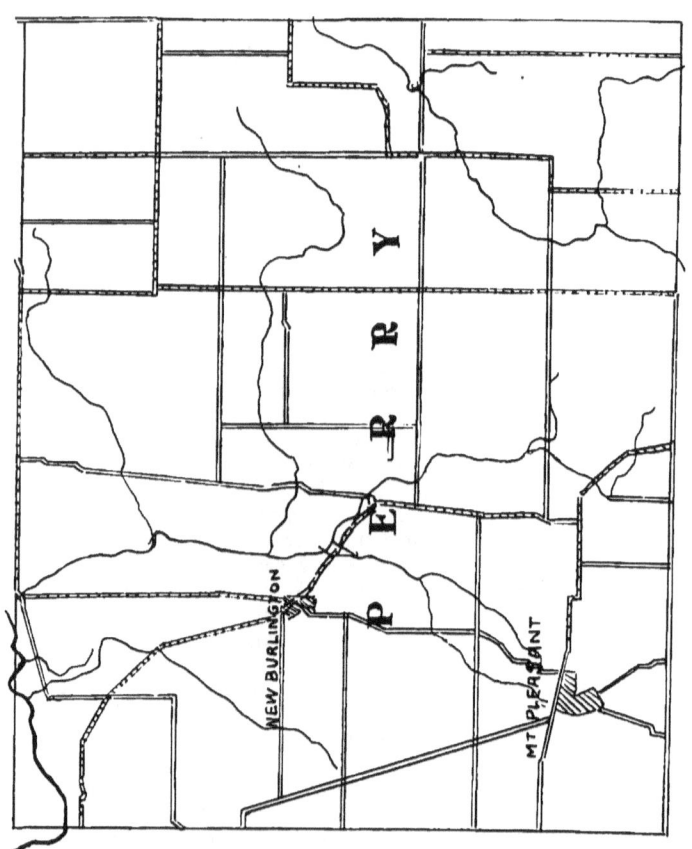

## PERRY TOWNSHIP.

The hilliest portions of the townships are in sections 3, 4, 5, 8, 9, 16, 18, 19 and 20, or in the central and southwestern sections of the township. The soil is a clay loam with an admixture of sand in some portions, and a sub stratum of gravel. Good gravel for making roads is found throughout the township. A large portion of the township was originally covered with a heavy growth of timber, consisting of various oaks, hickory, white and black walnut varieties of ash, beach, etc. A small portion of the territory is prairie, which we find along the small streams, and which the writer believes could be utilized to great profit in growing celery, as the soil seems identical with that in the Kalamazoo celery fields.

The largest water-course in the township is White river, which drains a small portion of the northwest corner.

Touching Section 32 it flows west along or near the township line between Perry and Liberty until reaching Section 31, where it takes a more southerly course through the northwest part of Section 31 and into Monroe township. The next in size is Prairie creek which enters the township in Section 19, flows east of north, draining Sections 19, 17, 8, 9, 4, 33 and 22, and empties into White river near the Liberty township line.

A tributary of Prairie creek, familiarly known as "Shave Tail," has its source in Section 1, and flows almost west to its mouth, near the southwest corner of Section 4, draining Sections 1, 11, 3, 9 and 4. Stony creek flows north through the center of Section 23, northeast across the southeast corner of Section 14, the noathwest corner of Section 13 and southeast corner of 12, into Randolph county. So there is not a tier of sections either running north and south or east and west which is not drained by one or more of these streams. This, in connection with the natural undulating surface of the land, makes drainage very easy, which the land owners have generally made very complete.

In matter of altitude Perry has the highest point in the county, that beng on the northeast quarter of the northwest quarter of Section No. 13, owned by Mr. J. A. Mills. Although there are other points of almost equal elevation in the township, one of them being just south of the village of New Burlington and near the home of Hon. John Linville. This hill has been denominated Bald Hill by some of our surveyors, and from which one can get a fine view of the surrounding country.

The first permanent settlers that we have any account of in Perry township, were Cornelius Van Arsdoll, James Lee, William Blount, David and Aaron Richardson, who came with ox teams, cutting their road most of the way through the forest to their intended future homes, where they arrived in April, 1820. Arriving at this season of the year gave them the advantage of the spring and summer weather in which to clear off ground and erect their cabins. Their food at this early day consisted principally of bread and meat. The bread being often obtained by mashing corn between two stones, placing a large stone on a stump, then using a smaller one as a pestel. The mashed grain was then sifted and prepared for baking. Game being abundant, the pioneer had no trouble in procuring meat, and the question was never heard at the table as to whether you would have roast beef or loin of mutton. But instead it was squirrel, wild turkey, venison or opossum.

The records show that but two of these first pioneers ever entered land in this township, they being Cornelius Van Arsdoll and Aaron Richardson. The former locating land in Section 31, February 16, 1829, and the latter in Section 8 in August of the same year. Why it was that the early settlers were so indifferent about securing their titles we of today can hardly realize; but it is presumable that they depended largely on their pre-emption rights.

Among the first settlers of this township was Goldsmith C. Gilbert, who settled on Prairie creek, in Sections 32 and 33 at an early period, but through neglect or want of means, failed to enter the land which he had improved, and a man by the name of Wilder Potter, stopping with him a few days, and learning that Mr. Gilbert had not secured his title went to Indianapolis and entered it for himself. This was the east half of the northeast quarter of Section 32, and the northwest quarter of Section 33. Thus many men were wronged out of their hard-earned rights.

Hospitality being one of the cardinal virtues of the early settlers, it was no uncommon sight to find from two to five families in one cabin of fifteen to eighteen feet square, the proprietor and his good wife sharing their home with newcomers until they could build their cabins. Not only in dividing their homes did they display hospitality, but in many ways, such as assisting them in getting out house logs, hewing puncheons for floors, raising their houses, rolling logs, etc. Many stories of adventure are told of the trips to the land office at Indianapolis. One which we now recall being of Aaron Cecil starting on horseback to Indianapolis to secure a tract of land in Section 32. It was a long, lonesome trip to make alone through the forest, the road or blazed path being around by old Strawtown on White river, below Anderson, in fact almost following the river all the way. Mr. Cecil started out, not dreaming that another settler wanted to enter the same tract, and taking his time, stopped over night on his way to rest himself and horse. But after he had been

## PERRY TOWNSHIP.

several hours on his journey, a neighbor (every one living within five, or even ten miles, was a neighbor then) heard of his errand, and wanting the same land, started on foot and traveled all night to get in ahead of Cecil. Just as he was going into the land office he met Mr. Cecil coming out, he having secured the title, not knowing how near he came being too late. Whether or not the footman secured other land we never learned, but we hope he did, for his efforts were surely worthy some reward.

Another instance was that of Samuel Simmons, who had improved land in Sections 5 and 32. Neglecting to make his entry it was entered from under him by Daniel Thompson and sold by him to Aaron I. Cecil in 1831, who entered 160 acres in Section 32 at the same time he purchased the Thompson tract. And thus it seems that in the pioneer days, as now, there were sharpers (or in other terms, dishonest rogues) on the lookout to swindle their fellow men out of their honest earnings.

We propose in these articles to give the original entries of lands and also the present owners by sections. Commencing at the northwest corner of the township, we find that section 31 was entered by Cornelius Van Arsdoll, George Ribble, Lewis Reese, Thomas Hacket and Garret Gibson, the first entry being made in November, 1822, and the last in October, 1830. The present owners of this section are W. W. Rees, Lavina Rees, James T. Page, J. Rees, Sr., W. R. Moore, J. M, Lenon and G. Hughes. White river flows in a southwesterly course through the northwestern part of the section. The Muncie and New Burlington free gravel road passes through this section east and west near the center. In this section was born one of the claimants to the honor of being the first white child born in Delaware county, being Isaac Van Arsdoll, son of Cornelius Van Arsdoll. The other claimant of this honor (which neither could have prevented had they so desired) is Rev. Scott Richardson, still living in Blackford county, Indiana, his parents living at the time in section 8. So Perry township certainly has the honor of being the birthplace of the first white child born in the county, as these gentlemen were certainly born, and both of them in Perry township.

The lands in section 32 were entered by Wilder Potter, Daniel Ribble, Daniel Thompson, Aaron Cecil,. John W. Cecil and George Ribble, the first of these entries being dated December 16, 1822, and the last September 1, 1833.

This section (32) is now owned by S. R. Cecil, W. R. Cline, S. E. Cecil, S. G. Cecil, L. Whitney, P. Whitney, S. and E. Jordan and John Rees, Sr. The section has two gravel roads through it.

Section 33 was entered by William Poff, Isaac Jackson, Martin Keesling, Wilder Potter and Jacob Marshall. The entry made by Wilder Potter was the first, December 16 1822, and was the tract of land before mentioned as that on which Goldsmith C. Gilbert had settled and improved. The last entry in this township was made by William Poff, March 12, 1836.

As shown by our latest authority the land in this section in now owned by M. J. Cline, Lewis Keesling, W. R. Cline and W. A. Cunningham. Prairie creek crosses the southwest corner of this section, and the Smithfield and Selma pikes the eastern part.

The first entry of public lands in section 35 was made by Loring Waldo on June 29, 1830, and was eighty acres, being the west half of the northeast quarter of the section. The balance of the section was entered latter on, up to August, 1834, by Michael G. Carver, Albert Robinson, Hilda Adkins and Peter Halstead. This section is now owned by M. Dunkin, A. H. Ratcliff, M. A. Murray, E. C. Clark, W. A. Clark, Lewis Keesling and A. C. Duncan. Good gravel roads extend along both the east and north lines of the section.

Section 35 seems to have been some later in getting into the market than the sections west of it, as the earliest entry of any of its lands were not made until July, 1830, and the last entry July, 1836. This section was entered by Henry Row, Joseph Derr, Ira Main, Thompson Stansbury and Peter Derr; the present owners bing M. C. Moore, M. Helm, G. Helm, W. S. Helm, C. Swingley, T. Brewer, J. Brooks, S. Helm, A. H. Ratcliff, L. E. Chenoweth, M. A. Andars and G. T. Helm. The Blountsville and Smithfield pike runs along the west line, and a gravel road on or near the north line of this section.

Section 36 is in the northeast corner of the township. The first entry of land was by Joel Drake, in August, 1833, and was only forty acres. Mr. Drake entered another forty acre tract joining the first, the following February, 1834. The balance of the section was all taken up in 1836 by Martin Dye, Alexander Nisbet, Henry Dye, James Barr, William Baird and Robert R. Barr.

This section is now owned by T. M. Amburn, J. L. Remel, E. Thompson, E. Sample, J. and D. Sample, E. and J. Brooks, H. Will, M. E. Cline and J. Brooks. It is well drained, laying as it does about middle way between White river on the north and Stony Creek on the southeast, and less than a mile from either of them.

The six sections above described being the north tier, is the only Portion of Perry township in Congressional township twenty, north. The other four tiers of sections being in township nineteen. The entire civil township of Perry, however, is in range eleven, east, the range lines being the township lines at both the east and west boundaries. The east line of Perry, being also the east line of range eleven, makes that point eleven times six miles, or 66 miles east of the base range line.

The first settlers who came to Perry township (the company headed by Mr. Cornelius Van Arsdoll) brought with them two Indians by the name of Jefferson (an Indian boy) and Kilbuck. They were very useful in cutting the road through the woods, which had to be done from somewhere in Wayne county to their destination. Old Beaver and Hunter are two well-remembered half-breeds of the early days, and as one of the old settlers remarked to me the other day, the only ones as he remembered that were considered drunkards in the settlement, although whisky was kept by almost every family and always plentiful at log-rollings and house-raisings.

A story is told of two poachers or thieves who harassed the early settlers until they were compelled to take the law in their own hands. The one was a colored man known as "Old Obediah," who lived on the north side of White river opposite Mr. Van Arsdoll and was noted as a chicken thief. To stop this the settlers chose John Reese judge, and Tom Hacket as constable, and convened a court in Van Arsdoll's log barn. The constable proceeded to arrest the accused, and after a short trial he was clearly proven guilty, but while the court was summing up the evidence the officer in charge of the prisoner purposely stepped to one side, when some sham friend (as the whole proceeding was a sham) suggested to the prisoner that "now is your chance," and away he went, closely followed by his dog and the yells of the pursuers, not hesitating for a moment when he reached the river (which was "high") but plunged in and was not seen in the neighborhood again for five or six years.

The other was a white man, known to the settlers as "Old Tom Hall," who was a noted bee thief, and who was arrested by Officer Hacket, tried by Judge Reese, and sentenced to two days' imprisonment in the "wolf pen." This was a pen built of heavy logs, covered with same, with a trap-door on top. This door was so arranged that the wolves would get into it to get the bate inside and would drop through, but could not get out. This pen was near the river, and also near the line dividing the east and west half of the northeast quarter of section 31, on land now owned by Mrs. Lavina Reese; and here the prisoner was kept the allotted time fixed by the court.

It is said that "Old Tom" afterwards, in sticking his arm into another man's corn crib after night, got his hand into a steel wolf trap, and was found standing there on the next morning, even not coming into breakfast when politely invited by the owner of the corn crib. For this offense he was again arranged before Judge Reese's court, but as he had suffered a broken arm by the accident (?) the court thought the penalty sufficient.

Game was plentiful in these early times and almost everyone was a successful hunter. Almost every settler kept his hunting dogs, besides a watch dog for his home protection.

One of the staple articles, much depended upon as an article of exchange for merchandise, was coon skins, and consequently coon hunting was much indulged in, and a good coon dog was very valuable. The hunter would start out after dark, peeling the bark off of a hickory tree and lighting it for a torch, he would strike boldly into the woods. His dogs, anxious for the sport, would at once get down to business, and soon the baying would announce to the anxious hunter that a trail had been struck. Mr. Coon, hearing the dogs after him, would soon take to a tree, (most generally a very large one) but as timber was of little or no value, the hunter would at once proceed to cut the tree, without any thought as to the owner of the land on which it stood. Then as the tree would fall, some one or more of the company would be delegated to hold the dogs to prevent them from running under the falling tree, until about the time it struck the ground, then letting them loose they would rush onto the coon, which would frequently "put up" a big fight. At other times the coons would evade the dogs an succeed ind reaching and climbing another tree, in fact, the writer has helped cut the third tree for one coon.

The experienced hunter could tell the moment the game was treed by the baying of the dogs, and you would hear the joyful exclamation of "he's treed." He could also tell you if the dog was running any other game than coon. As I have often heard the remark, "that dog's on a rabbit track," and the dog was very apt to get a whipping for so far forgetting his dignity as to trail a rabbit when out for coon. Among the noted coon hunters of Perry township was Garret Gibson, who entered the west half of the southwest quarter of section 31, in 1830, lived in the township many years and has many relatives living here now.

Section No. 1, in Perry township, was settled and the land entered by William King, John Fetters, Bowater Bates, John Connor, William Locke, Thomas Clevenger, William Baird, Norris Flemming and Joseph Whitacre. The first of these entries was made by John Connor October 31, 1822, and the first or earliest entry made in the township. This

HOME AND STORE OF ELI W. WALRADTH, Iasel, (Old Mt. Pleasant). Perry Township.

WM. BARNES,
(Deceased). A pioneer carpenter of Mnncie.

MRS. EVELINE WACHTELL
BARNES,
Of Muncie.

THE WACHTELL BLOCK,
West Washington street, north of Court House.

## PERRY TOWNSHIP.

was the east half of the southeast quarter of the section, and is now owned by L. Lindsey, S. Reese and S. M. Warner. The last entry in the section was made by Joseph Whitacre in March, 1837. The present owners of section 1 are R. Brewer, J. J. Fetters' heirs, H. Fetters, S. M. Warner, A. Reese, L. Lindsey, M. E. Cline, W. Terrel, J. E. Clevenger and T. G. Clevenger.

Section No. 2 was entered by Robert R. Barr, Henry Way, Andrew McAlister, William Dilts, James Barr, John Brooks and Nelson Thayer, in the years of 1832-35-36 and 37, and is now owned by P. A. Helm, H. Kennedy, J. M. Lenon, M. H. McCormick, E. J. Halstead, P. R. Clevenger and J. L. Ullom. The Blountsville and Smithfield free gravel road runs along the west side of this section. The Christian church stands near the southwest corner on section 11, and school No. 1 near the northeast corner on section No. 1.

All the public land in section No. 3 was taken up in six entries, four of which were made in 1830 and the other two in 1836. The parties making these entries were William M. Clark, Lyman Halstead, Peter Halstead, Joseph Walling, Samuel Halstead and David Hoover. The present owners of the lands of this section are W. A. Clark, C. Clark, G. W. Keesling, L. E. Doughty, John Williams, Jr., and W. C. Scott. This section has good roads along the east, south, half of the west, and through the center east and west. School No. 2 is near the west line of the section, in section No. 4.

Section four might be termed one of the early settled sections of the township, as the first entry of land in this section was made in December, 1822, but a short time after Mr. Conner made his entry in section one, and was made by James Bryson. The other settlers entering land in this section were Joseph Walling, David Hoover, William N. Rowe, John Will, Louisa Thayer and William J. Cecil.

This section is now owned by John Williams, Jr., Wm. J. Williams, W. and B. Gilmore, A. R. Holloway, George W. Keesling, and J. B. Cecil; A road runs through the section, north and south, near the center, and Prairie creek crosses the west side.

The earliest land entry in section No. 5 was dated October 9, 1826, and was made by Daniel Thompson. From then until October 25, 1834, all the land in this section was taken up by Aaron Cecil, Benjamin Walker, George Ribble and William J. Cecil. Relatives of some of the first settlers still own and occupy a greater portion of this section.

The present owners are S. G. Cecil, Z. W. Cecil, J. B. Cecil, S. and E. Jordan and John Rees, Jr. The southeast quarter of the section joins the village of New Burlington, from which place a gravel road runs north through the section; also the Muncie and New Burlington free gravel road angles across the section.

Section six was entered in the years 1830 to 1836, inclusive, but the records show no entries in either 1833 nor 1834. These entries were made by Samuel Cecil, Joseph Keesling, James Cecil, John VanArsdol, Daniel Keesling and Henry Mulkins, and now owned by J. Rees, Sr., M. C. Will, S. and E. Jordan, A Keesling, John Rees, Jr., John Will, R. Rees and C. Cunningham. This section we find short of 640 cares, as in fact, are all the sections of the township bordering on Monroe.

Section seven was entered in the years 1834 and 1836, and all but two of these entries were made in the year 1836.

The names of the parties taking this section from the government were James Cecil, David Robinson, John Kirkpatrick, Sr., William Drum, Isaiah Gandy, Samuel Hutchings, Joseph R. Pratt and Keder Homan. This is also a fractional section and now owned by Jane Felton, H. Templin, L. Rees, O. Ladd, John B. Jackson, E. D. Jackson, G. W. Helmick, Jacob Keesling, E. J. Jackson and James Carmichael. A good road passes through the center of the section, east and west; another angles across the western half and another along the greater part of the north line.

The public land in section eight was entered by Aaron Richardson, Benjamin J. Blythe, Solomon Johnson, Calvin Cecil, James Cary, William Cecil, Almron Spencer, William Drum and Ephraim Cary, in the years of 1829, '31, '32 and '36.

The lands are now owned by S. Jump, J. B. Cunningham, T. P. Iron, J. and W. Williams, A. Shockley, E. Cary, R. J. Carey, C. W. Cecil, James Carmichael and W. R. Moore. The village of New Burlington occupies a portion of the northwest quarter of the northeast quarter, and school No. 4 is located on the southwest quarter of the northeast quarter. This section is in a high state of cultivation, with good roads.

Section nine was entered by William Powers, William R. Roe, Eli Hoover, William Baltimore, William J. Cecil and Stephen Bunnell, during the years of 1829, '30, '31 and '35. The eastern portion of the section is high, or hilly, and along Prairie Creek, which drains the western portion of the section, is low, rich prairie land. The land is now owned by A. B. Cunningham, W. and B. Gilmore, F. M. Gates, A. L. Gates, A. G. Gates, L. G. Gates, J. and B. Cunningham, J. H. Shroyer, N. Howell and S. Carmichael. The Muncie and Blountsville pike crosses the section and school No. 9 is on the southeast corner.

## PERRY TOWNSHIP. 15

The government land in section ten was entered by John Buck, Samuel Halstead, William Locke, William Ball, Joseph Fifer, Thomas Edwards, Martin Hoover, Henry Hart and Stephen Bunnell, during the years from 1831 to 1837, and is now owned by I. W. Swingley, C. Swingley, E. H. Valentine, J. Hawk, R. B. Linsey, J. C. F. Thornburg, P. A. Helm, O. F. Bowers, W. L. Linsey and A. J. Blount. This is the only section in the township that can lay claim to a good road on each of its borders and entirely surrounding the section.

Section eleven was entered by Moses Hudson, Benjamin J. Blythe, George Holloway, Charles Miller, Paul Way, John Buck and Henry Way, in the years 1832, '33, '34 and '36. The present owners are E. C. Sutton, H. A. Sutton, G. W. Keesling, T. C. Reese, J. A. Mills, J. C. Turnboldt, W. A. Jordan, L. and R. Gates and O. O. Linsey. The Christian church is located on the southwest corner; gravel road along the south and west lines.

Section twelve borders on Randolph county, and is the center of Perry township, north and south. Its lands were entered by Thomas Clevenger, Norris Fleming, John Thornburg, Jacob Branson, Joseph Whitacre, Solomon H. May, Samuel Rooks, Evan Jay, John Helms, Henry Hill and Ephraim Emmons, and is now owned by John Linsey, L. Linsey, S. M. Warner, S. Hackman, L. Gilmore, T. C. Reese, J. Mills and J. Thornburg. School No. 8 is on the south quarter and a cemetery on the northwest corner.

The earliest entry of land in section 13, Perry township, was made June 4, 1822, and the last on February 1, 1837. The original purchasers were Benjamin Carr, Edward Thornburg, Sr., Isaac Thornburg, Joseph McClurkin, Isaac W. Beeson, Alexander Thornburg and John A. Locke.

The present owners of this section are G. H. Thornburg, E. W. Thornburg, L. Gilmore, A. Gates, J. H. Thornburg, R. B. Lindsey, J. A. Mills and C. E. Trees. The highest point of elevation in the county is in this section, in the west half, and near the center of the section north and south. The section has three gravel roads and the northwest part is crossed by Stony creek.

Section No. 14 was entered by James Warren, David Stephens, James Livingston, Robert Hindman, William Locke, Michael Wolfe, Jackson Brewer and Isiah Templin. These entries, with the exception of the one made by Isiah Templin (1835) were all made in the year 1836.

The present owners of land in this section are M. and A. Yockey, R. B. Lindsey, S. Hindman, C. E Trees, J. C. Thornburg, A. Yockey, M. Cunningham, J. E. Fletcher and D. Fletcher. The section is surrounded by gravel roads with the exception of three-fourths of a mile. Stony creek crosses the southeast corner of this section.

The lands in section 15 were entered by Michael Wolfe, William C. Ball, Henry Way, James Hart, Jesse Pugh, Jonathan Warren, William Locke and Leonard Stump in the years of 1835-36 and 37; and are now owned by I. S. Clevenger, J. Clevenger, I. V. Thornburg, J. E. Fletcher, S. A. Thompson, D. Fletcher, A. G. Gates, A. H. Hiatt, R. P. Shanklin, L. Gates, C. Hart, F. M. Hewitt and William Beall. School No. 6 is located on the southwest quarter and the section has gravel roads on the south and east lines.

As early as 1803 there were petitions presented to our national congress, asking for changes in our system of disposing of public lands, whereby would-be purchasers of small tracts could be accommodated, and where sections were before sold, they could be divided and sold into half sections, half sections in quarters, quarters in eights, result of which was to cause a rapid settling up of government lands, the government, at the time of the settling of Delaware county selling land in quantities of forty acres or more. Another wise provision was the reservation of one thirty-sixth part of all public lands, (or one section in each township) which the government gave in perpetuity for school purposes. Then for convenience, it was determined that section 16 (it being near the center of each township) should be designated and reserved as such school section. For our purpose, suffice it to say that the Indiana State Legislature passed all sections numbered sixteen in this State into the hands of officials whose duty it became to rent, sell, or otherwise dispose of these sections for the benefit of the schools of the respective townships in which they were located. This explanation, we trust, fully accounts for section numbered sixteen never being entered, but sold to settlers by the officials having the proper authority, and the purchase money used for the education of the children of the township.

Therefore, section 16, in Perry township, was sold on August 14, 1830, as follows: East half of northeast quarter, 80 acres, to Samuel Harvey, at $2.50 per acre; west half of northeast quarter, 80 acres, to John Armentrout, at $2.50 per acre; northeast quarter of southeast quarter, 40 acres, to Israel Shoemaker, at $1.25 per acre; southeast quarter of southeast quarter, 40 acres, to Leonard Stump, at $1.25 per acre; west half of southeast quarter, 80 acres, to Leonard Stump, $1.87½ per acre; northwest quarter, 160 acres, to John Reese, at $1.20 per acre; east half of southwest quarter, 80 acres, to Jesse Delaney, at $1.75 per acre; northwest quarter of southwest quarter, 40 acres, to Stephen Bunnel, at $1.25 per acre; southwest quarter of southwest quarter, 40 acres, to William

PERRY TOWNSHIP. 17

H. Underhill, at $1.25 per acre. Thus the entire section sold for the sum of $890. While that may seem a small amount for a section of land in the rich region of Perry to us, yet the amount would go further toward educating the children of the township than many times that amount would now.

The present owners of land in section 16 are E. D. Jackson, A. Hiatt, R. P. Shanklin, L. Hewitt, F. M. Hewitt, J. H. Reese, L. Johnson and Thomas Marshall.

The pike running from Muncie to Blountsville (the old State road) passes through the section near the center, and Scott's run crosses the eastern portion. The eastern portion is convienient to two school houses; No. 6 being near the southeast corner and No. 9 near the northeast corner of the section.

Section No. 17 was settled early in the twenties, and its land taken up in 1823 to 1836. These entries were made by Solomon Sanford, William Underhill, William Bunnel, Hervy Bates and Jesse Jackson.

The present owners of 17 are L. A. Linville, L. Odle, M. J. Felton, L. Johnson, G. M. Reese, J. B Howell, J. Jackson, R. Felton, F. H. Linville, J. Linville, James Carmichael, J. S. Hutchings and James H. Jackson.

The road from New Burlington to Mt. Pleasant passes through the section near its center, being on the half section line from the north line to the center, at which point it angles to the west of south. Another road crosses the section east and west on the half section line.

1834 is the earliest entry of land in section 18, and during that and the two succeeding years all the public land in the section was entered by Martin Galliher, Thomas C. Anthony, Jesse Jackson, Isaac Branson, Elijah Harrold, Morgan Thornburg, Joseph Cheeseman and Jonathan Thornburg.

The present landlords of section 18 are E. D. Pommel, M. Masterson, D. Jackson, F. H. Linville, S. J. Hutchings, James H. Jackson, Lewis Keesling, Jacob Keesling, P. Turner, O. F. Nelson and Mrs. H. Shuttleworth. A road crosses the section east and west on the half section line, and another almost north and south, east of the center.

Section 19 is the southwest section of the township. This section was entered by Mahlon Branson, John Lewis, Samuel Poff, Peter Dragoo, Isaac Branson and Robert Franklin from 1830 to 1836, inclusive, and is now owned by Lewis Keesling, P. H. Chalfant, S. J. Dragoo, M. Taylor and O. C. Dragoo. The village of Mt. Pleasant is located on the line between this section and section 20.

Section 20 was entered in the years of 1833-35-36-37, by

John Armantrout, Isaac N. Delaney, William Honnell, David Fetrick, Elias Burkett, Henry Riggs, William Heaton, Abraham Slover and William P. Mathews, and is now owned by R. Felton, E. Reese, Elijah Felton, M. Shockley, G. Chalfant, J. S. Huffman, W. A. Acker, J. Acker, P. H. Chalfant and P. Oxley.

The first public land in section 21 was entered as early as September, 1829. Others in 1830-31-33-34-35 and 36. The names of the parties availing themselves of homesteads in this section at government prices were Leonard Stump, James Lindley, Thomas Keener, Hosea Sisk, Joseph Cowgill, Hervey Bates, William Lindley, Rachael Dummit, Daniel Kessler and Charles Lindley. The land is now owned by A. M. Ofterdinger, R. Marshall, M. Marshall, S. Parks, E. Bird, E. Marshall, T. Marshall and H. Acker. The Muncie, New Burlington and Blountsville pike (old state road) passes through this section, while other good roads run through and along the borders of the section.

Section 22 was entered by John Elliott, Ebenezer Elliott, Leonard Stump and William Locke, all of whom made their purchases in 1836, from March 7 to December 16. This section has gravel roads on the east and north lines. The land is now owned by W. Lindsey, D. and A. Fletcher, J. S. Jordan, W. A. Jordan, John Daugherty, W. E. Daugherty, C. Howell, G. Paul, C. Daugherty, William Beall and A. J. Cross.

Section No. 23 was entered in the years from 1829 to 1836 by Tarah Templin, John Lenington, Eli Fox, Robert Templeton, John Elliott, Michael Wolfe, Isaac Blount, Calvin Ball and Robert Worrell. One of these first purchasers, Eli Fox, was the possessor of the shortest name we ever remember of having seen or heard, six letters spelling both his first and last name. The owners of land in this section at this time are William A. Jordan, H. Ofterdinger, J. A. Jordan, John Daugherty, M. C. Worl, and S. M. and S. Linville. This section has two gravel roads running north and south, one on the west line, the other eighty rods west of the east line.

Section 24 is the southeast corner section of both the county and the township, and its lands were entered in 1832-35-36 and 37, by Hugh McCune, Lemuel Hamilton, James Lindley, Jr., William C. Swan, Abraham Lenington, John Beckelshymer, Isaac Wrightsman and Samuel Bedwell, and are now owned by J. H. Thornburgh, James Davidson, B. Bird, C. E. Trees and William A. Jordan. This section has one gravel road that passes through the section north and south, eighty-three rods west of the east or the Randolph county line. School house No. 7 is located on the northwest corner. Perry township has nine school districts, and each have substantial brick school houses except No. 1, which has a new frame building. School building No. 1 is in section No. 1, building No. 2 in section No. 4. No. 3 in section 32, No. 4 in section 8, No. 5 in section 20, No. 6 in section 15, No. 7 in section 24, No. 8 in section 12 and No. 9 in section 9.

### THEN AND NOW.

Then, the forest covered old Liberty's lands;
   Then, the red man roamed at will;
Then, the chieftain met his warrior bands
At the place where the modern mansion stands,
   On the sunny slope of the hill.

Then, the hunter came from the rising sun,
   His home on the eastern shore;
With muscles of iron, and trusty gun,
And built his home where the waters run,
   Where the red man romas no more.

Then, his family came his cabin to cheer,
   Then, the latch-string hung at the door,
Which said to the passing pioneer:
"Come in, you are always welcome here;"
   But he's gone, we see him no more.

Now, orchards bloom on every hand,
   Foretelling the coming fruit;
Now, towns and villages dot the land;
Now, people dress in garments grand
   Instead of the buckskin suit.

Now, carpets cover the parlor floor
   Where once the puncheons lay;
A silver bell on the great front door.
Must we stop at this? Is there nothing more?
   Are we wiser and better than they?

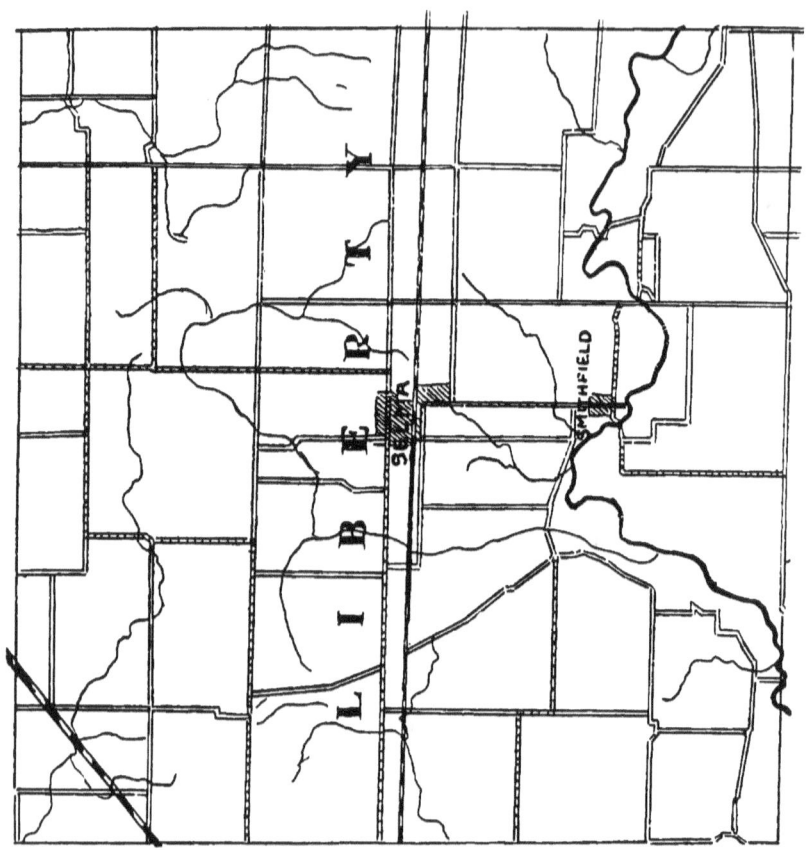

# Liberty Township.

Liberty township lies in the east tier of townships of the county, and is, therefore, in range 11, east. It is six miles or sections square and all in township 20 except the north tier of sections (31 to 36 inclusive) which are in section 21. The township is bounded north by Delaware township, east by a portion of Randolph county, south by Perry and West by Center township. With the exception of the southern portion, in the vicinity of White river, the surface of the land is generally level, although enough rolling for drainage. The different varieties of oak was the prevailing timber in Liberty, although other varieties common to this part of the country were found in many parts of the township.

The first settlements in Liberty township were made, as is usually the case, along the water courses. In this case there were three land entries made in the township in 1822, all three being in sections 21 and 28, in the neighborhood of White River, just below the old town of Smithfield. The first of these entries was made by James Jackson, November 11, 1822, and was the east half of the southeast quarter of section 21, and now owned by Arthur S. Cecil.

The oldest town or village in Liberty, and in fact one of the oldest in the county, is the village of Smithfield. The name was given to a small collection of houses which stood here long before the town was surveyed and laid out into town lots by the original owners of the land (David Stout and William Duncan). Smithfield is one of those quaint hamlets so often seen in this age, which has relapsed from a more honorable condition, by reason of railroads and other thoroughfares, coming just close enough to miss them. Early in the fifties the Bellefontaine and Indianapolis, (now the Big Four) railroad, was built and it passed about a mile north of Smithfield. This sounded the death-knell of the village, and although there was quite a business done here for several years thereafter, the new town of Selma sprang up on the railroad, and business gradually left the old town until now it has become more valuable for cornfields than it is as a town or trading point. We think the first merchant in Liberty township was Jeremiah Fenner. He was located at Smithfield in the general merchandising way at an early date, and after a number of years sold his stock and good will to a Mr. Garrison. Thomas Leonard opened a store here a few years later, then William Lewis in the same store-room. Mr. Lewis afterwards sold goods in the new town of Selma. Probably the oldest cemetery or "graveyard" in the township is one which is located about half a mile west of the site of Mount Tabor Methodist Episcopal church. The deed to this land has been lost or mislaid, and we are unable to give the doner's name. However, as the land was entered by Jacob Payton in 1832, it is fair to presume that he donated the land as was usual in such cases. About the year 1839 a young son of John W. Baughn died and was buried on the home farm in section 36, this being the northeast section of the township. About one year later, 1840, Mr. Baughn donated this piece of land for a public burial place for which purpose it has been used ever since, and Mount Pleasant Methodist Episcopal church was afterwards erected near this cemetery.

Much progress had been made in other directions before even a partial system of education had been adopted in Liberty township. As late as the year 1831 the township was without schools, which was nine years after the first land entry was made, and in that year William J. Moore was sent by his father, John Moore, to Wayne county, Indiana, where his uncle lived, the object of his visit being to attend one of the schools of that county, but upon his arrival he found the school closed from some cause, and on foot he was compelled to trudge home again, wiser by experience, but not more so by education, or as the settlers use to say "Book larnen." How much this circumstance had to do with the first school in Liberty township we can not say, but certain it is that John More founded the first school room after the return of his son from Wayne county. A short time previous to this Mr. Moore had purchased an 80 acre tract of land adjoining his home place of William Downing, on which there was an empty cabin. This was converted into a school house, and a subscription was raised by the settlers who had children to attend school, and Samuel Collier (father of Mrs. A. F. Patterson, of Muncie), was employed to teach the first school in Liberty township, which was a two-month term.

In the winter of 1832 and 1833 a cabin on the land of Asahael Thornburg was converted into a school house and Anderson R. East taught the school during that and the succeeding winter. In 1839 Amos Meeks taught a school in a cabin in the northeast part of the township.

These early schools were supported entirely by subscription, and the first steps toward the establishment of free schools were taken by appropriating the congressional fund of the township for the maintenance of free schools. For a number of years the old buildings were made to do duty under the new regime, until the accumulated funds warranted them in erecting new and better school buildings. These appeared here and there, one by one, until Liberty stands

## LIBERTY TOWNSHIP.  23

well up in the list for good schools, all of which has had a marked effect for good on the morals of the community.

Perhaps the first election ever held in Delaware county was the presidential election of 1824, when the candidates were Adams and Jackson. At this time, Delaware was a part of Randolph county and this election was held at the cabin of William Williams in Liberty township. The total number of votes cast was about twenty.

Liberty was first settled (like most of the country) by squatters and hunters, who never became land owners, but kept moving on west as the country became settled up and game consequently more scarce. These forerunners of civilization deserve and are accorded much praise by a greatful posterity, yet it is a fact much to be regretted that while our early pioneers were carving enduring monuments to their memories from the dense forests, they thought so little of what they were doing, as to leave no records from which a history of their settlement and movements could be made, therefore, the only source of information open to us is the store-house of memory.

The north tier of the sections in Liberty township is in congressional township 21. The balance of the township sections 1 to 30 inclusive being in township 20 and all in range 11 east. Commencing at the northwest corner of the township, we find section 31. This section was entered in 11 different tracts by eight different parties. The first of these entries was the east half of the northwest quarter (80 acres) entered by Lewis Smith November 20, 1832, and now owned by J. H. Satterfield and P. C. Hirons. After this entry by Mr. Smith the government lands of this section were purchased by Jefferson Cox, John Guthrie, Stewart Cecil, Monroe Goff and John Dragoo in 1835, and Jefferson Cox, John Moody, Jesse Holland and Monroe Goff in 1836. The present owners of the land in section 31 are J. H. Satterfield, P. and S. Hirons, Samuel Bell, P. C. Hirons, S. Cecil and C. E. Reed. The section has three and a half miles of public roads, one and one-third of which is free pike. The L. E. & W. railroad crosses the section from the southwest to northeast and Muncie branch of Prarie creek drains the section. Lying east of 31 is section 32. There were no entries of public land in this section until May 30, 1836, when Thos. Points entered 40 acres in the southwest quarter, after which time all the remainder of public land in the section was purchased by the June following, by Joseph Newman, John Newcom, George Moody, Thomas H. Weirman, John Moody, Jesse Holland and Samuel Moody.

At present (1899) the land owners in section 32 are L. & W. Goontz, L. A. Goontz, E. M. Thornburg, J. Jenkinson,

P. C. Lillie, P. C. Hirons, M. M. Moody and A. Miller. The L. E. & W. railroad crosses the northwest corner of the section, about a mile southwest of DeSoto station.

The section has three and a half miles of public road, one mile of which (that on the south line) is free pike. School No 3 is located in the southwest corner of this section.

East of section 32 is section 33. John Sparr entered the northeast quarter of this section (160 acres) on December 22, 1835. William W. Orr, of Muncie, now owns this tract. In 1836 the entire remaining lands of the section were purchased of the government by Thos Zarner, Joseph Newman and Thomas Bloom.

The present land owners in section 33 are William W. Orr, F. H. Pittenger, F. Hitchcock, E. Evans, L. A. Goontz, S. S. Williams and N. Wood.

Section 34 was entered in the years 1835, '36 and 37, as follows: By James Orr, Adam Boots and William Henry Williams in 1835; Ila Lake and Wm. H. Williams in 1836; Robert Lake and Pendroy in 1837. At present the land owners in section 34 are J. and C. Orr, J. H. Orr, Wm. W. Orr, G. T. Orr, N. Truitt, J. S Hopping, P. E. Mott and L. Mott. School No. 2 is located near the west center of this section, just across in section 33. The section has three miles of public road, two and a half miles of which are free gravel pike.

Section 35 lies just east of section 34. Its lands were entered in 1835 by John Dinsmore (southwest quarter), and in 1836 by Daniel Fox, William Woods and Samuel Lewellen. At present the section is divided up into small farms and are owned by S. R. Strong, A. Shroyer, P. and A. Pittenger, L. S. Sparks, J. A. Shroyer, M. J. Murray, I. K. Ketterman, M. R. Sparks, J. E. Campbell and W. Orr's heirs.

Section 36 lies in the northeast corner of Liberty township. It was entered in 1836 and 1837, in small tracts, there being twelve entries made by eleven parties, as follows: In 1836 by Samuel S. Swain, David Fox, Samuel Malcolm, Solomon Rohrbaugh, John W. Baughn, Elijah Reeves, Samuel Lewellen and John Hines, and in 1837 by James Sparr and Thomas Gough.

Section 36 is now owned by J. W. Meeks, A. F. Meeks, J. and T. Mills, S. A. Tharp, W. W. Current, S. R. Strong, S. A. Leavell, M. Leavell, P. and S. Pogue, J. H. Baughn, A. B. Hoover, J. A. Shroyer and M. S. Tharp. The section has some four miles of public road, about one-half of which is free gravel pike.

Section 1 is the east section of the north tier of sections in Township 20. On February 19, 1833, Benjamin Irwin Blythe entered the fractional northwest quarter of this sec-

## LIBERTY TOWNSHIP.

tion. Subsequently, by act of Congress of June 23, 1836, the balence of the public land in section 1, together with all of section 2 (also fractional) was reserved for school purposes. Section 1 is now owned and generally occupied by Oliver Jones, S. C. Bartlett, S. Ketterman, A. Ketterman, D. A. Stephens, M. S. Tharp, Joseph Meeks and A. B. Hoover. This section has nearly three miles of public road, and is very thoroughly drained by the headwaters of Campbell's creek.

Section 2, lying west of section 1, is owned at present by N. Ketterman, I. K. Ketterman, W. C. Swander, W. and H. Swander, A. C. Dragoo, W. H. Hitchcock, D. A. Stephens and William H. Murray. The section has three miles of road, one of which is free pike. School No. 1 is located near the northeast corner of the section, in the corner of section 35.

Section 3 was somewhat late in getting into market, as its lands were all entered in the years of 1836 and 1837—during the first of these years by James H. Neal, who made three entries, and in 1837 by Moses E. McConnell, Meeker Shroyer and John Givan. The present land owners of section 3 are J. H. Hopping, N. Truitt, D. R. Hopping, J. and M. Shroyer, J. C. Huffman, M. F. Mason, N. J. Shroyer, J. Searls, S. and E. Whitney and J. Hitchcock. This section has two and-a-half miles of public road, the Albany and Selma free gravel pike passing north and south through the center.

Section 4 was first entered by John Morrison on July 24, 1834, after which time there were no further entries until 1836, when purchases were made by James H. Neal, James Huffman, George Barton, Jonas Huffman and Samuel M. Kinsley. In 1837 the entries of the section were completed by John Morrison and John Givan. Section 4 is now owned by T. B. Small, F. Hitchcock, J. Searles, G. W. Sayers and W. H. Phillips. This section has 2¼ miles of public road, 1¼ of which is free pike, and school No. 10 is located in the southwest quarter.

Section 5, like section 4, was first entered in 1834. However, the pioneer of section 5 was William Bromfield, who entered a 40-acre tract at that time (October 22, 1834). The other parties purchasing in this section were Joseph Howrey, in 1835, and George W. Miller, William Broadrick, William L. Gough and Willis Ball, in 1836. This section is now owned by G. and L. Miller, A. Miller, John Shafer, W. H. Phillips and E. M. Gough The section has free gravel pike on both its north and south lines, with a public road on a portion of the west line.

Section 6 joins Center township. Its lands were entered

in 1834, by Reuben Preston, and in 1836, by Reuben Preston, John Kinsley, Washington Heck and Dr. Samuel P. Anthony. The present owners of section 6 are P. M. Carpenter, A. Harmon, S. Holt, A. H., Gough, C. C. Hirons, M. E. Bell and John A. Jones.

Section 7, Liberty township, lies three miles east of the north part of the city of Muncie and adjoining Center township. The first of its congress lands ever purchased of the government was by Charles points on June 18, 1833, and was the east half of the southeast quarter, 80 acres, and now owned by the heirs of Milton Truitt and J. R. Sprankle. During the year 1835 entries were made by Joseph Rash and Willis Hance. In 1836 the remainder of the public lands in this section were taken up by Henry Phillips, John Richey and Washington Heck.

We find the land owners at this time to be A. Gough, L. F. Miller, C. C. Hirons, Milton Truitt's heirs, J. and O. Jones, J. R. Sprankle and J. S. Wood. This section has the Centennial pike on the north, and the Selma pike on the south line.

As early as May 27, 1831, there were two entries of government land in section 8, the one was the northeast quarter 160 acres by Eli Babb, and the other was the east half of the northwest quarter 80 acres by John Robinson. In 1833 one entry only was made and that by John Barton. In 1834 but one entry by John Richey. In 1835 one entry by Ranzel Barton, and in 1836 two, one by Thomas Sweetman, and the other by Peter Clark. The land lords of section 8 at the present time are M. and W. Hufford, W. H. Phillip's, E. T. Babb's heirs, E. M. Gough, L. F. Miller, Delaware county (for infirmary) and Milton Truitt's heirs. This section has four miles of public roads, two miles of which is free gravel pike. The north half of the section is drained by Hog creek, a tributary to White river.

Section 9 had but one land owner prior to 1836. This was William Barnes who entered the east half of the southwest quarter (80 acres) on January 3d, 1834. This tract is owned at present partly by J. F. Jackson and partly by W. H. Burtt. In 1836 entries were made by Aaron Stout, John Neal, Gilbert Winsett, Ranzel Barton and Charles Melone and the last public land in the section was purchased by William M. Clark on December 6, 1838. Section 9 is owned in small farms generally by R. S. Arbogast, L. P. Arbogast, J. H. Hitchcock, G. W. Sayres, J. M. Putney, C. Sholtz, S. E. Dotson, J. E. Neal, Jr., J. F. Jackson, and W. H. Burt. The section has five miles of public road, that on the south line being the Muncie and Selma free pike. The southeast corner of this section joins the town of Selma.

## LIBERTY TOWNSHIP.

The east half of section 10, 320 acres was also reserved for the use of sahools by an act of congress passed June 23, 1835. The west half was sold to Isaac Barnes, John Neal and Daniel Lutz in 1837 and the last 80 tract to John McConnell April 6, 1837.

Section 10 is now owned by J. W. Bortsfield, C. Sholtz, T. Barnes, J. McCall, S. E. Dotson and the town of Selma, a portion of which occupies a small portion in the southwest corner of the section. The section has nearly five miles of road, the Albany and Selma pike crossing the center north and south.

All of section 11 was entered in the year 1836 by four persons and all entered in the month of August. Isaac Dunn entered the southeast quarter and the northwest quarter, and John A. Gilbert the southwest quarter August 13. Thomas Wallace entered the west half of the northeast quarter August 17, and John VanBuskirk the east half of the same quarter August 20. Eleven is now owned by A. C. Dragoo, J. Shrack, A. B. Hoover, W. H. Murray, J. A. Fowler, M. J. Gunkle, A. A. Yates, J. Pittenger, T. J. Simmons and N. Jones, Jr.

Section 11 is surrounded by public roads, having one on each section line.

All the public land in section 12, Liberty township was purchased of the government on the same day, August 19, 1836. Joseph Brandon purchased the northeast quarter, 160 acres, Jacob M. Johnson, the southeast quarter, 160 acres, and Peter Clyne the west half, 320 acres.

This section joins Randolph county and its present owners are R. Meeks, J. Meeks, J. Simmons, N. Jones' heirs, C. Jones, W. H. Pierce, L. J. Reed and S. F. Shrack. The section has public roads on the north, south and west lines.

Section 13 lies south of section 12, and also adjoins Randolph county. The lands of this section were also all taken up in 1836. Levi Bowersby entered the northwest quarter on June 13; George Dickey the southwest quarter August 26, and the southeast quarter the same day; John VanBuskirk entered the east half of the northeast quarter August 20, and Lewis Kendall the west half of the same quarter August 26.

The section is now owned by N. Jones' heirs, and C. Jones, H. Yates, J. W. Goings, S. Jones, J. M. Patterson, H. B. Murray, I. E. Crampton, G. M. Dunkin, M. J. Patty, and J. M. Davis. The section has public roads on the north and west; also east and west, through the center. The Big Four railroad crosses the northern part of the section in an east and west direction.

Section 14 was purchased of the government in 1836 and

1837. During the first mentioned year the purchasers were: Eleazer Coffeen, Benjamin Plantz and Daniel Ellenberger. In 1837 purchases were made by Lewis Shroyer and John McConnell. The section is now divided up into small parcels and owned by R. L. Vaught, B. Stonebreaker, N. Winget, M. J. Gunkle, G. and G. Goings, W. Moore, E. Simmons, L. R. Black, J. Winget, L. A. Winget, W. Dunkin, Jr, B. F. Dunkin and J. Dotson's heirs. The section has public roads on the north, east and west; also through the center, with the Big Four railroad running through the northern part.

School No. 6 is located on the east side of the section, near the half section line.

Section 15 was entered in small tracts, there being eleven entries in all, and all, with one exception, were made in 1836. The entries during this year were made by Henry Ellenberger, Daniel Ellenberger (2), David Mays, Aaron Marshall, George Dickey, Chester Searles, William Weir (2) and Gilbert Winset. The entry in 1837 was made by William McConnell. Section 15 is now owned by William Hanna, J. and N. Hutchings, A. E. Hoover, J. Greenwalt, E. J. Price, N. E. Black, D. C. Sweeny, J. Dotson's heirs, William Lewis, and the greater part of the town of Selma, which town lies principally in this section. The section has five miles of public roads besides the streets of the village.

Section 16, as in all other townships, is the school section, and as such was sold to the highest bidders on May 12, 1832, and brought the minimum price, $1.25 per acre, making the total receipts for the section $800.

The parties purchasing this section were: Jacob Earhart, 80 acres; William Barnes, 40 acres; Samuel G. Campbell, 160 acres; William Stansbury, 40 acres; William Poland, 40 acres; Frederick Goings, 40 acres; James F. Davis, 80 acres; A. R. East, 160 acres.

The present owners of this school section are: R. Dunkle, S. J. Williams, J. Goings, M. W. Campbell, J. Jackson, C. Carmichael, J. W. Goings, W. Bortsfield, and N. Black, E. G. Campbell and D. C. East. The section has some four miles of public road, and one mile of the Big Four railroad in the northern part.

Section 17 was entered as early as 1833 and as late as 1837. The entries in 1833 were made by Joseph Humphreys, William Payton, Jr., and Jacob Payton, in 1835; by Frederick Goings, in 1836; by George Dickey, John Morgan, Lewis Kendall and Alexander Addis, and in 1837 by John Norris. We now find this section owned by W. H. Campbell, J. W. Goings, W. H. Burtt, L. Skiff et al., C. Hed-

HOME OF J. C. HUFFMAN,
Two miles north of Selma.

RESIDENCE OF J. F. MASON,
Stock dealer, two miles north of Selma, Albany pike.

rick, M. Cowley, D. C. East, M Whitney, H. Whitney, H. Graham and J. C. Watt.

The section has three miles of public road, that on the north line being free pike. School No. 4 is located in the northwest corner of the section.

The first entry of land in section 18 was made on the 24th of August, 1829, by Elijah Casteel. Then followed the entries of Washington Downing, in 1830; David Hamer and Joseph Mulkins, in 1832; James Tilden, in 1834, and John Guthrie, in 1835. The present land owners in section 18 are: J. S. Graham, S. A. Graham, P. Graham, C. and V. Bullock, A. Guthrie, Catherine Meeker, J. C. Watt, Charles W. Cecil, J. M. Graham and William Ribble.

The section has a free pike on the north, and also one on the south line, and a public road on the east line. The Big Four railroad runs east and west through the northern part.

Section 19, Liberty township, lying east of, and adjoining Center township was entered in the years 1831-'32 and '33. John Moore was the first pioneer land owner of this section, he entering the northwest quarter (fractional) 147 5-100 ares, and the west half of the northeast quaater 80 acres on February 2, 1831. In 1832 entries were made in the east half of the section by Reuben Preston and William Payton. In 1833 the southwest quarter was entered by Jacob Payton, Jr., and Joseph Dungan.

The present land owners in section 19 are J. C. Watt, Charles W. Cecil, C. Guthrie, P. Guthrie, Z. T. Williams, J. R. Koons, G. Fulhart, D. Rees; Jr., D, H. Simmons and J. L. Simmons.

The section has three miles of public road 1¼ miles of which is the Muncie and Smithfield free gravel pike. The Mt. Tabor cemetery is on the south line of this section near the southeast corner.

Section 20 was entered in the years of 1831 to 1839, as follows: In 1831 by James Truitt, Reuben Preston, Thomas Whitney and Lewis Smith. In 1832 by Thomas Hamilton, Asaiel Thornburg and William N. Smith. In 1833 by Thomas Hamilton, 1836 by Parker Truitt and John Smith, and in 1839 by David Rench.

The present owners of these lands are Jane Lenon, Walter A. Cecil, M. Whitney, J. Babb, E. C. Gough, Jesse Truitt, O. S. Lenon, J. C. Hoover and J. Snider. This section has three miles of road, also 1¼ of which is free pike.

James Jackson entered the east half of the southeast quarter of section 21 on the 11th day of November, 1822. This was among the earliest purchases in the county, and the second entry ever made in what is now Liberty township.

This tract is now owned partly by Jane Lenon and partly by Walter A. Cecil.

After the advent of Mr Jackson in this section, entries were made in 1825 by David Stout, in 1827 another by James Jackson, in 1828, another by David Stout in 1829 and 1830 by Parker Truitt, also in 1830 by Andrew Collins. In 1833 by John Stout and in 1835 the last of the section was entered by James Truitt.

Section 21 is now owned by A. S. Cecil, M. M. Hopping, Jane Lenon and Jesse Trnitt. The section has about three miles of public road, and is well drained by the White river passing through the east, central and southern parts.

Section 22 is the section in which is located the old town of Smithfield. This section was settled early. The first entry was made by David Branson and Morgan Thornburg in 1923. In 1824 entries were made by David Branson and Thomas Cox. In 1829 by William Wire and James Jackson. In 1936 entries were made by John Richardson and Abraham Bush. Section 22 is now owned by J. Dotson's heirs, J. S. Dunkle, J. and N. Hutchings, William Lewis, W. Bortsfield, H. Hutchings, J. L. Hutchings, W. Dunkle, F. N Cannady and the town plat of Smithfield. White river crosses the southeast and southwest corners of the section, which is also well supplied with public roads.

The first entry of public land in section 23 was made by John G. Decas, January 9, 1824. After this other entries were made in 1827 by Asa M. Thornburg, in 1829 by John and Solomon Stout, and Levi Bawlsby, in 1832, by John Rush Deeds, in 1836 by Eleazer Coffeen, Christian Life, John Richardson and Loring A. Waldo, and in 1837 by Landrine Rash and Thomas Rash. The section is now owned by L. D. Wright, W. Dunkle, Jr., W. Bush, J. S. Dunkle, H. Spangler, E. Ceeil, A. D. Spangler, O. Sherwood, and M. Lesh. White river passes through the section in nearly a west course generally, although meandering around considerably and somewhat crooked. School No. 7 is located near the southeast corner of this section.

Section 24 was settled in 1823 to 1837. The land was purchased in 1823 by George Blalock; in 1829 by John Connor; in 1830 by Michael Mayer; in 1835 by James Barr and Tnomas Wallace; in 1836 by Joseph Lewis and Samuel Cray, and in 1837 by Lewis Shroyer. This section joins Randolph county and is owned by Joseph Meeks, J. C. Naylor, J. Cline, T. Naylor, W. H. Naylor, W. Stephens, C. E. Sutton, J. G. Cecil, et al., and D. Brooks, et al. The section has but 1½ miles of public road. This section is well watered by White river in the southern and Phillips creek in the northern part.

## LIBERTY TOWNSHIP.

Some six years before any other purchase of public land was made in section 24, John Fowler entered an 80 acre tract in the northeast part of the section, this was on April 4, 1825. After which time entries were made by Michael Pepper, in 1831; John B. Bailes in 1832; John Conner in 1833; John Gardner in 1834, and Henry Clyne, Isaac Cline and John Pennington in 1836. This is the southeast corner section of Liberty township, and its lands are owned by S. E. McAlister, J. Clyne, J. G. Cecil, D. Brooks, et al., J. W. Odle, M. and J. Grable, S. Kegrice, J. O. Gable and J. Will.

The section has nearly four miles of public road, most of which is free gravel pike. The first entry of the public domain in section 26 was made by Levi Bawlsby in 1829. Then followed the entries of Peter Cylne and Lowring A. Waldo in 1831, Peter Clyne, Uriah Bulla and Jacob Thornburg in 1833, John Gardner in 1834, and Samuel Williams and Isaac Clyne in 1839.

The section is now owned by J. Fredline, J. O. Gable, John J. Cline, H. E. Patterson, M. C. Cline, et al., S. Greenwalt, C. and M. Carmichael and George Parrott.

The public land in section 27 was entered by Peter Halstead and Lowring A Waldo in 1830; David Stout in 1831, Norse Main in 1832; William Williams, Sr., George Turner, Jr., Jonas Hammer, Francis Collins and Joseph Shields in 1836.

Twenty-seven is now owned by P. C. Spangler, A. D. Spangler, H. Parrott, F. N. Cannady, M. A. Eckberg, J. C. Williams, Z. T. Dunkin, J. T. Stiffler, M. Dunkin, G. F. Dunkin, A. C. Dunkin and L. L. Denny. The section has 3½ miles of public road, and White river passes through the north part of the section for a distance of half a mile.

One of the first entries of land ever made within the present bounds of Liberty township and among the first in the county, was that of the west half of the northwest quarter of section 28, 80 acres entered by William Blunt. Sr., December 9, 1822. The other lands of this section were entered by Wilder Potter in 1822 (but seven days later); William Barnes in 1826; William Pallen in 1831. William Barnes in 1832; Samuel Cecil in 1835; James H. Cecil and William Barnes in 1836, and Henry Bates and William I. Poff in 1837.

The present land owners in section 28 are Arthur A. Cecil, Z. T. Dunkin, A. R. Lenon, O. S. Lenon, L. L. Denny, G. A. Ribble, I. B. Cline and M. Marley. White river crosses the northwest, and school No. 10 is located in the sontheast corner of this section.

In section 29 Wilder Potter was the first landlord entering the east half of the southeast quarter, December 16, 1822.

Then William Stansbury, John Smith and Asael Thornburg in 1830 John Richey in 1831; Thomas Wilcoxon, Isaac DeWitt, John Smith and John W. Cecil in 1832. At present 29 is owned by O. S Lenon, C. W. Collins, Walter A. Cecil, B. Frank Smith's heirs and W. Ribble, et al. White river angles across the the southeast corner of this section, affording good natural drainage.

Alson Ashley and Henry Bolton jointly entered the east half of the southeast quarter of section 30 on May 30, 1823. After this entries were made in this section as follows: In 1828 by Samuel Simmons; in 1830 by Thomas Crawford and Henry Bolton; in 1831 by Samuel Simmons; in 1832 by Jacob Payton, Samuel Hutchings and Henry Bolton, and in 1834 by Samuel Cecil. The present owners of section 30 are: Walter A. Cecil, D. Rees, L. W. Rees, B. Frank, Smith's heirs, E. and M. Rees, H. Shroyer, S. J. Guthrie, C. Fullhart, R. Lenon and J. M. Lenon. School No. 9 is located near the northeast corner, and the famous Inlow Springs are in the northwest corner of the southwest quarter of this section.

---

### "OLD PIONEERS."

Sometimes as I sit in a thoughtful mood,
And view the spot where the old elm stood
At the side of the road, near the end of the lane,
My thoughts run back in childish strain;
And I see myself 'mid griefs and joys,
At play with neighboring barefoot boys.
But all things seem to have changed with the years,
Save the tie that binds the "Old Pioneers."

Are these the boys we played with then?
These thoughtful, sober, gray-haired men?
And are these the girls of olden days
Who joined us in our milder plays?
Yes, these are some who are left from then,
These womanly women, and manly men;
But many have gone with the passing years
And broken the circle of " Old Pioneers."

The cabin looms up in the distance yet,
Where father, and mother, and children met,
Surrounding the fire on the earthen hearth,
The dearest spot on all the earth.
Where, after the evening prayer was said,
And the little ones tucked in the trundle-bed;
God's blessing came down in them olden years,
And brought sweet sleep to the " Old Pioneers,"

I see that mother as she sits at her loom,
And the father as he shapes the hickory broom,
Thus the work went on of a winter night,
The cabin lit up by the log-fire light,
Or the tallow-dip, or great pine knot,
For the hearts were light in the toiler's cot;
And they wanted no dazzling chandelier
In the humble home of the "Old Pioneer."

We may talk of improvements that time has made,
Through great inventions, through science and trade,
Of the wonderful changes we witness since then,
Of conquest by sword, and productions of pen,
Yet it comes to me as a crowning thought,
That the greatest of all great works e'er wrought
Since the days of Adam, through all the years,
Is the characters built by our "Old Pioneers."

The girls who lived in the cabin then
Became the mothers of the kings of men;
They instilled in their sons that spirit bold
That we read in our starry banner's fold
As it kisses the breeze, and is held on high
By patriot hands that never die;
Though stained with blood, and drenched with tears,
Thou art ever the pride of the "Old Pioneers."

## Delaware Township.

All of Delaware township lies in township twenty-one and range 11 east. It is five miles north and south, and six miles east and west, containing thirty sections, numbered from one to thirty inclusive. It is bounded on the north by Niles township, east by Randolph county, while its southern boundary is the north line of Liberty, and its west line the east line of Hamilton township.

The greater part of the township is rolling, with the exception of the southeast portion which is quite level in its general aspect, although the entire township is easily drained, there being a number of streams with a sufficient fall for drainage, while in some places, excellent mill sites are obtainable. The principal water course of the township is the Mississinewa river, which enters the township in section twelve, near the northeast corner, runs almost west then southwest, northwest and north, draining sections 12, 2, 3, 9,

10, 16, 17, 8, 7, 6 and 5, passing out of Delaware into Niles township,, one and one-half miles east of the northwest corner of Delaware township.

While the Mississinewa drains the northern part of the township, much of the eastern portion is drained by Mud creek, and the southern and southwestern portion by Campbell's creek and its tributaries. Formerly Delaware was very heavily timbered with the varieties of oaks, hickory, ash, walnut, etc., while much poplar was found in places. In evidence of this statement we might state that Black's mill, built in 1845, is all weather-boarded with poplar siding, and still in a pretty good state of preservation. The land in Delaware is a mixture of clay, gravel and loam, very productive of all the field crops usually grown in this latitude, and we frequently find very productive soil on the tops of the highest hills, it being what is known as a black gravel soil. Besides being heavily timbered, Delaware township abounded in small hills filled with rich deposits of gravel and sand, which has been of untold benefit to the people of the township for building purposes and road making, which fact has been fully realized, as it is seldom we find any mud-road in the township. Good buildings prevail generally, and the inhabitants themselves seem to have plenty of "sand."

Before the lands of this township were placed in the market, and prior to the time when the white men began to settle upon them, a white man by the name of John Boyles, (but more familiarly known to the first settlers as "Jack," or "Jacky Boyles,") took up his residence among the Indians, (by whom the land was held) about eight miles northeast of Muncie, at a point on the Mississinewa river is where his cabin (and afterwards his mill) were located. As to the time of his settling it seems impossible to obtain data, but this much we learn, his wife has been heard to say, that she entertained the original surveyors, when they were employed locating the county and township lines, which work was done in 1822. As to how long they had lived here prior to that date we have no means of knowing. Mr. and Mrs. Boyles had both been married prior to their union with each other, he having three daughters and two sons, and she three sons by a previous marriage. Her former husband was a man by the name of Dunn, but any history previous to the facts here stated seem to be entirely in oblivion. His object in settling among these wild people is hard to guess, as from all accounts, he did not belong to that class known as "Indian traders." Living among these people, he contracted many of their habits and fell naturally into their mode of living. Mr. Andrew Black, who remembered him well, says he never knew the water too cold to cause Mr. Boyles to even hesitate when wishing to cross the river, but that he would wade through without seeming to notice it.

It is said by a recent writer that he carried many scars on his person, which he said had been received in fights with the Indians. Mr. Boyles erected a mill here on the Mississinewa river. The mill was built out in the stream, near the west end of the mill-dam, was very crude in its construction, and of none of the "five best known orders of architecture." So perhaps the only special claim it has to notoriety is its being the first of its kind in the country.

An anecdote told by some of the first settlers is that on one occasion a settler went to the mill to get some corn ground, but seeing no one around, at last heard a dog barking somewhere below, and finding his way beneath the building discovered one of Mr. Boyles' hounds, his mouth at the meal spout, eating the meal as fast as the mill ground it, and barking up the spout for more. However, as slow as it was, there is no doubt that it was faster and more convenient than grating the corn on a grater, or pounding it between two stones, as many were compelled to do. This mill stood on the west side of the river, about seventy-five rods above where the Albany pike bridge now crosses the Mississinewa and nearly opposite the present "Black's Mills." The land on which Mr. Boyles settled was the east half of the northeast quarter of section 7, and which was formally entered by him on July 25, 1832. The river runs nearly north through almost the entire length of this 80-acre tract This land was subsequently purchased by John Black, on which he erected the present mill in 1845, and which has become as well known as any institution in the county. A few rods east of this mill is the section line of section 8. Mr. Black desiring to obtain a site for his residence, traded three sheep skins to James Thomas for an acre of land east of the mill site and just across the section line in section 8. This was the first of Mr. Black's possessions in No. 8, of which in later years he was principal owner and which is nearly all owned by his relatives still.

But to return to the history of the first settler, (John Boyles). The last known of him, his son William took him to Wisconsin, where he (William) had gone some years before, since which time he has never been heard from by his former neighbors.

Among the early settlers of Delaware township was also Andrew Kennedy, who, late in the year of 1827 settled on the land where the town of Albany was afterwards located.

Here Mr. Kennedy made some improvements, which he subsequently sold to William Venard (by the settlers pronounced vinyard) who in turn purchased the land of the government on the 3rd day of October, 1832. This was the northeast quarter of the southeast quarter of section 2 (40 acres) and lies in the southwest corner of the streets that form the road running west to Black's mill, and the one running north, or the Eaton pike, the two old roads passing through the town Here, in 1833, Mr. Venard subdivided his land into town lots and founded the village of Albany, the corporate limits of which now cover nearly two sections of land. Mr. Kennedy after selling his improvements to Mr. Venard, settled in section 15, and on November 23, 1835, entered the northwest quarter of the southwest quarter of the section (40 acres) where he spent the remainder of his life. In 1830 Daniel Jones settled on the south half of the northeast quarter of section 2 (80 acres) joining Mr. Venard's tract. He entered this land on November 30, 1831. At the first election after the organization of the township, Mr. Jones was elected a justice of the peace, which position he and Benjamin Drummond jointly filled for several years, and though strange it may seem to officers at present, both subsequently resigned.

Among the next settlers were Isaac Martin and Thomas and Adam Wilson, Mr. Martin entering the north half of the northwest quarter of section 5 (80 acres) which is now owned by H. N. and S. Williams This entry was made November 30, 1831. While in June the same year Thomas Wilson had entered the south half of the same quarter; same section (5). However, according to our records, the first land ever entered in Delaware township was the east half of the southwest quarter in section 19, which was entered by Henry Harmon on the 18th day of October, 1830.

This 80 acre tract is now owned by Daniel Pittenger, and Corners, at what is known as the "five points" on the middle Albany and Muncie road. Among other early settlers and those who became well known in after years were James Dean, John W. and Reuben Strong, Frederick and Lewis Stoner, in section 12; Adam Keever in section 13; Joshua Bantz in section 10; Solomon Boots in section 11; William Black in section 4; Ezra Bantz and Jacob Pendroy in section 1; David Bright in section 3; Joseph O'Neal and Jonathan Bergdoll in section 11; Joseph Godlove in section 16; Daniel Cochran in section 17; James Campbell and Joseph Orr in section 24; William Bartlett in section 25; James Orr and Adam Boots in section 27; Nicholas Pittenger and Daniel Richardson in section 28, and many others coming a few years later.

The land office at which the Delaware township lands were entered, was at Ft. Wayne, a distance of some sixty miles by the route that must be traveled. As there was no accommodations to be had on the road with perhaps the single excep-

## DELAWARE TOWNSHIP. 37

tion of the home of one settler, who had located on the Salimony river, not far from the present town of Montpelier, therefore going to the land office to transact business in those days was no easy matter, and there were in the community but few men with the knowledge of the route, time to spare, and courage to undertake the trip. However, as is usually the case, proper characters seem to come forth to suit every occasion, and so in this. Two men, of whom we have heard much, and of whom we have some personal knowledge, were often employed on these errands of trust and importance. We refer to Jacob Pendroy, of near Albany, and Joseph Luckey, who lived in the northwest part of the township.

Mr. Luckey was a very quiet man, illiterate, so far as books were concerned, but intelligent, and the soul of honor. Mr. Andrew Black states that the first time his father (John Black) saw Mr. Luckey he engaged him to enter land, handed him his money without any hesitancy, feeling perfectly satisfied that he was honest, courageous and capable. He added that but with few words Mr. Luckey threw his trusty rifle across his shoulder and strode into the forest in the direction of Ft. Wayne, returning in due time with his business all in good shape. Mr. Luckey was a noted woodman and a successful hunter. He afterwards emigrated to the state of Missouri. Jacob Pendroy entered many tracts of land for settlers in Niles, as well as in his own township, and like Mr. Luckey, always in a satisfactory way.

One of the first roads opened for public travel in Delaware township was from Deed's Mill at Smithfield, to the village of Albany. This road ran parallel with, and one mile west of the county line. It was opened in 1833, but was both ill shaped and ill kept until it was formally surveyed, straightened, and improved generally, in 1840 Another of the early roads was that from Muncytown via John Boyles's mill, and terminating at Granville. This road was on or near the present line of the Muncie and Granville pike, never getting perhaps more than a half mile from that line. Near Muncie it crossed White river at the present Elm street bridge crossing and recrossing the line of pike several times.

All the records from which could have been gleaned the necessary information touching early road making, as well as other early history of the township, were destroyed by fire, and the oldest record now extant, begins with the year 1853. The first road therein mentioned was one for which a petition was presented to the trustees at a meeting of the board on the 3rd day of June of that year. The road was to "begin at the Albany state road and run south on the section line to the road leading from Sheller's shop to the county line." A committee consisting of Joseph Godlove, John Shafer and Samuel

Thomas were appointed to view the road, and on June 25, 1853, made their report, "that in their judgment the road would be a public benefit," and it was accordingly ordered opened. Other roads followed this with similar histories.

As near as we can ascertain, the first stock of goods brought to the township and offered for sale to the public, was in the year 1834, when Granville Hastings opened a store in a building near the present site of Zehner's mill in section 16. He came from Wayne county, Indiana, and one of his first steps after arriving here was to make preparations for the erection of a mill at this point, and it is said that among his merchandise he brought a quantity of flour, an article which in those days was regarded as quite a luxury, and not to be indulged in except on stated occasions, such as weddings, or the reception of special personages, the ministers at quarterly meetings, and for the purpose of an occasional pie or dumplings and crust for chicken pot-pie.

Mr. Hastings employed a number of men to dig a race and construct a mill-dam, paying them a barrel of flour for a month's work. He completed his saw mill, but died before completing his grist mill.

The next store in the township was that opened by Uriah Pace at Albany in 1836, in a little log building that has long since disappeared. Speaking of Mr. Pace, reminds us of an anecdote that was told in 1852, when Franklin Pierce was the candidate on the Democratic ticket for president, and William R. King for vice-president. It was said that an old gentleman, who lived north of Albany, inquired of a neighbor as to who was nominated. (Now, it happened that Bennett King lived just east of Albany, and Mr. Pace was frequently called Piere) so the neighbor informed the inquirer that the candidates were Pierce and King. After some thought the gentleman said: "Well, I don't know much about Bennett, but I expect he will make a good vice-president, but I am well acquainted with Uriah and know him to be a good man, so I shall vote the ticket straight." Shortly after Mr. Pace opened his store John Mitchell opened a little grocery, at which was sold the first liquid refreshments in Albany.

In 1838 William Krohn, an intelligent German, came to Albany and engaged in merchandising for a number of years. He was an enterprising merchant, and kept a stock of goods much superior to that found in small villages in the early times. Mr. Krohn finally sold his goods business and practiced law in the community during the remainder of his life.

About 1841 or '42 Jacob Powers established a store in Albany, but sold to his clerk, Abraham Shank, shortly afterwards, who continued the business about a year, and left for other parts. Abel, Elisha and Samuel Bergdoll opened a store in Albany about 1836, but retired from the business a few years thereafter.

The first physician of the township was Dr. Isaiah Templin. Besides, we are told that Mrs. Boyles occasionally looked after professional calls in this science, and her right to do so was perhaps never questioned by an examining board.

While the township was yet very sparsely settled, ministers of the Methodist Episcopal church were sent out as missionaries by the conference, and held services at private houses throughout the settlement. About the year 1835 a class of this denomination was organized at the home of Jacob Pendroy, in the south half of the northwest quarter of section 1, and continued to meet at his house and at the houses of the other members of the class for three or four years. A log house was then built on a portion of John W. Strong's farm for the combined purpose of church and school, but as yet the church had no regular pastor. After a few years, however, the meeting place was transferred to Albany, where about the year 1848 the society erected a frame church building in the south part of the town. In the meantime the class had been given a place in the Granville circuit and regular appointments for preaching.

In 1876 Andrew Black donated a lot in section 8 upon which Delaware Chapel was built (and a society formed also by the Methodist Episcopal denomination), at a cost of about $1,200. This is a neat frame building, pleasantly situated on the Albany pike near Black's mill.

Union Chapel, also a Methodist church, was erected about 1845 on land owned by John Pittenger and donated by him to the society. This was a frame building, and was occupied until 1870, when it was replaced by a brick building. Early in the fifties a Methodist Episcopal class was organized in the eastern part of the township, and about five years later erected "White Chapel" on the northwest quarter of section 23, and about two and a half miles south of Albany.

For a number of years after the first settlement of the township there were no public burrying grounds, (or graveyard) and the cemetery near Granville, in Niles township, or Bethel, north of Albany, was used as the resting place of the Delaware dead, or they were laid away on some retired spot of the home farm. At an early date there were several interments near the junction of Mud creek with the Mississinewa river, and this afterwards became a public burial ground, but many who were buried here were afterward removed to the cemetery donated to the township by Alfred B. Strong.

In 1850 Wm. Black deeded a piece of land in the n. w. corner of section 4 to the County Commissioners, to be used as a public burrying ground. The first person buried here was a young son of Joseph Stafford, and the second was Mr. Stafford's wife. Another cemetery is at Union Chapel, north of the village of DeSoto, and still another, the "God Love Grave Yard," on the northwest quarter of section 16.

Schools in Delaware township, like in most new countries, were crude, but effective, and indulged in for a few weeks each winter, provided some one could be found with the required capabilities for teacher, which was a reasonable knowledge of "reading, writing and ciphering" as far as the "single rule of three" or (simple proportion). He must also possess a good, strong right arm and plenty of courage to back up his edicts. It has been said that the first school in the township was taught by Joseph Godlove in his kitchen. As to whether he had any other rooms in his house than the kitchen we are left to guess. These were the days when on Christmas the school teacher was expected to treat or take a ducking, and it is said Mr. Godlove refused to treat his school til he saw the hole cut in the ice, when he changed his mind; perhaps he intended to treat anyhow, but wanted to see how far his school would carry their demands. It was a common practice in these early times for the school teachers to board by turns with the patrons, and in order to equalize matters he was expected to board the most where the greatest number of pupils were sent from. While this arrangement was just, it was not always pleasant, as the teacher generally had some choice as to his boarding house, but, poor fellow, he was supposed to say nothing, but patiently bear his troubles. The weak the teacher was to board at our house was always looked forward to with much interest. Mince pies were baked, "crulls" were fried, the best apple bury was opened, and a general talk had between the mother and children as to proper conduct in the presence of the teacher. And, oh, how proudly the mother would sit, the bright knitting needles flashing in the firelight, as they were dexterously plied by her nimble fingers, while she listened to Mary and John rehearse their lessons to the "teacher." And, now, will some one tell us why a boy in the forties or fifties obtained as practical an education in two to four winters, of sixty-five days each, as they do now in nine or ten years, of six to nine months each? We pause for a reply.

In the year 1846 the cabin in which William Venard first settled, near the center of what is now the town of Albany, was converted into a school house, and a three months term of school taught by a man whose name has been forgotten.

In the following year (1837) the first building erected expressly for school purposes was built on the farm of Adam

Keever, some two miles south of Albany. This was a hewed-log building, much superior to the buildings in which the schools had been held formerly. This house became noted as being the first representative of the free school system in Delaware township, for, in the winter of that year the term began, and the public money, or "congressional fund," belonging to the township, was appropriated to pay the teacher. But unfortunately, this fund only proved sufficient to meet the expenses of one-third of the term (or one month) and the remaining two months salary was made up pro rata by subscription, as was usual in such cases. This was the manner of conducting the public schools until the present free school system was inaugurated, conformably to the provisions of the revised constitution of 1851. The first houses under the new system were erected in 1855, three in number. One in District No. 2, near the southwest corner of section 4, on land entered by Samuel P. Anthony, now owned by John N. Wingate. One in District No. 6, in the northeast corner of section 23, one mile east of White Chapel church, on land now owned by M. S. Whitehair. One in District No. 8 on land now owned by C. W. Confer, one mile east of DeSoto station. At a meeting of the trustees, held June 30, 1855, it was agreed that Enoch Current and John W. Bortsfield should build the school houses in Districts Nos. 6 and 8 for the sum of $275 each, and that John H. Ellis build the house in District No. 2 for $290.

The enumeration of the children between the ages of five and twenty-one years in the township in 1859 showed a total of 405. During the winter of that year the writer taught the school in District No. 2, sixty-five days for sixty-five dollars, so you see the salary was easily calculated. However, if the wages were low, our living was not expensive, as we had excellent board and lodging at the home of Andrew Black at a cost of $1.25 a week. The pioneer school teacher is gone. (If still living, he is like the little boy in Sunday school said, when asked by his teacher in regard to his father's business. His reply was that he was a Christian, but he did not work at the business of late years.) And while some of their practices would be considered unreasonable and severe at this time, yet we should remember that desperate cases demand desperate remedies, and that great reformations are accomplished gradually.

Delaware township at present (1899) has eleven school districts, each provided with good substantial buildings, all of which are built of brick except two recently built, which are frames. One of these (No. 11) is in the village of DeSoto in section 28, the other (No. 9) is in the northwest quarter of section 29, and one mile west of DeSoto.

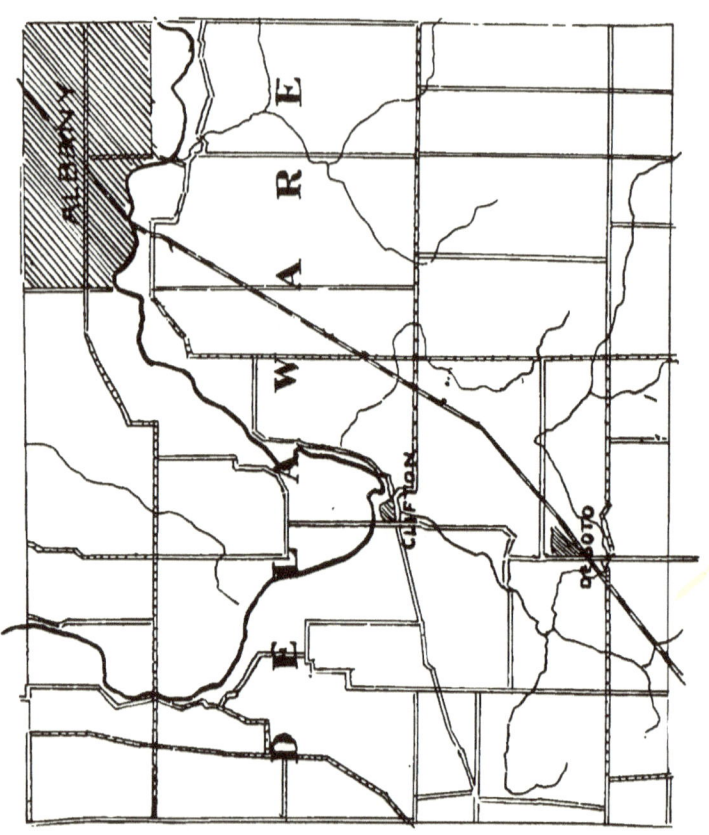

## DELAWARE TOWNSHIP. 43

Section No. I in Delaware township was entered between August 13, 1832, and November 23, 1835, by Abraham Custer, Reuben Strong, Lewis Stoner, John W. Strong, Jacob Pendroy and Ezra Bantz. The entire section is now within the incorporate limits of the town of Albany, although much of the land is owned by individuals, and land and manufacturing companies, yet it is all laid out in blocks of ten to the mile, making one hundred square blocks in the section, and while there are many buildings on the northwest quarter of the section, yet the greater portion of the section is unimproved as a town or village. The L. E. & W. railroad crosses the northwest corner of the section, and has its station, or depot building, about half way between where the road enters and leaves the section.

The first entry in section 2 was made by David Jones on November 30, 1831, and on March 26, 1836, (in less than five and one-half years) the last of the public land in the section was taken up by Absalem Boots The other purchasers of these lands during the period intervening were John Dinsmore, William Venard, Reuben Strong, John Quinn, Stephen Venard. Morrison Quinn, Emson H. Venard and Henry S. and Joseph Eron.

The section is also almost covered by the corporation of the town of Albany, the exception being that portion of the section lying south af the Mississinewa river, which passes in a westerly course through the section, cutting off about one fifth of the section on the south This portion of the section so cut off, and not being platted, is now owned by A. Strong, J. Bantz, jr., and J. L. Bartlett, et. al. The northeast quarter of this section is the original site of the town of Albany.

In section 3 Francis Venard entered forty acres in 1833, October 7, after which time there were no more entries recorded until 1836, in which year the balance of the section was taken up except one forty and a fractional eighty acre tract, which was entered the following year, 1837. The names of the purchasers in this section after Mr. Venard were Ralph Stafford, Susanna Thomas, Joshua Bantz, Robert Malcom, George Mills, Martin Depoy, David Bright and Henry Judy.

Section 3 is now owned by J. R. Stafford, James Stafford, H. Pact, E. Rautledge. R. E. Current, G. H. Current, J. Bantz, jr., M. L. DePoy, M. F. Davis, J. Pace and J. A. Strong.

The Mississinewa river crosses the southeast corner of the section and the Albany and Mississinewa free gravel pike crosses the section.

The public lands in section 4 were entered in the years of 1833, '34, '35 and '36 by William Black, McCoy Malcom,

Morrison Quinn, Joseph Godlove, William Martin and Samuel P. Anthony.

This section is now owned by William Black (youngest son of the original owner) J. A. Strong, R. Rautledge M. Richey, and John N. Wingate. The Albany and Mississinewa pike is on the south and a portion of the east line of the Peterson and Black pike on and near the west line. School No. 2 is located on the south side of the section at thehalf section line.

Three eighty acre tracts were entered in section 5 as early as 1831, three in 1833, one in 1834, and the remaining eighty acres in 1836.

The parties securing these lands were Archibald Dowden, Isaac Martin, Thomas Wilson, John Thomas Wilson, William Thomas. David Sutton, and Adam Wilson. The greater part of section 5 is high, rolling land, with a gravel soil. The present owners are G. W. Younce, J. F. Black, W. R. Bryan, George A. Stafford, H. J. Williams, and H. N. and S. Williams.

The Mississinewa river enters the section from the west about one hundred and twenty rods north of the southwest corner, running in an easterly direction to within forty rods of the center, where it turns north and leaves the section at the half section line on the north side. The Albany and Mississinewa pike runs along the south line, the Peterson and Black pike on and near the east line, a public road north and south through the center, and another along the north half of the west line.

Six is the northwest section of the township, and was entered in 1831, '34 and '36 by Israel Martin, Thomas Williams, William H. Green, Benoni Wilson, Adam Wilson, William Thomas, Ezekiel Thomas, and John Baldridge.

William H. Green was of English stock. His father emigrated to America before the Revolutionary War and became a soldier in the Colonial army. William H. was born in New York State, and while a young man came to Athens county, Ohio. He served in the war with England in 1812. Came to Delaware county and entered the north half of the northwest quarter of section 6 (this being the northwest corner of the township) on August 4, 1836. We understand that Mr. Green had a very correct family history, running back for many generations, but shortly after settling in his new home his cabin was destroyed by fire, and these, with many other important papers, were lost. Some time after this he lost his wife by death, and afterwards married the Widow Duddleston (mother of Isaiah Duddleston, the present trustee of Niles township), with whom he lived until his death, which occurred about 1856. Mr. Green was the

HOOSIER MANUFACTURING COMPANY,
Albany, Ind.

father of the late Jackson Green, of Hamilton township, and grandfather of Dr. George R. Green, of Muncie.

The present owners of section 6 are L. W. Davis, J. Harshman, J. I. Gray, T. W. Goodrick, James E. Stafford, and William H. Stafford.

This section is about surrounded by public roads, with the Muncie and Granville pike passing through it from north to south end of center. The Mississinewa crosses the southeast corner of the section in a northerly direction. School No. 3 was first located on the south line of section 6, but is now in section 7, some 40 rods south of the section line.

Section 7 in Delaware township can lay claim to the first white settler in the township, if not the first in the county, in the person of John Boyles As we have heretofore stated, Mr. Boyles was here in 1822. As to how long he was here prior to that time it seems impossible to ascertain. Mr. Boyles, however, did not enter his first purchase of public land until July 26, 1832. Why he delayed so long we can only guess—perhaps he concluded that no other white man would ever settle here and he would virtually own all the land and remain "monarch of all he surveyed."

Besides John Boyles the persons entering land in section 7 were Lloyd Wilcoxon, John Batreall, jr., Archibald Dowden, William Boyles, Squire Boyles, Charles Francis Willard and Jefferson Walburn,

This section is now owned by Andrew Black heirs, James E. Stafford, John H. Stafford, David Justice, J. N. Lewellen, Moses Clark, D. E. Brammer and Elisha R. Wingate.

The Mississinewa river enters the section near the middle of the east line, and running slightly west of north passes into section 6. On this stretch of river is where John Boyles built his mill, and is also where Black's mill is situated.

Section 7 is well provided with roads, many of them angling and crooked, but of so long standing that they have become a fixture, yet the section has three miles of straight road, on section lines. School No. 3 is on the northwest quarter on the Muncie and Granville pike.

The land in section 8 was entered as early as 1832, and as late as 1836, by William Moody, Wilson Lennon, William Thomas, Andrew Wilson, Robins Wilson, George Richeson and John Funderburg.

The present land owners in section 8 are R. F. Brammer, J. F. Barrett, Andrew Black heirs, D. A. Black, E. J. Smith, O. and T. Saunders and John H. Stafford. The section has the Albany and Mississinewa pike on the north line, and a public road on the east. The Mississinewa river runs in a north of west course, almost entirely across the south half of the section.

Section 9 was entered in 1833-34 and '36 by Stephen Berry, jr., Moses Canan White, David Sutton, Reuben Eppert and Silas Sparr, the junior after the name of Stephen Berry caused some family troubles and litigations. As many thought it to be a clerical error, and that the intention was to enter the land in the name of Stephen Berry, sr., the father of the younger man, who was a boy at the time the entry was made. Be this as it may Stephen Berry, jr., held his title.

The section is now owned by J. and W. Krohn, J. Holloway, E. C. Holloway, A. Black heirs, D. A. Black, R. E. Allen, John W. Goings, E. J. Smith, W. R. Allen, M. Cline and M. Pershing. The section has about four miles of road, that on the north line being the Albany and Mississinewa pike. The Mississinewa river crosses the southeast corner in a southwest direction.

Section 10 was entered in 1832, '33 and '36, by Joshua Bantz, John Quinn, David Bright, John Bantz, Martin, Henry Bright, John Sparr and John H. Taylor.

Section 10 is now owned by John Bantz, Jr., J. N. Wingate, M. L. Depoy, E. J. Sparks, C. M. McNeily, E. Black, H. M. Marquell, J. McNelly, Samuel Marquell and John W. Goings.

The section is well supplied with public roads, the greater portion of which are free gravel pikes. The Mississinewa river crosses the northwest corner of the section in a southwest course, and the Lake Erie & Western railroad crosses the southeast corner, running parallel with the river.

Solomon Boots, one of the first settlers, entered the east half of the northeast quarter of section 11, on the 12th day of November, 1831. This eighty-acre tract crosses the Mississinewa river at the northeast corner and joins the present town of Albany. It is now owned by A. T. Dehaven. The other tracts were entered in 1832, '34, '35 and '36, by John Quinn, Joseph O'Neal, Alfred Lee, Adam Keaver, William Custer, Jonathan Bergdoll and Joseph H. Hulse. The section is now owned by J. T. Dehaven, J. Khron, Brown and Bergdoll, J. N. Wingate, and John and William Krohn. Section 11 has pike on west and a portion of the north line, public road on the east and crossing northeast quarter. School No. 20 is located in the north part.

One-half of section 12 was entered in 1832, and the other half in 1833. John W. Strong and James Dean entered 160 acres each in 1832. Mr. Strong entered another 80-acre tract in 1833, and his brother, Reuben Strong, and Lewis and Fredrick Stoner each entered an eighty.

All the original owners of section 12 settled on and im-

## DELAWARE TOWNSHIP. 47

proved their land, lived here up to an old age, and raised their families on the lands they redeemed from the forest.

The present owners of section 12 are E. and E. Strong, C. A. Mason, G. R. Strong, A. Strong, Eliza Strong, A. T. Dehaven, S. M. Strong and J. R. Holloway.

This section joins the town of Albany on the north and Randolph county on the east. It has a public road on the west, three-fourths of the east, and east and west through the north half. The Mississinewa river crosses the north half of the section in a westerly course.

The earliest entry in section 13 was made on the 1st day of September, 1832, and the last of the public lands were entered March 18, 1837. The purchasers of land in section 13 were Nehemiah Burden, Abner Woolverton, Adam Keever, James Campbell, Levi Boots and James Dean.

Like section 12 this section was entered by actual settlers who at once, after securing their title, commenced to improve their land, and proved by their after life that they had come to stay.

Section 13 is now owned by W. J. Burden, A. T. Dehaven, J. and J. Hartzell, S. Campbell, C Bartlett, N. A. Devoss, J. Friddle and C. E. Marquell. Mud creek drains the section by crossing the southwest corner in a northwesterly course, and again crossing the northwest corner in a northeastern course. Section 13 has a gravel pike on the south line, and public roads on both the east and west line.

Section 14 was entered in the years of 1832 to 1836 by Adam Keever, Joseph Templer, Eli Thornburg, and Stephen Kennedy. The first of these entries was made by Adam Keever, being the east half of the northeast quarter (80 acres), and now owned by A. T. Dehaven. This entry was made on September 1, 1832.

The section is now owned by A. T. Dehaven, John and William Krohn, E. J. Selvey, C. E. Stafford, A. Carter, S. J. Shroyer and L. Marquell. Section 14 has a free gravel road on both the south and west lines, also a public road on the east side.

The first public land entered in section 15 was on the 5th day of August, 1834. On that day John Puckett entered the northeast quarter of the southeast quarter (40 acres), being the north half of an eighty acre tract now owned by L. Marquell, and on the same day Joseph H. Hulse entered the west half of the same quarter, a tract now owned by E. Bartlett. The remainder of the section was entered by John Bantz, Solomon Rohrbaugh, Samuel P. Anthony, John H. Taylor, Martin Forbes, John Kennedy, Andrew S. Kennedy and Granville F. Hastings. The present owners are D.

Michael, J. and W. Krohn, John W. Goings, H. Boots, J. Boots, J. F. Dowden, E. Bartlett and L. Marquell.

This section has gravel pikes along the east line, and north and south through the center, with a public road along the south line. The L. E. & W. railroad angles through the central part of the section.

Section 16, as in all townships of the county, was set aside for the benefit of public schools, and was sold by the commissioners as follows:

November 10, 1833, to Joseph Godlove, 251½ acres at $2.50 and $3.00 per acre.

Same date to George F. Hastings, 265½ acres at $1.25, $2.00 and $3.00 per acre.

November 20, 1833, to Robert Malcom, 38½ acres at $1.24 per acre.

December 3, 1833, to David Jones, 40 acres at $1.25 per acre.

October 17, 1834, to Samuel Calaway, 38½ acres at $2.00 per acre, making 634 acres in the section, aggregating $1,739.10.

The present owners of section 16 are John W. Goings, L. Godlove, J. L. Allegree, A. L. Godlove, Joseph Godlove, I. G. Boots, F. Shroyer's estate and H. Zehner. The horseshoe bend of the Mississinewa river is in this section, entering the section one hundred rods west of the northeast corner, runs south, then east, then south and southwest until within eighty rods of the south center, where it turns north, then west, then north of west, and leaves the section at the half section line on the west side, running a distance of one and three quarter miles in the section, and leaving it three-fourths of a mile from where it enters. School No. 5 is located in the southeast corner of this section, Zehner's mill in the south center, and the Godlove cemetery in the north center.

All of section 17, except eighty acres, was entered in 1836. Of the eighty acres entered prior to that time forty acres were entered on November 21, 1833, by Edward Marshall, and forty acres on June 10, 1834, by Joseph Baird. The parties entering in 1836 were Abraham Godlove, Daniel Cochran, Philip Cochran, Thomas Martin and Ebenezer Halstead.

The present owners are Joseph Godlove, Andrew Black's heirs, M. M. Friddle, H. Zehner, A. Cline, S. Shroyer, W. Dewitt, John H. Stafford, S. A. Holloway, O. J. Saunders, Charles Marsh and William Hitchings. Section 17 has about two miles of public road, but these have so many angles and elbows that we find them very difficult to describe. The

Mississinewa river crosses the northwest corner of the section in a northwesterly course.

Two eighty acre tracts in section 18 were entered in 1831, two forty-acres in 1833, and all the remainder in 1836. The purchasers of this land were Elizabeth Friend, William Custer, Henry Huddleston, Isaac Martin, A. Custer, William Pence and Philip Cochran. The section is now owned by S. A. Holloway, D. E. Bramer, J. W. Hamilton, A. M. Peterson, William Hitchings, M. H. Dick and J. Shafer. Section 18 has a public road along the south and half of the east line. The Muncie and Granville pike crosses the section; also a public road on the west (which is the township line), and the west half of the north line. Thus 18 is well supplied with highways.

We find the early history of our county so closely interwoven with the lives and biography of the early settlers and their families, that it is very difficult to separate them. Therefore the history of Delaware township is, to some extent, the lives of her first settlers. We mention this fact, trusting that our readers will pardon us for the occasional, seeming divergence, from historical facts of personal mention.

We now come to Section 19. The first entry of land recorded in Delaware township was the east half of the southwest quarter of this section (80 acres). This entry was made by Henry Harmon on October 19th, 1830. The north half of this tract is now owned by Adam Sheller, and the south half by Daniel Pittenger. The remainder of the section was entered in 1834, '36 and '37. Thus it will be seen that three years intervened between the time Mr. Harmon made his purchase until he had any neighbors, so far as government land purchase was concerned, for the next purchase after his was that of Daniel Pittenger on October 20th, 1833, just three years and one day later. Besides Mr. Harmon and Mr. Pittenger the purchasers of land in section 19 were Elijah Reeves, James Russell, Stephen R. Martin, Thomas Albin, John Pepper and William Stansberry.

The present owners of the land in section 19 are E. W. Hitchings, William W. Green, Adam Sheller, H. Allison, N. Sheller, E. J. Pittenger, J. Cullen and Daniel Pittenger. These landlords in section 19, with but one or two exceptions, are either the old pioneers or their children. This is perhaps as hilly a section of land as there is in the township. This section has more than five miles of public roads bordering or passing through it, and school No. 4 is located in the northeast corner. The west line of this section is the township line, dividing Delaware and Hamilton townships.

On November 17th, 1832, Benjamin Drummond and Uriel Fox each entered forty acres of land, composing the south half of the southeast quarter of section 20. The forty entered on that date by Mr. Drummond, corners up to the present station or village of DeSoto, and the M. E. church is located on the northeast corner of the tract. After these two entries there were no other purchasers of public land in the section until 1836, in which year the remaining government land was all taken up by John Godlove, Benjamin Drummond, Ebenezer Halstead, Aquilla Hensley, George McCullough, Robins R. Williams and John Pepper.

The owners of section 20 at the present are W. Dewitt, W. Polhemus, John Marks, Adam Madill, A. Sheller, William Hitchings, T. and M. Wilcoxon, A. M. Peterson and J. H. Sheller. Campbell's Creek crosses the southeast corner, and the section has a gravel pike east and west through the south half, a public road on the west line, and another angling through the northwest part.

In section 21 an eighty and a forty acre tract was entered in 1834, and the remaining unpurchased part of the section was all taken up in 1836 The first purchasers of land in this section were Jonathan Rardon, Jacob Sellers, Glass Ross, Sam'l Thomas, Christopher Humphreys and John Pittenger.

The owners of realty in section 21 at present are R. E. Taylor, E Pittenger, T. and F. Myers, J. H. Pittenger, J. Pittenger, F. Shroyer's estate, T. E. Myers and Adam Madill. The section has two and one-half miles of public road. The Lake Erie and Western railroad crosses the southeast, and Campbell's creek the northwest corner.

On March 12th, 1835, Daniel Perrine entered the north half of the northeast quarter of section 22, (80 acres). Seventy acres of this tract is now owned by A. Canter, and ten acres by J. Boots. All the remaining land in this section was taken up during the year 1836, by Stephen Kennedy and Michael Beeghley.

The present land owners in section 22, aside from those above mentioned, are J. H. Canter, E. S. Dowell, L. M. Dowell, D. Young, G. H. Byrd, W. A. Schofield, John Madill and R. Friar.

Section 22 has a public road along the north and half the south line, with a gravel pike north and south through the center. The Lake Erie and Western railroad crosses the northwest corner of this section.

One hundred and sixty acres of section 23 was entered in 1835 by Solomon Rohrbough and John Boots, four hundred and forty acres in 1836 by Solomon Rohrbough, Benjamin Manor, Martin Boots and Elias Beeghley, leaving one forty acre tract, which was entered November 21, 1837, by Thomas Berry.

The present owners of this section are M. S. Whitehair,

## DELAWARE TOWNSHIP.

A. Boots, A. M. Pittenger, A. Evans, L. M. Dowell, C. E. Dill, C. Bergdoll, J. C. Friddle, W. Progue, James Dill and W. Hitchcock. The section has two miles of public road north and south, also one mile of pike on the north line. White Chapel M. E. church and school No. 6 are located on this section.

Like section 23 section 24 was settled and the government land purchased in the years 1835, '36 and '37. Many of the first owners of this section were well known, and are still remembered by our citizens. They were James Campbell, James Dean, Joseph Orr, George Iman, Solomon Rohrbough, James Pendroy and William Woods.

The titles to the lands of this section have changed hands until none of the original names are now represented in the present owners, who are L. Booker, S. G. Selvey, J. Hiatt, M. S. Whitehair, G. S. Whitehair, H. C. Whitehair, B. Selvey. John Bartlett and A. Evans.

Like section 23 this section has two miles of road north and south, and one mile of pike east and west on the north line.

Section 25 is the southeast corner of the township. The section has public roads both north and south through the center, also on the west line. This section was entered in the years of 1835, '36 and '37, by William Bartlett, Solomon Rohrbough and Samuel and Edwin Johnson. The name of Bartlett, (a very common one), is the original name found among the landlords of this section. At present we find the title of the lands in the names of J. L. Bartlett, John Bartlett, Jos. A. Lewellen, C. and M. Sloniker, J. Meeks, A. Meeks, E. Bartlett, L. H. Cowgill and S. R. Strong.

In section 26 the public land was purchased in the years of 1834, '35 and '36, by Solomon Rohrbough, Warren Mann, Joseph Humpreys, William Jameson, Thomas Jones and James Johnson.

The section is owned at this time by M. and A. Evans, James Dill, W. J. Brewington, M. Bartlett, S. Rohrbaugh, S. R. Strong, F and A. Pittenger, A. Shroyer, J. A. Shroyer, T. W. Bartlett and M. A Orr. Twenty-six has three miles of public road. School No. 7 is located on the east half of this section.

Section 27, another one of the south tier of sections, is well drained by the head waters of Campbell's creek, which passes diagonally across the section from southeast to northwest. It has good roads crossing each other at right angles in the center of the section, and another along the west half of the north line. This section was all purchased of the government from September 21, 1835, to October 15, 1836, by James Jones, Jabesh Jones, David Lewellen, James Orr, Justice Kitterman, Ila Lake and Adam Boots.

Twenty-seven is now owned by L. M. Dowell, George Swander, L. Dean, J. and C. Orr, P. Payton, John Madill and A. H. Anderson

William E. Pendroy entered 40 acres of land in section 28 as early as October 27, 1832 (this forty is now owned with other lands by A. and L. Devoe), after which time there were no other entries recorded for the section until 1836, in which year the remainder of the section was all entered by Thomas Humphreys, Jesse McCray, Nicholas Pittenger, Daniel Richardson, Ila Lake, Uriah Lenon and John Moody.

The land owners in section 28 are C. W. Confer, E. B. Pittenger, J. and F. Myers, M. E. Ogle, J. Young, J. and C. Young, I. Pittenger, B. and E. Evans, E. Evans, A. H. Anderson, A. and L. Devoe and Adam Madill. This (28) is the only section in the township with two district schools. No. 8 is located in the east center of the section and No. 11 in the northwest corner, in the village of DeSoto. The L. E. & W. R. crosses the northwest corner of the section, where now is the village or railroad station of DeSoto.

The first entry of land in section 29 was made in 1833, and the last in 1837. The parties securing these lands were Jacob C. Harmon, Thomas Harmon, Josiah Wade, Henry Pittenger, Wilson Lennon, Uriah Lennon, Jacob Furrow and Thomas H. Weirman. The sction is now owned by B. Marks, A. Sheller, Isaac Worley, N. Lennon, N. Tomlinson and L. Cheesman, G. M. Wilson, J. Sheller, J. W. Myers, and P. C. Lillie. The section has three miles of public road and the railroad crossing the southeast corner.

Thomas Crawford entered a tract in the northwest quarter of section 30 as early as 1832. but for the following three years there were no other entries recorded, and not until 1837 was all the public land taken up in this, the southwest section of the township. After Mr. Crawford's purchase the remaining public domain of this section was purchased by Thomas F. Wilson, Daniel Pittenger, James Sparr, William Dragoo, John B. Goff and Benjamin Dragoo.

The section is now owned by N. Hurtt, Daniel Pittenger, Z. Shreve, Isaac Worley, W. W. Shrewe, G. Payton and William Reed.

## SNOW, BEAUTIFUL SNOW.

The snow, the snow, the beautiful snow
How we old boys love it, you know,
For we remember how we used to go
To Christmas dance or Christmas show.

And how we hitched old "Dobbin" or "Gray,"
To the pole jumper we called a sleigh,
Which we made with the ax in half a day
When other boys were out at play,

Then, wrapped in our mother's blanket warm,
To protect our body from outward storm,
Whilst within, our blood in a whirl,
We started out to get our girl.

We got her, of course, and then—oh, dear!
We cared no more for snow storm drear.
We sat so close in that jumper sleigh
(Because she couldn't get away).

Since then, whenever I see it snow,
The blood in my veins begins to flow
Just a little quicker, or faster, you know,
And I think of the nights of long ago,

When I took my sweetheart, Kittie or Kate,
To spelling school, and came home late,
And tied old Grey to the post by the gate,
And told him to be content and wait,

And then we went in by the kitchen fire,
I, frightened to death for fear of her sire,
But braced right up, for through a door
I heard the sound of her papa's snore.

Then, oh, how happy were Kitty and I,
She got some milk and apple pie,
And big red apples, a half a score,
And still her papa continued to snore.

And now I am getting old you know,
But I love the pure and beautiful snow,
It brings to my mind that younger life,
And I love my sweetheart—she's my wife.

       \*    \*    \*    \*

We sit by the fire, my wife and I,
And hear the merry bells go by,
But we never think "what might have been,"
For we are happier now than then.

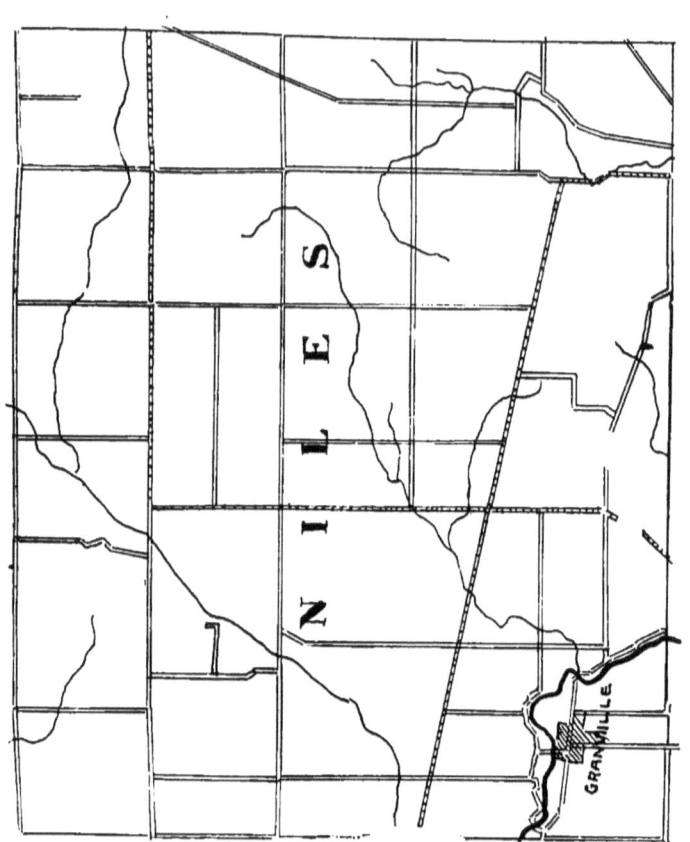

# Niles Township.

Niles township is all in congressional township, 22 north, and range 11 east. It is the northeast township of Delaware county, bounded north by Blackford county, east by Jay county, south by Delaware township and west by Union township. In dimensions, Niles, like Perry, is five tiers of sections north and south, and six tiers of sections (or miles) east and west.

Niles was originally a heavy timbered township, having been densly covered with several varieties of oak, ash, hickory, black and white walnut, beach, and in some localities, poplar or (as the Yankee would call it) white wood. But as has been the case in most all parts of our county, much of the best timber was cut off, rolled into "log heaps" and burned before its real worth was appreciated or perhaps we should say, before it had much value.

A former historian tells his readers that the "eastern and southern" portions of Niles is quite level while the northern and western portions are hilly. This writer certainly never traveled through Niles, or lost his reconing as to lines and locations. In fact the only portions of Niles that can be called other than level, is the southern part of the township, say the two southern tiers of sections, sections 33 and 34 are the most hilly, and while the Ellis and Gregory hills in these sections are somewhat difficult to cultivate in places, and necessitates some meanderings in road making, yet they are filled with untold wealth, not gold, but of the best of sand and cleanest of gravel. The product of these hills will be highly appreciated by any one driving over the fine gravel roads of Niles to-day who waded through the mud in the same part of the county forty or more years ago.

Niles township is drained by the Mississinewa river, Essley, Half-way and Mud creeks. The Mississinewa river crosses the southwest corner of the township, crossing section 32 in an almost north direction, thence turning west passes along or near the line dividing sections 30 and 31 and passes out into Union township. Essley's creek has its course through sections 12, 11 and 10, thence in a southwest course, touching sections 9, 17, 10 and 19, where it runs into Union township and reaches the Mississinewa just above the town of Eaton. Half-way creek is a short but beautiful little stream, having its source about the center of the east tier of sections in 24 and draining sections 25 and 36, passing out into Delaware township, dividing the town of Albany into east and west Albany, and emptying into the Mississinewa at the south side of the town. Mud creek is a small stream, (now almost entirely ditched) heading in section 14, passing through sections 23, 22, 21, 28, 29, 35 and 32, where it finds its superior and loses its identity.

The soil of Niles township is very productive and well abapted to the growing of all the cereals, as well as to clover, timothy and other grasses.

Perhaps owing to the fact that Niles being remote from the old State road running from Richmoud in Wayne county to Marion, and on to Peru and other towns along the Wabash river, is the cause of the public lands not being taken up so early as those in other parts of the county. But be the cause whatever it may, Niles was not settled up until several years subsequent to settlements in other localities. The first settler we have any account of in the township was a man by the name of Hessenflow, who built a cabin on the banks of the Mississinewa river, near where the village of Granville was afterward located, but as we have no account of him thereafter, he probably felt too crowded when neighbors began to locate within five or ten milss of him, and sought wider fields still farther west, as many have been known to do.

The first entry of land in Niles township was made by Samuel Gregory, May 3, 1831, being the west half of the southwest quarter of section 34. Here Mr. Gregory made his home, reared a large and respected family, some of whom are among our prominent citizens of today. Mr. Gregory subsequently entered other lands in the township, and adjoining his first entered tract where he lived until his death, sometime in the sixties, an honored and highly respected citizen. The other parties making entry in 1831 were Isaac Martin, Samuel Kite, William Battereal and John Battereal in section 32, and Peter Thomas in section 31. In 1832 there were eight entries recorded, four of them being made by Philip Stoner, Philip Essley, William Custer, and Reason Iams In 1833 there were twenty entries recorded, 1834 but twelve, and twenty in 1835, while in 1836 there were one hundred and thirteen entries, or nearly one-half of the entire township was taken up this year. After this time entries were less frequent until May 23, 1839, when David Smith entered the last of the Niles township public lands, the north half of the southeast quarter of section 28, now owned by M. Saunders and others. While there are but few of the old settlers living today, many of their posterity are still citizens of our county.

A great majority of the pioneers of this township came from Ohio, direct to their new homes, although other States did much toward furnishing the strong arms and brave hearts to fell the forests, and furnish to their followers this goodly heritage.

Commencing at the northwest corner of the township,

## NILES TOWNSHIP.

we find that section 7 was entered by Stephen Hayward, Thomas N. Sinks, Ephraim Sinks, George Leedom and Jonathan Ballenger. This being the north section of the west tier, we find a shortage of acres, as is the case in all the sections bordering on Union township. The lands of section 7 are now owned by J. A. Jernegan, W. Matthew, E. Edwards, James Edwards, E. B. Lozier, W. R. Toll, A. M. Craig, M. A. McClain and James Holcroft. This section has three public roads, on its north, east and south lines.

Section 8, lying next east of section 7, and along the Blackford county line, was entered, as was section 7, in 1836 by William J. Knight, William J. Essley, John C. Corbley and John Black, and is now owned by R. and A. Stafford, C. Robbins, J. W. Andrews, J. A. Jarnegan. This section has public roads on the north, south and west.

Section 9 was entered in 1836 and 1837, all of it being taken up in 1836 except the the northeast quarter, which was entered by John Thomas in 1837, the balance of the section having been entered the year previous by James Wooster, John Black and George Huffman. In the fall of 1857 the writer assisted in building one of the first frame chool houses in the township, on the southeast corner of this section, on land entered by George Huffman. This school house has disappeared and a modern brick edifice has superceded it, but was built south of the section line on the northwest corner of section 15. Section 9 is now owned by J. E. Stoner, T. H. Racer and others, J. E. Racer, W. C. Brundrent, A. N. Foorman and George Huffman. This section has public roads on the north and east, a gravel pike on the south, and a road north and south through the west half. Essley creek runs through the section.

Section 10, like section 9, was entered in 1836 and 1837 by William D. Field, George Huffman, Dennis Wilson, Jacob Huffman, John Constant and John Mellit. The land in section 10 is now owned by H. Weaver, J. S. Manor, S. F. Huffman, Samuel S. Selvey, J. Shatto, H. Bales and J. E. Storer. Section 10 has public roads on the north, east and west, and a free gravel pike on the south, thus having a public highway on each section line. Essley creek runs nearly west through the north half of the section.

Section 11 was taken up by settlers in the years of 1836 and 1837. The purchasers of its lands from the government were John Buckles, Joel B. Low, Eldridge Addison, William Bell and Valentine Bone. Now owned by G. A. Buckles, John Buckles, J. Crowell, L. Grannon, M. J. Hartley, S. Ritter, J. Ritter, S. C. Davis and N. J. Weaver. Like section 10, it is surrounded by public roads, with a graveled pike on the south line, and drained by the headwaters of Essley creek, which runs north of west through the section.

Section 12 is the northeast corner of both the township and county. It is a full section containing 640 acres, and was entered in 1836, '37 and '38 by Joseph Heaton, Adam Reader, Samuel P. Anthony, John Buckles, Hugh Campbell, Noah Shearly and James Peterson. The present owners of section 12 are H. Bantz, the Dunkirk Land Company, J. and C. France, J. Brotherton, C. E. Rogers, J. Buckles, J. Beal, N. G. Weaver, J. Armstrong, W. Manning, and W. B. Wilson. Gravel road on both north and south and public road on west line.

The pioneers of not only Niles, but of all the townships of Delaware county, have passed away. The log-rollings and and cabin-raisings are things of the past, yet the fruits of the labor of the pioneer are still with us. With us in a healthy, pure-blooded posterity, who have sprung from an honest and industrious ancestry, who employed their minds and bodies in building homes for loved ones.

How often do we hear the remark regarding some man who has climbed high on the shining ladder of fame from an humble starting point, whose parents were considered poor, piling up logs and brush by day and burning them by night, that "he is a self-made man." This is a great mistake. He, of all men, is not self-made; he has had all the advantages of poverty. Dare any man in the face of all the evidence say that poverty is not an advantage to the child? I think not. It may be an inconvenience to the parent, but surely a blessing to his posterity. Poverty, with honesty and industry, has been the incentive that has brought to the surface all the true greatness in our day and generation, because of the want of anything better the pioneers of this country lived on plain food. Their evenings were spent around the fireside with their families.

Their clothing consisted of plain, but substantial material, home woven, and home made. Their children grew up to manhood and womanhood with correct habits of industry and economy, and their after lives but proves the advantages of (what the world calls) poverty. The present generation, who have sprung from the pioneers of our county, should ever feel thankful that their parents were poor, that they have been reared by those whose best advice was their examples of right living, and that the many "vices and superfluities" of life were not know nor practiced by their ancestors. Of all men, I envy most the man who has lived on the same broad acres from his boyhood, who cultivates the fields where in youth, his father and mother lived and died. I can im-

## NILES TOWNSHIP. 59

agine no sweeter nor happier way to spend one's life than in the country, out of the mad race for money and place and power, and as a wise man has said, "out of the dusty highway where fools struggle and strive for the hollow praise of other tools." To the young farmers of our beautiful county I would say there is no reason why farmers should not be the kindest and most cultivated of all men. There is nothing in plowing the fields to make men cross, cruel and crabbed. To look upon sunny slopes covered with daisies, does not tend to make men unjust. And ever remember that he who labors for the happiness of those he loves, invariably and unwittingly elevates himself. But farming was not the first occupation of the first settlers of Niles Township Their first occupation was that of building cabins and clearing the ground that they might have shelter, and cleared land to cultivate. The task of providing for their families (for most of them had families) until the land was prepared for the first crop grown, was a momentous question with most of them, as ready cash was a scarce article and the necessaries of life, to say nothing of its luxuries, very hard to procure. As we have before stated in these articles, they depended upon grated or pounded corn for bread and game for meat. Instead of coffee, tea was made from broken twigs of the wild spice bush, or, as still done, from the bark of the sassafras root, for which we acknowledge our foundness still. Sugar and syrup were obtained more readily, as the settler did not have to wait for anything but for the first bright days of spring, or as we used to say, for sugar making weather, then preparing his troughs, which was done by cutting a tree into pieces about two and a half feet long, spliting them into halves and hollowing out the pieces thus obtained, thus forming a receptacle for the sap obtained from the sugar or hard maple tree by "tapping" them at the proper time.

If there are any of my readers who have never enjoyed a night at a "stirring-off" in an old-fashioned sugar camp, you have missed much of the sweetness of this life.

Section No. 13 in Niles township is the east section of the second tier from Blackford county and joins Jay county on the east. This section was all entered in 1836 and 1837 by Banlin Smith, John Buckles, Nathaniel Poor, James Peterson, Hugh Campbell and William Shrack. This section is now owned by Perry Steel, A, Fowler, F. M. Selvey, Sarah A. Lucas, W. A. Wilson, J. L. Bales, W. R. Routledge and W. Frank. It is well supplied with good roads. The Dunkirk and Moore pike on its north line, Green street on the west, a section line road on the south and the Albany and Dunkirk road through the eastern portion.

School No. 1 is located on the northeast quarter or this

section. It has long been known as Green Street school, from the name given the road running by it. This road has borne the name of Green Street for many years, in consequence of almost all the settlers taking up or purchasing the land along the road were formerly from Greene county, Ohio. The writer taught this school in the winter previous to the breaking out of the Rebellion in 1860-61. The school house was then a frame building, and stood where the brick edifice now stands. Although the country was comparatively new, yet at that early day there were many pupils in school. My recollection now is that the enrollment was eighty-three pupils. But one fact I remember distinctly, and that is that James Bales, Amos Hummer and John Beal furnished the school with twenty-one pupils—seven each.

Section 14 was entered in 1836 and 1837 by James Peterson, Elisha Bartlett, Richard Higman, Nathaniel Polk, William Lee, Daniel Fisher and Hugh Campbell.

The land in this section is now owned and mostly occupied by G. Michael, A. C. Rook, Joab Thornburgh, S. Michael, Jonathan Bales, Peter McNelly, R. Cunningham and Adam Shirk. This section has had a public road on each of its borders for more than forty years, the road on the north line now being a free gravel pike.

The land in section 15 was entered in 1835 and 1836, the south half of the section being entered by George W. Stafford and Samuel Sprinkle in 1835 and the north half by Richard Higman and John Constant in 1836. That portion entered by Messrs. Stafford and Higman was improved soon after the entry was made while the tracts taken up by Sprinkle and Constant was mostly unimproved for a number of years.

The section is now owned by D. Bales, E. Bullock, Samuel S. Selvey, J. and A. Garr, C. Bales and heirs, S. Bales and heirs, and Peter McNelly. School No. 5 is situated on the northwest corner of this section. Section 15 has public roads on the northeast and south, also through the center east and west

Section 16 being donated to the township by the government for school purposes, was sold by the commissioners on November 2, 1838, to the following purchasers in eighty-acre tracts.

Morton C. East, William Richardson, Andrew Black, James Black, Mary Gorton and James McMillan. The purchase price paid at this sale was $1.50, $1 62½ and $1.75 per acre. The tract purchased by James McMillan was for some cause forfeited, and afterwards the title was perfected and the land resold to Thomas Klugh at an increased amount of $97.50. Section 16 is now owned by H. Weaver, A. C. Weaver, D. B. Moore, Mrs. D. B. Moore, C. H. Manor, W.

INTERIOR OF DR. S. A. MARTIN'S DENTAL PARLORS,
Upstairs, 118 S. Walnut St., Muncie.

DAVID CAMMACK,
Postmaster, Muncie.

ARTHUR C. PERSHING,
Trustee, Center Township.

H. Richey, J. and S. Fudge, J. and E. Racer and W. Fishback. Sixteen has roads along its north and south lines, and a free gravel pike through the center north and south.

Section 17 was entered in 1834 to 1839 by John Black, Rachael Chandler, Ralph Stafford, John Barley and John D. Heighway, and is now owned by J. W. Black, T. J. Robbins, C. A. Barley, E. Black, J. R. Black and C. H. Manor, School No. 6 is located on the northwest corner of this section. Roads run along the north and south lines and through the west half.

The land in section 18 was all entered in 1836 and all by Ezra Wasson, except eighty acres, which was taken up by Thomas Moore the same fall after Mr. Wasson had made his purchase in June.

The section is now owned by A. N. Foorman, A. M. Robbins. J. W. Long, J. W. Cochran, M. Hayworth and J. Herron and C. A. Barley. That portion of the section bordering on Union township is fractional, or short in acreage. The section has public roads on the north, south and west, also north and south through the center.

NOTE.—Through the kindness of R. S. Gregory I am enabled to give information relative to Mr. and Mrs. Ralph Shaw. They were English people, he a bright, scholarly young man, but unfortunately for a young man in England, was poor. She was a daughter of one of the noblemen of the country. Winning her affections while they were quite young, they concluded to marry and hide themselves in the "new world," knowing they could never get the consent of her father to their union. So, about 1835 or 1836, they proceeded to carry out their former plans, came to New York and started for the then "far west." On March 16, 1836, he entered two forty-acre tracts of land in Niles township, near Granville, before mentioned. Here Mr. Shaw and his royal-blooded wife lived happily together, and both being well educated, taught school at different times and different places. Early in the fifties, Mr. Gregory remembers Mr. Shaw and his wife coming to his father's house with the statement that they had just received the news from England that Mrs. Shaw's father had recently died, and before death, (or his representatives after his death) had relented of the hardness toward the American daughter and her husband, and had invited them to return to England to receive her share of the estate, which they hastened to do. Mr. Shaw, being a scholar and a gentleman, besides having added largely to his store of political knowledge by his sixteen or twenty years residence in Delaware county, was (shortly after returning to England) elected to the honorable position of mayor of Southport, in which capacity he served until his death which occurred about 1875 or 1876.

The character of the pioneers of our county is properly within our range. They lived in a region of exuberant fertility, where nature had scattered her blessings with a liberal hand. Their liberties, the vastness of their inheritance, the dense forests, the many improvements constantly going forward, combined with the bright prospects of a glorious future in everything that renders life pleasant, deeply impressed their characters and gave to them a spirit of enterprise and independence of feeling, and a joyousness of hope. They were a thorough combination of characters, conditions and opinions. Coming as they did from various states of the union and older settlements of our own state, they found themselves here in the wild forests, and became cheered with the hope of being able to build up a family, an honor to themselves, and a fortune founded on honesty and industry, from new elements. And thus they settled down beside and with each other. All now form one society, feeling a dependence upon one another, borrowing and loaning, back and forth, not only the "newspapers," but the common utensils of the kitchen, frequently going a mile or more through the woods, by the blazed trail, to borrow a peck of flour or corn meal, that the family might subsist until the father returned from the mill, miles away, where he had gone, with oxen and cart, or, perchance, on horse back, with the sack of grain across the horse, and the time of his return depending on the number of grists that were in before him, as each had to await his turn. His return thus depending on uncertainties would often cause much anxiety to the mother and children in the lonely cabin at home, when darkness would close in and the winds beating upon the rude home, bringing unwelcome sounds, accompanied by the howlings of hungry wolves.

These were the dismal, desolate phases of pioneer life. But the years passed on and the pioneers continued their toil, ever sweetened with hope, submitting patiently to hardships, until the light of a glorious civilization and prosperity dawned on them in waving fields of golden grain and luxuriant meadows. Comfortable dwellings have risen on or near the old cabin site. And might we not appropriately term this the noonday of prosperity? In the place of the blazed pathway or trail through the forest we have the smooth gravel pike, bordered on both sides with substantial fences or hedges, behind which are finely cultivated fields of grain, rich pastures with their occupants of fat, sleek thoroughbred stock, or orchards of delicious fruits. On every hand we may observe this wonderful transformation. Let us, then, thank God, emulate and endeavor to imitate the pioneers of Delaware county. And thus having the promises already fulfilled, continue in the industry and perseverance of which we have had so glorious an example.

Section 19, in Niles township, was entered as early as 1832 and as late as 1836. The first owners of land in this section were Philip Stoner, Philip Essley, James Black, Elisha Essley, Jesse Essley, Junius McMillan and Stephen Butlar. The section is now owned by J. D. Hance, C. L. Smith, J. Roberts, J. W. Long, F. R. Foorman and W. C. Hance. This is another fractional section, being in the west tier. Essley creek crosses the south half, a road on the north side, and north and south on the half section line.

As early as 1833 settlers began to see the advantages of the rich soil in section 20, and four entries of land were made during the year. These were made by James Black (making three of them) and Francis A. Essley. The balance of the land in section 20 was entered in 1835 and 1836 by William Constant, Elisha Essley, Cyrus McMillan, Jeremiah Priest and James L. Veach. The present owners of section 20 are: C. H. Manor, Z. Stanley, jr., S. J. Stanley, C. L. Smith, W. C. Hance and Z. Stanley, sr. Essley creek crosses the northwest corner and good roads run along the north line and through the center of the section north and south.

Section 21 at the center of its east line is the center of Niles township. The public land of this section was entered in 1835, 1836 and 1837 by Alfred Barnett, William Lee, David Mason, Frederick Thornburg, Andrew Wilson, Albert Boyd and David Moore, and is now owned by James D. Weaver, D. N. Peterson, L. L McDaniel, J. R. Black, R. Champ, E. E. Miller, L. F. Smith, D and W. Frank, M. Vincent, S. E. Stanley, S. D. Frank and William D. Barley. A good road borders the north, east and half the south lines, and a free gravel road crosses the section north and south on the half section line.

Section 22 was all entered in the year of 1836 from March 7 to August 27, or within six months, by Jacob Moore, James Bolton, Augustus A. Root, Loxley A. Rickand and Samuel T. Kyle.

By giving our readers the facts connected with the settlement of a quarter of this section they can form a pretty correct idea of the lives of early settlers generally.

Loxley A. Rickard, in company with Daniel Bosman and Richard Higman and their families, left their former homes in the state of Delaware in the year 1835, and plodding slowly westward with their teams and covered wagons, fording deep streams or camping on the banks until the waters would fall, they finally arrived in Ross county, Ohio, where they remained during the following winter. Then again starting westward they arrived at Muncytown (now city of Muncie) about the first of August, 1836. Here they arranged to leave their wives and children until they could select their future homes. Striking out to the northeast, they finally selected land in Niles township, Mr. Rickard in section 22, Mr. Bosman in section 23 and Mr. Higman in sections 14 and 15. The next object was to secure their title of the government. To do this they employed a man by the name of Pendroy, who had settled in section 35 the previous year and was now considered an old settler, to proceed to the land office at Ft. Wayne and make their entries for them. Their title secured, they at once went to work to build their cabins that they might bring their families to their new homes. Mrs. Rickard states that their cabin walls were erected and the roof put on when they moved out to their home. The cabin had no floor or chimney. A large stump stood in the center of the room, against which they built the fire of cool evenings. Their fire for cooking was made against a log outside the cabin. Some large slabs, or puncheon, were split from logs and lain across the back end of the cabin to keep their bedding off the damp ground. The old lady adds that "we got on very nicely, but were a little crowded at first, as Mr. Higman and his family stopped with us the first night, as his cabin was not quite so nearly completed." And just such lives were being lived all over this county.

The land in section 22 is now owned by A. Devoe, O. H. Devoe, F. S. Fosdick, A. N. Bosman, W. D. Barley, and W. and Mary Shirk. There is an open road on every section line surrounding section 22, and has been for more than forty years.

Section 23 was all taken up in 1836, except a forty acre tract, which was entered as late as October 6, 1838, by Isaac Spence (father of our townsman, N. N. Spence), the balance of the section having been purchased by Thomas Berry, Ezra Porter, Daniel Bosman, William Scott and Ira Ingraham. The present landlords of 23 are Adam Shirk, A. and E. Wilson, J. B. Bosman, J. Mendenhall, W. Foorman, W. Campbell, C. P. Cole, C. W. Andrews, and P. Archibald. Section 23 is also surrounded by open roads of many years location.

The public land in section 24 was purchased of the government between the first of April and last of December, 1836, the original purchasers being Amos Wooster, Nathaniel Dickson, Adam Michael, and Isaac Mailten. Twenty-four is the most eastern section of the middle tier and joins Jay county. The section is now owned by H. and M. Miller, M. Shatto, W. H. Maitlen, Adam Shirk, W. Harrison et al.

RESIDENCE AND FARM BUILDINGS OF ELISHA R. WINGATE,
An old citizen and farmer of Delaware township, 7 miles northeast of Muncie,
on the Granville pike.

RESIDENCE OF R. S. GREGORY,
East Washington Street, Muncie.

## NILES TOWNSHIP

Twenty-four has roads on the north, south and west, also the Albany and Dunkirk road crossing it north and south.

Public land in section 25, Niles township, was entered as early as 1833. The natural drainage furnished by Halfway creek, which passes through this section and section 36, south of it, was possibly some inducement to the prospector, as most of the public land being level, was considered wet land prior to the clearing up and draining. The first purchasers in section 25 were Samuel Kyle, John Dinsmore, Daniel Dean, Jr., John Wilson and William H. Houston. The first of these entries was made by John Wilson, who settled on the west half of the southeast quarter of the section. This eighty-acre tract is well watered by Halfway creek which passes through it. Here Mr. Wilson settled and reared a large and respected family, many of whom are still living in the county.

Besides clearing up a fine farm, Mr. Wilson instituted a tannery in early days. Crude, of course, as compared with that industry of our day, but nevertheless a great blessing to the community at that time. Here the settler brought the pelts of game and hides of animals, and in (which was a long) time had them converted into leather. When the leather was received, the next process was to call the family together, and to have each one to stand with the heel of the foot against the door post, a small stick placed lengthwise under the foot was cut off at the end of the big toe, thus obtaining the exact length of the foot. Sometimes a string was placed around the instep to get the measurement of the foot in circumference, but most frequently the length only was taken, and whoever went to the shoemaker's would have to remember if "Mary" or "John," as the case might be, had a high or low instep.

Sometimes it would happen that the measure would be lost on the way to the shoemaker. One instance, I remember, where the elder brother was sent with the measures and lost one, fearing to come home and report it, he concluded to cut another stick as near like it as he could, and the difference was never known until long afterwards when he volunteered to tell it after finding that the shoes fit the one his guess measure was for as well as the others. Small tanneries were quite numerous in the early days of our county. Another of these useful manufacturers was that of Ralph Stafford. This was located about a mile above Black's mill, on the southside of the Mississinewa river. Mr. Stafford once told me of a man who had brought him a beef hide that he wished to sell. Mr. Stafford said the hide was quite wet, the man stating that he had dropped it in the river when crossing in the canoe. Mr. Stafford placed the hide on the scales, and it being so very heavy excited his suspicions, and unrolling it he found the hair filled with sand. It seems that the owner had saturated the hide with water, then taking it by the tail had dragged it through the sand until it became many times heavier than it naturally was. But, like many do, he overdid the natural so far that he missed the sale entirely. Mr. Stafford afterwards (in 1853) bought a farm and removed his tannery west of Black's mill, on what was then the upper Granville road, now Muncie and Granville pike, where he farmed and operated his tannery for many years.

The present owners of the land in section 25 are A. Gray, A. Bales, H. Shirk, E. Berry, R. Berry, J. A. Bales, C. Baldwin, R. M. Bartlett, M. Bryant, C. Wilson and G. M. French. Section 25 has a road on the north and also west line, another a part of the way through the section north and south on the half section line, and another on and near the south line.

Section 26 was all entered during the months of March and May, 1836, by John Blakely, Sarah Kimball, Robert Kimball, John W. Vincent and John Shrack. The land in section 26 is now owned by J. A. Bales, P. Frank, E. E. Frank, C. Baldwin, M. Bryant, James W. Wingate, A. S. Wilson, G. and M. Wilson, D. C. Frank and I. F. Andrews.

One of the first organized churches in the township has its house of worship in the southeast corner of this section. We allude to the Bethel Methodist Episcopal church. Some time in the year 1836 Rev. Wade Posey, a missionary of this church, organized a class at the house of Eli Anderson, who had settled about a quarter of a mile south of where Bethel church stands. This class consisted of seven members, and here in this cabin these faithful few met and worshiped for three or four years, until about 1839 or 1840, when their increasing numbers made the erection of a church building a positive necessity. John Shrack, one of the members of the class, donated a lot in the southeast corner of this section (it being the southeast corner of his land also), on which was erected a hewed log house of worship, or the "Bethel church." Some years later this first building was entirely destroyed by fire, but not discouraged, the members with commendable energy very soon erected another house similar to the first, on the same site. This second Bethel church stood, and was used for worship, until 1859, when it was torn away, and the present (Bethel) neat and commodious church took its place. "Bethel" has ever been a prosperous society, in a prosperous community, and many pleasant recollections of the writer linger about old Bethel. Long may she flourish and cast her influence for good on the coming, as she has on the passing generation.

On the lot donated for this church the first cemetery (or grave yard) was established, and the first person buried here was Mrs. John Kyle, who died in 1837.

Section 27 was also entirely taken up during the year 1836, with the exception of the southwest quarter, which was entered on December 4, 1835, by Jeremiah Veach. The other three-fourths of the section was purchased by William McCoy, Jacob Moore, Robert Kimball, and William Foster. The present owners are F. M. Wingate, W. A. Jones, C. M. Mann, P. W. Vincent, M. A. Wilson, J. Ball, T. Wingate, J. A. Wright, J. S. Fudge, J. and W. Krohn, and James W. Wingate. The Albany and Eaton pike angles across the southern part of the section, and there are good roads on the east, west and north lines.

Section 28 was purchased of the government by settlers in the years from 1832 to 1839. Those securing land in this section were George Shearon, Samuel Martin, David Smith, John Lewis, Robert M. Boyd, Israel Martin, William Custar, Robert Huston, Noble Gregory, Glass Ross, Henry Shearon, and Stephen Berry.

About the center of this section, in a pleasant grove, is where the famous "Gregory camp meetings" were held for a number of years, and here during weeks in August each year assembled the worshipers of God (and mammon). They erected substantial wooden tents, (they forming a hollow square) came with their families, brought their provisions and bedding, and thus spent many pleasant days in the cool grove, mingling with kindred spirits in the worship of God, and social friendships. And while this was the programme at the "camp ground," the "grocery wagons" (for that is what they were called) would locate two miles away (required by law), near the village of Granville, and there do a lively business vending ginger-bread, cider, melons and candies. Wrestling, jumping and not infrequently fighting was indulged in, so that within two miles you could see the two extremes of morals, even in those early days of long distances.

Section 28 is now owned by William D. Barley, L. F. Smith, E. E. Miller, C. Miller, M. R. Smith, S. and G. Low, T. and C. Walburn, T. and G. Sanders, M. Saunders, S. Williams and M. A. Wilson. Section 28 has two good gravel pikes passing through it and crossing each other at almost right angles near the center. Section 29 was entered in the years 1833–34–5 and 36, two hundred and forty acres being entered in 1833, one hundred and sixty acres in 1834, eighty acres in 1835 and a hundred and sixty acres in 1836.

These entries were made by John Blakeary and John Thomas in 1833, Samuel Clark in 1834, James Robinson and James Hetton in 1835, and by Charles Redding and James Hetton in 1836. These lands are now owned by M. Topp, L. Clark, C. C. Edgington, W. C. Hance, F. S. Wingate, E. B. Wingate, Crooks and Wolf, J. A. Barley, A. N. Bosman and M. R. Smith. Section 29 has a public road on the south and greater part of the west line, through the center north and south, and the Albany and Eaton pike passes across the north half of the section. In section 30 the public lands were taken up as early as 1832, and each year thereafter until the last entry was made in 1836. The purchasers of the public domain in this section were Thomas Hillman, Ralph Shaw, Willis Hance, William Gregory, John Gregory, Reason Iams and Norris Venard. The present land owners in section 30 are Joseph D. Hance, S. J. Peterson, W. Peterson, Calvin C. Crooks, C. Boyd and Crooks and Woolf. This section lies across the river and just north of the old village of Granville. Section 30 has public roads on the east and south; also through the center north and south, and the Albany and Eaton pike across the north half. The Mississinewa river drains the south part of the section, crossing the section line twice, and not being more than sixty rods from that line at any point.

Section 31 is the southwest corner of the township, and perhaps the first settled part of the surrounding country. The first entry of public land in this section was in June, 1831, but squatters had located along the banks of the Mississinewa river several years prior to that date. The land in section 31 was all entered in the years of 1831 to 1836 by Peter Thomas, John Gregory, William O'Neal, John Engard, Jonathan Ruggles, John Battereall, Andrew Battereall and Jacob Battereall. The village of Granville, the only town or village in the township, is located in this section. Granville is the successor of Georgetown, which was situated a short distance above Granville on the Mississinewa river, but from some cause refused to grow to a large city, and was finally submerged into its more prosperous rival. It is stated that Price Thomas, (grandfather of "Budd" Thomas, one of our ex-police commissioners of Muncie), hewed the logs for the first house in Georgetown, in 1833. John Gregory, (uncle to Ralph S. Gregory of Muncie), purchased the west half of the northeast quarter of the section, On April 17, 1832, and in 1836, divided a portion of his purchase into town lots, thus founding the village of Granville. Afterward Peter Thomas, (whose purchase joined that of Mr. Gregory's on the east, the line being where the Muncie pike now enters the village), also laid out town lots, and Granville soon become a thriving town, known for many miles around for its commendable enterprise, and questionable practices, for Granville, like many of our more modern places, had all kinds of people, and many anecdotes are told of its early days. And while the morals might have been somewhat slack in some things, yet honesty was always strictly guarded, and dishonesty summarily punished. A fellow was arrested on one occasion for horse stealing, taken before Squire ———, of Granville, the evidence heard, the prisoner found guilty, sentenced to the state prison for ten years, tied to a horse, and with a constable in charge started for Jeffersonville. Arriving at Muncietown, some one inquiring the circumstances of the constable, was told that he was on his way to the penitentiary with the prisoner who had been sentenced by Squire ———'s Court at Granville. The constable was finally persuaded to turn his victim over to the county sheriff until the Squire could change his papers to committal in the county jail pending trial by a higher court, where more money could be expended and less justice had. Granville is situated in one of the most fertile and picturesque spots in Delaware county. As a commercial point it has passed through many changes of prosperity and adversity. She has had her taverns, blacksmith and wagon shops, dry goods and grocery stores, her schools and churches. The two last named still remain, but most of the others are gone. Eaton, two and a half miles northwest, and Albany four miles east, both being situated on railroads, have taken the life away from Granville and left but little in a business way, save the postoffice and not much of that.

The owners of land in section 31 at present are C. Boyd, Crooks and Woolf, Eli Peterson, S. Michael, M. J. Berry, S. A. Smith, J. C. Long's estate, W. Peterson, H. Duddleston, R. Duddleston and L. W. Davis. Section 31 is well supplied with public roads, kept in good condition, is one of the hilly or rolling sections and well drained by the Mississinnewa river.

Section 32 was also one of the early settled sections of the townships, one half of its lands being entered in 1831, the remainder in subsequent years to 1836. The entries in this section were made by Alexander Price, John Sutton, Samuel Kite, John Battreall, Isaac Martin, William Battreall and William Downing. Section 32 is now owned by J. L. Ray, J. F. Peterson, E. H. Valentine, Crooks and Woolf, Eli Peterson and H. J. Williams. 32 has good roads and is well drained by the Mississinnewa, which crosses the west portion of the section.

Section 33 is perhaps the most hilly section of land in Niles township. The "Ellis hills" are in the southwest quarter of this section and are rich in their deposits of sand

and gravel. They derive their name of "Ellis hills" from the fact that Capt. John H. Ellis at one time lived here. He was at that time a carpenter and erected many frame houses built in the northeast part of the county. He afterwards lived in the village of Albany, where he served for a number of years as justice of the peace, and employed his spare time in reading law. Came to Muncie a short time before the beginning of the war of 1861.

In 1862 Captain Ellis assisted in raising a company of men, of which he was elected captain, mustered into the service as Company B, 84th regiment, Indiana Volunteer Infantry, at Richmond, Ind , September 3, 1862, served with his company until killed in battle at Chickamauga on the 20th day of September, 1863, just one year and seventeen days after being mustered. The command of Company B was then given to the captain's son, Frank, who served with his regiment and was mustered out with it June 14, 1865, and who has held several positions of trust and profit in Delaware county in subsequent years.

This section (33) was first purchased of the government by James Gregory, William Lee, Alexander Price, Andrew Battreall, Jesse Clark, William Downing and Samuel Gregory in the years 1831, '34 and '36. The present land owners are Samuel Gregory, B. M. Williams, J. and L. Anderson, J. L. Ray, J. F. Peterson, G. W. Younce, John F. Black and N. Peterson. The Peterson and Black free gravel pike crosses the section north and south, a public road east and west and another on the north of the west half.

Section 34 was taken up in the years 1831, '36 and '37. The original purchasers were Robert Kimball, George Huffman, Jacob Peterson, Samuel Gregory, Michael Hedekin and Joseph Stafford. Near the center of the northwest quarter of this section once stood the old "Gregory school house," where Ralph S. Gregory, N. N. Spence, and many other bright and able speakers received their first drill in oratory at the debating societies that met here on winter evenings to discuss such questions as "Whether the negro or Indian race had the greater cause of complaint against the white race?" "In which is most pleasure to be obtained, pursuit or possession?" "Which is the mother of the chicken, the hen that lays the egg or the hen that sits on and hatches the chick?" "Does the hen cackle because she has laid the egg, or does she lay the egg just to have something to cackle about?" and such other important questions that would be invented by the fertile brain of the Niles township youth from time to time. This section (34) is now owned by James Wingate, E. Fishback, M. Wright, Samuel Gregory, James R. Stafford and Joseph R. Stafford. Section 34 has less distance of public road than any section in the township, there being less than two miles of road touching the section, and there is no section perhaps better prepared to furnish gravel to make good roads than is section 34.

Section 35 was taken up by Eli Anderson, Thomas Vincent, John Shrack, Adam Keaver, John Dinsmore, John Mann and Eli Pendroy. These lands are now owned by W. T. Bartlett, R. Flanery, M. Vincent, Jas. W. Wingate, D. M. Bell, C. N. Bartlett, E. L. W. and C. Bartlett and F. and A. Cline. Near the center of the east line of 35 where halfway creek runs into this section for a short distance are the "haunted hills of half-way," where supersticious people used to see ghosts and hobgoblins, almost as scary as themselves but the fact that such foolish notions are things of the past is another proof of the advance of civilization. The Albany and Eaton pike crosses the east and north portions of this section.

Section 36 is the southeast corner of the township joining Randolph county on the east and the corporation line of the village of Albany in Delaware township on the south. The public lands of this section were entered by Isaac Pavy, John Boots, Eli H. Anderson, Jacob Noggle, Warren Mann and Ezra Bantz in the years of 1833,' 34 and '36. The holders in section 36 at present are D. M. St. John, J. J. Hoak, F. P. Anderson, R. M. Bartlett, F. and A. Cline, E. L. W. and C. Bartlett, B. W. and D. J. Manor.

The schools of Niles township are located as follows: No. 1 northwest quarter of section 13, No. 2 southeast quarter section 26, No. 3 southeast quarter section 27, No. 4 (Center) southwest quarter section 22, No. 5 northwest quarter section 12, No. 6 northwest quarter of section 17, No. 7 northeast quarter section 30, No. 8 (Granville) northeast quarter section 31 and No. 9 southwest quarter of section 20. The school buildings are all substantial brick buildings and the schools right up in the front of Indiana schools, which means among the best in this or any other country.

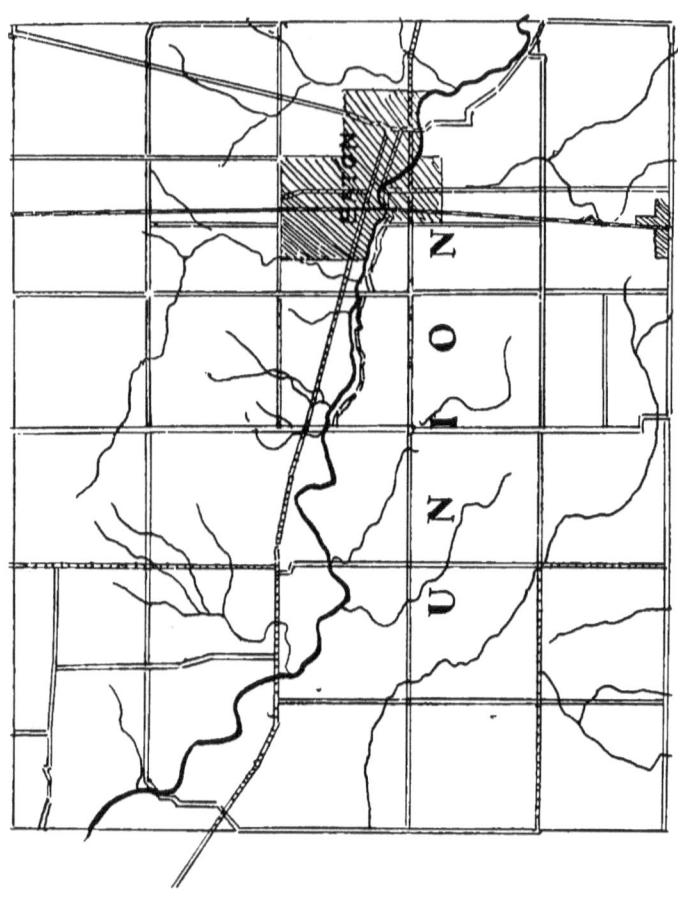

RALPH S. GREGORY,
Attorney at Law, Muncie, Ind.

## WHEN "PHIL." AND I MET.

[TO P. L., ROYERTON, IND.]

Say, "Phil," do you remember the time
   We met 'neath the forest boughs?
When you was hunting the old roan mare
   And I was hunting the cows?

That was nearly fifty years ago,
   Yet I remember it well.
And how you placed your ear to the ground
   To catch the sound of the bell.

We had no introduction, "Phil,"
   No meaningless words, and bows,
When you was hunting the old roan mare
   And I was hunting the cows.

I've wandered through halls of Congress, "Phil,"
   And listened to music rare,
But I'll never forget the boy I met,
   Who was hunting the "old roan mare."

The friendships made 'neath the forest shade
   Are fresh in my memory still,
Though the castles I reared, have disappeared,
   Since I hunted the cows with "Phil."

The clothes we wore, were not from the store
   Of a fashionable tailor, I vow,
But you and I know that fashion and show
   Never found a "roan mare," nor a cow,

And now, friend "Pnil,', as we pass down the hill,
   May we keep up our "hunting" no less,
And if we shall find a contented mind,
   Our lives will have been a success.

# Union Township.

Union township is the north township in the center tier, or district No. 2. In dimensions it is five miles north and south, and six miles east and west, containing thirty sections, and in round numbers 19,200 acres of land. The township is bounded, north, by a portion of Blackford county; east, by Niles township; south, by Hamilton, and west, by Washington.

The Mississinewa river enters the township on the east, about one mile north of the southeast corner, and flowing through the township at an angle of about twenty-five degrees north of west, leaves it almost a half mile south of the northwest corner, thus dividing the township in nearly equal parts. In former years, and before the waters of this river became polluted by the offals of manufactures located farther up the stream, the Mississinewa, through this township, was noted for its beautiful scenery, clear waters and fine fish. The land along the river is a series of rolling bluffs, low enough to be easily accessible, and high enough to be pretty, while back from the river, on either side, the land becomes somewhat low and flat, and before drainage became so universal, were considered wet lands. However, at present, and in fact for a number of years past, artificial drainage has become so general, and these lands being ditched have become the most productive, and, consequently, the most valuable lands of the township.

Union was originally covered with heavy forests of the several varieties of oak, hickory, walnut, poplar, etc., on the high lands along the river, and elm, ash and other varieties on the lower lands. Besides the drainage given the township by the Mississinewa passing through the center, the township is further drained by Pike creek in the southwest part, and several small creeks and branches in the north. The soil of Union does not differ materially from that of the adjoining townships. Black loam, with a substratum of clay, and clay intermixed with sand, are the prevailing features of the soil.

It perhaps sounds strange to the present citizen of Union township, especially of not more than middle age, to read of the former navigation of the Mississinewa river. However, it is a fact that boats for carrying freight were built and sent down the river loaded with the products of the country along the stream as early as 1838, and for a number of years afterward. The first of these voyages we have any account of was made in 1838 by Jacob Gump and Joseph Snider. Their vessel was not fashioned after the model of our Trans-Atlantic steamships, nor was it so commodious or comfortable as our modern floating palaces on the Hudson, the Mississippi or the Ohio rivers.

The boat of these early settlers was a flat-boat, fifty or perhaps sixty feet in length, four feet wide and three feet deep. On this was placed one hundred barrels of flour, two barrels of lard, three barrels of linseed oil, together with a quantity of bacon, coon skins, ginseng, and in fact anything the settlers could gather up that would bring cash in the market to which the craft was bound, which in this case was Peru, Indiana, some sixty miles down the river, and a short distance below where the Mississinewa empties into the Wabash river. The pilot of this boat was one Abraham Gray, who was supposed to know the river, although we do not suppose he had a regular United States license, as pilots are now required to hold before being allowed to take charge of the steering apparatus of a boat.

The crew consisted of four men, each of whom manned an oar. The trip down was supposed to consume two days, and as it was not considered safe to navigate at night, the boat was tied fast to a tree, the crew went ashore and cooked and ate their supper, rolled up in their blankets and slept until morning, when, after a hearty breakfnst, they would resume their voyage. Reaching their journey's end, they sold their cargo for cash, sold their boat to some one who wished to proceed still farther down the river, made what purchases they could carry, and then started for home on foot, where they would arrive in two or three days, to the delight of waiting wives and children, and the envied of all the neighboring boys. And why not? Had they not been on a long voyage and had safely returned?

Among others who ventured their hard earnings on the river in flat-boats was John Black, who found his first flour market, the product of his mill above Granville in Delaware township, at Peru and points along the river. This process of marketing was kept up until late in the forties, when the big feeder dam was placed across the river near Peru, which put an end to navigation above that point.

So far as we have been able to gather the facts, the first school ever taught in Union township was by Miss Susan Handley, in a cabin which stood on the southeast quarter of section 24, then owned by Junius McMillan, and now owned by F. R Foorman. This school was taught by Miss Handley in the winter months of 1836 and 1837, sixty-two years ago. Her salary was contributed by six of the citizens who were patrons of the school; these were Wilson Martin, Junius McMillan, William Essley, Philip Stoner, Aaron Mote and Francis Harris, who paid $1.50 for each pupil he sent.

In 1837 a log house was built on the land then owned by Aaron Mote, now by D. A. Barley, on the northeast quarter of section 23. This house was built especially for school purposes and was perhaps the first school house in the township. During the winter following (1837) William Campbell taught school in the new school house. During the same winter (1837 and '38) Robert Wharton taught school in a cabin on the northeast quarter of the northwest quarter of section 19, on the land of Havilla Green. This forty acre tract is now owned by Liberty Ginn, and lies one mile west of school house No. 6. This was the first house known as the "Green school house."

About this time the township was divided into school districts, but the expenses of the schools were still paid by the citizens who patronized the schools, and this condition prevailed until 1840, when the first money obtained, from the sale of section 16, became available, and while the public fund thus created was sufficient to meet the current expenses, public education was as free as under the present system, but this fund was limited, and nearly every year became exhausted before the close of the term, in which case it was usual for the patrons to subscribe prorata of their individual means for the purpose of meeting the expenses of the school to the end of the term. But the new system which was inaugerated in 1852 marked an important epoch in the history of public education in Union township, and instead of the meager advantages that characterized the schools prior to that date, a course of study was adopted that was calculated to prepare the student for any ordinary business in life. And about this time a standard of qualification was established, and teachers were selected after a rigid examination. Union is now divided into eleven school districts, and in each of these is a modern brick building for school purposes which would have appeared a palace to the pupil of the thirties and forties.

In 1836 David Shilder entered the east half of the southeast quarter of section 15, in Union township, but subsequently sold it to John B. Babb. Mr. Babb was one of those handy men who could turn his hand to various kinds of work besides clearing land and farming, and, in 1841, while engaged in walling a well for a Mr. William Tippin, who lived on the northeast quarter of section 15, on land entered by Joshua Shideler, in 1835, a stone accidently fell from the top of the well thirty-six feet, striking Mr. Babb on the head, fracturing the skull, from the effect of which he lay unconscious for six days, but finally recovered and lived many years afterwards, a useful citizen to the community.

The first mill built in the township, and in fact one of the first in the county, was built by Francis Harris on the west half of the northwest quarter of section 25, Mr. Harris having purchased the land of the government on February 16, 1831. This first mill was crude in construction, the building being of round logs, and the mill-stones or buhrs being dressed out of "nigger heads," which were and still are found in abundance all along the river. For a bolting chest a hollow sycamore log did duty, and a harmonious crudeness characterized all the departments. Mr. Harris continued in the milling business for some eight or nine years, when he sold out to Frederick Carter, Caleb Carter and Thomas Johnson. About 1847 the firm of Carter & Johnson erected a frame building on the same site, in which they placed two run of buhrs and a sash, or perpendicular saw, for sawing

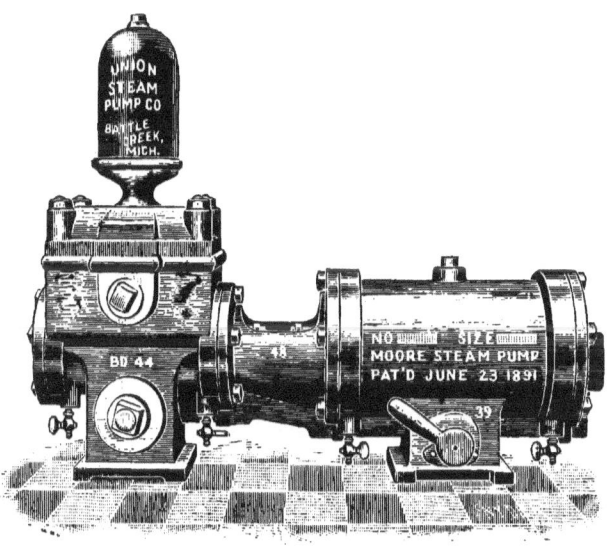

GEO. KEISER & CO., S. HIGH STREET.

EATON PARK,

CHAS. BROWN, Manager.

An ideal place for Sunday School and Society picnics. Splendid scenery, good boating, bathing and fishing. Go once and you'll go again. Open day and night.

GEO. R. MANSFIELD,            CHAS. GOUGH,
Clerk Delaware County Circuit Court.      County Surveyor.

lumber, for which there began to be a great demand. Shortly after the erection of this mill, the firm sold out to Charles and Gerge Carter, and soon after this transaction the mill was destroyed by fire. The Carter Brothers rebuilt their mill at once on the same site and operated it successfully for a number of years, in fact until one of the firm (George) died, when his brother Charles purchased his deceased brother's interest, extended the race some distance farther west, erected a new saw-mill, and afterwards a four-story flouring mill. The mill is located in the southern part of Eaton, and is known as the Carter mill, a monument to the enterprise and industry of one of Union's oldest citizens. About 1845 David Studebaker erected a saw-mill on the west half of the southeast quarter of section 22, just below the point where the Studebaker pike crosses the Mississinnewa river. By turns this mill was converted into a flouring, carding, and finally general woolen manufacturing mills.

The first church organization we have any account of was at the residence of John Ginn, who came to the township in January 1830. Mr. Ginn was a native of Ireland, emigrating first to Pennsylvania, from thence to Morgan county, Ohio, and from there to Delaware county, Ind., where he spent the remainder of his life, a well respected and honored citizen. The church organization referred to occurred about 1833, when seven or eight adherents to the tenets of the denomination, under the pastoral labors of Rev. Robert Burnes, were united as a class of the Methodist Episcopal church. At nearly the same time, another class of the same denomination, was organized at the cabin of Tristram Starbuck, who was one of the first settlers, and who made the second entry of land in the township. Mr. Starbuck lived in section 22, and Mr. Ginn in 18, so it only being some two or three miles from one of these class headquarters to the other, they eventually united, and Richard Craw, one of the members, donated a lot of ground from his farm, upon which they built a log church, and named it "Mount Zion."

Among the early prominent members of this church were Martin Brandt and wife, James Rutherford and wife, John Gorthop and wife, Leonard Cline and wife, Phillip Keller and wife, Richard, William and John Craw and their wives, Mr. and Mrs. Tristram Starbuck and Mrs. Isaac Cox. The log church, "Mount Zion," continued to serve the purpose of worship until 1867, it was superceeded by the present brick edifice.

The Christian church of Eaton grew out of an organization formed at the home of Robert Long, east of Eaton, in 1839 or '40. Like most church meetings, this organization first met at the cabin homes of the settlers, then at school houses., in summer time when the weather would permit, in the groves.

Among the early ministers of this church were Ebenezer Thompson, Elder Montford, Amos Wilson, George H. Babb, Benjamin Martindale, Samuel Hendricks, Elijah Martindale and Thomas Wiley. In 1858 Charles Carter donated to the society the lot on which was built the Eaton Christian church.

The German Baptist church was organized in 1840 at the home of Jacob Gump, just south of the present town of Eaton, where their meetings were held for a number of years. In 1855 they bought a lot of James Long on the east half of the southeast quarter of section 23, and south side of the river, and in the same year erected a substantial frame house for worship.

Union township has but one town and a half, all of Eaton and half of Shideler are in this township. Eaton dates back to 1870, when the railroad from Muncie to Ft Wayne was completed, but was incorporated in 1873. The population in that year was one hundred and fifty-eight.

Although a comparatively new place, yet Eaton will be noted in history for many generations as the pioneer gas town of Indiana. Early in the fall of 1886 the first gas well in Indiana was drilled in at Eaton. This well was about forty or fifty feet east of the railroad, and a few hundred feet south of the river.

Several years prior to this date, W. W. Worthington, then superintendent of the Ft. Wayne and Southern Railroad, together with George W. Carter, a business man of Eaton, concluded to drill at this point for the purpose of ascertaining if there was not a strata of coal underlying this territory, but after sinking their drill several hundred feet, struck gas, but did not know what they had found; but from the roaring noise produced by escaping gas, and the stench of the same, concluded that they were perhaps encroaching on the territory of his satanic majesty, and at once abandoned their project. However, in after years when gas had been discovered in the country about Findlay, Ohio, and excursions were made to see the wonderful discovery, Mr. Carter being on one of these excursions, at once recognized the important fact that it was nothing more nor less than natural gas that he and Mr. Worthington had drilled into, and at once commenced work, reopened their former operations, and in doing so opened the way to the most grand results of any discovery ever made in this or any other country. And now the hundreds of factories, and thousands of operatives and armies of laborers look to the unpretentious village of Eaton as the starting point of their great success.

The first land ever bought of the government in Union

## UNION TOWNSHIP.

township was purchased by Nimrod Jester on the 7th day of May, 1829 (80 acres), being the west half of the southwest quarter of section 22, and now owned by William Cox. Six months and six days after this purchase, or on the 13th day of November of the same year, the second entry in the township was made by Tristram Starbuck, it being also 80 acres, and the west half of the northwest quarter of the same section and joining Mr. Jester's entry on the north. Thus it will be seen that the ouly land entered in Union township prior to 1830 was 160 acres, a strip one mile long, north and south, and eighty rods wide, east and west, with the Mississinewa river crossing near the center.

Many adventures were had by the early settlers of this as well as other localities, which have never been given the public through print. One, which now occurs to our mind, was that of Jackson Green, then a young pioneer hunter. Mr. Green was out deer hunting, and his dogs coming close onto a large buck near the Mississinewa river, just above the Carter dam, the deer being pretty well run down, and perhaps thinking that he could the better defend himself, took to the water. Mr. Green coming up feared to shoot for fear of killing one of his dogs, they being in the water around the deer. So, leaving his gun on shore, he started to the assistance of his dogs, and the deer started for him, he caught the deer by the antlers and a desperate conflict ensued, the deer rearing and striking at him with its sharp hoofs, and he in turn endeavoring to drown the buck by twisting his head and throwing him on his back and drowning him, which he finally succeeded in doing after sever attempts, and when almost in despair, wishing all the time that some one would come along to "help him let go."

The first land entered in section 7 in Union township was the west half of the southwest quarter. This entry was made by John Ginn on May 1, 1830, and the last entry in the section was made by John Reasoner on October 9, 1835. The others entering land between these dates, in this section, were Josiah McVicker, William Jobes, Isaac Swisher and John Hamilton.

The present land owners in section 7 are Eli H. Roderick, J. W. McVicker, William Craw. M. E. Waters, E. M. Stiffler, E. Johnson, M. Butcher, J. E. Edwars, (trustee) and Liberty Ginn.

The section has a public road east and west through the north half, and another along a part of the south line. The Mississinewa river crosses the southwest corner of the section in a northwest course.

There were no entries recorded in section 8 until October 23, 1833. The original purchasers of this section were Leonard Cline, John Seekors, John Reasoner, Jr., Nathaniel and Henry Skinner, James Chenowith and Isaac Swisher. The land owners of this section are now W. H. Pursley, Eli H. Roderick, J. W. Long, O. P. Dunn, D. Smith, Sr,, J. R. McVicker, E. Roderick, G. Waters and William Craw. The section has a gravel pike along the east line, also public roads on the south line across the north half, and three-fourths of the way across the west half. School No. 5 is in the southwest quarter of this section.

Section 9 was entered in 1835, '36 and '37 by John W. Pyke, Isaac Miller, Ashford Roberts, John Flummer, William Adsit, John Reasoner, Sr., and Letice Shideler.

The present owners of section 9 are E. Holden, H. Smith, W. H. Pursley, M. M. Barnes and Isabel Adsit. This section has a gravel pike along the west line, and public roads on the east and south.

Section 10 was all taken up in 1836, Jacob Shideler entered the southeast quarter May 23, 1836, Jacob Gayman the north half September 20, 1836 and William Adsit the southwest quarter November 21, 1836.

The section is now owned by H. Strong, Jonathan Smith's heirs, J. Lambert, P. W. Dunn, W. and M. Haynes and H. Smith.

Section 10 has public roads on the east, south and west lines. The Smith ditch crosses the southwest quarter, running south of east.

Section 11 was also entirely purchased of the government in the year of 1836 by John Lambert, John Gayman, Abraham Gray, Abraham Shideler, Archibald Ray and Daniel Haynes. The last named gentleman, Mr. Haynes, is still living in his old neighborhood, a true specimen of the old pioneer. He has perhaps seen as many "ups and downs" of pioneer life as any man in the state, and is now living a quiet, retired life, well known and respected by a large circle of friends.

This section is now owned by J. L. Lambert, A. Campbell, W. Campbell, Alexander Dunn, O. Campbell, M. Jester, G. Haynes, B. F. Haynes, M. L. McGrath, S. A. Haynes, and J. Martin. Section 11 has public roads on the east, south and west lines. The L. E. & W. railroad passes through the section about thirty-five rods east of the center, and school house No. 2 is situated in the southeast corner of the section.

Section 12 is the northeast section of the township and its lands were entered in the years of 1835–36 and '37 by Ephraim Link, William Shearon, Aaron Mote, Patrick Carmichael and John Lambert.

This section (12) is generally divided into small farms, there being some sixteen owners of land in the section. They

## UNION TOWNSHIP

are E. Blazier, W. R. Toll, G. W. Bosman, S. J. Peck, A. and P. Carmichael, J. L. Lambert, S. J. Guthrie, N. S. Gothrup, P. Schetgen, J. L. Ferguson, W. W. Holdren, Lewis T. Bosman, O. and S. Carmichael, and G. W. Blodgett.

The section has public roads on the south and west, and the old Fort Wayne road crosses the section at an angle of about fifteen degrees east of north.

Section 13, lying south of 12 and adjoining Niles township on the east (as also does section 12), was entered in 1836, except three 80-acre tracts that had been entered the previous year by John McLain, Archibald McLain, and William Ray. Those buying in 1836 were John McLain, Aaron Mote, and Samuel Mote. The section is owned at this time (sixty-four years after the first title was given) by G. W. McLain, Charles McLain, P. Schetgen, R. and H. McLain, S. Scott, S. Younce, D. P. Orr, E. and S. Morris, L E. Wasson, E. S. Babb, and A. N. Foorman. Thirteen is surrounded by public roads, with the old Fort Wayne road angling across the eastern part.

In 1835 Hiram Cochran and Peter Shideler each secured an 80-acre tract in section 14. Then during the following year, 1836, Mr. Shideler entered another 80, John Van Buskirk an 80, Abraham Shideler 240, and David Shideler an 80, which consumed all the land in the section.

Fourteen is now owned by J. K. Cochran, R Cochran, M. L. Brandt, A. S. Chitty, J. L. Martin, D. Brandt, M. J. Morris, H. Holmes, H. E. McLain, B. McLain. D. Haines, and John Babb.

This section lies north of and adjoining the town of Eaton. It has public roads on each section line, and also north and south through the center One of the land owners of this section who now lives in Eaton, and is engaged in merchandising, we think should be mentioned in this connection, for a history of Union township, without mention of David Brandt would be incomplete. Mr. Brandt is not only a pioneer of the township, but may well be considered one of the pioneer business men of the county, and one of the oldest, if not the very oldest, merchants, in the county. He was engaged in business a half mile east of where Eaton is (at "Hen Peck") long before there was any Eaton, is now over eighty years old and still actively engaged in business. Mr. Bandt came to Union township nearly sixty years ago and has been a leader in all things pertaining to the interests of the community ever since.

Section 15 was entered in 1836, with the exception of one 80-acre tract taken up by Joshua Shideler, in July, 1835. The persons securing the lands in this section were Joshua

Shideler, Abraham Shideler, David Shideler, Peter Shideler, Benjamin Harris, Sarah Rardon, and Nancy Rardon.

The title to the lands in 15 is now held by Robert L. Brandt, F. J. Carter, H. Smith, W. S. Bell, J. S. Clouse, D. Babb, M. O'Conner, and E. Taylor. Section 15 has a public road on each section line.

Adjoining section 15 on the west is school section 16, which was sold on November 11, 1836, to three individuals, as follows: Caleb Sharon bought the northeast quarter at $2.50 per acre, the east half of the southeast quarter at $2.00 per acre, the west half of the southeast quarter at $2.50 per acre; Mr. William Adsit bought the southwest quarter at $4.00 per acre, and John Craw bought the northwest quarter at $2.25 per acre, the entire section thus bringing the sum of $1,760. The owners of land in 16 at this time are J. T. Nottingham, W. A Michael, R. Walters, Carrie Adsit, H. Holdren and William Cox.

Section 16 has public roads on the east and north lines, a gravel pike on the west and the Albany and Jonesboro pike touches the southwest corner. School house No. 3 is located in the northeast corner of the section.

Section 17 was entered in the years 1833 to 1837. The persons securing the public domain in this section were Samuel Skinner, William Craw, Elizabeth Flummer, Maria Sarah Flummer, Richard Craw, Samuel Lyle Black and Elijah Collins.

The freeholders of Section 17 are now O. P. Dunn, J. R. McVicker, H. and H. Crow, H. Meyer, R. E. Craw and Jesse Nixon. This section has free gravel pikes on the east and south, public roads on the north and north and south through the west half. The Mississinewa River crosses the southwest corner of the section. All the balance of the section lies on the north side of the river.

Section 18 joins Washington township on the west, and lies east of the village of Wheeling one mile Eighteen was an early settled section. The first entry in this section was made by John Ginn on November 30, 1830. This was the east half of the northwest quarter. Mr. Ginn made subsequent entries in the section in 1832 and 1833. However, the last of the public land in section 18 was not entered until May 26, 1836. The persons besides John Ginn securing land in this section: were David Ashby, Havillah Green, John W. Harter and Liberty and Joseph Ginn.

There are but three land owners at present in this section, and all are well known throughout the county. They are R. E. Crow, Jesse Nixon and Liberty Ginn.

Eighteen has a pike crossing the south and southwest part, a public road along a portion of the north and also

## UNION TOWNSHIP.

across the northwest corner. The Mississinewa crosses the northeast corner, cutting off about one-third of the section.

Section 19 lies south of 18 and also joins Washington township on the west. Its lands were entered in 1833-'35-'36 and '37 by Havillah Green, Sarah Ginn, John W. Harter, Moses Hinton, Reason Tiffin and Thomas and George (Jr.) Carter.

The land of this section is owned at present by Jesse Nixon, Liberty Ginn, M. E. Turner, C. L. Johnson, M. Thompson, Andrew Johnson and W. Spitler. Nineteen has public roads on the east, south and west. Also the Albany pike on the northeast corner where is located school house No. 6.

Section 20, just east of and joining 19, is another river section all of which seem to have had an attraction for the first settlers. Twenty was entered in the years of 1832 to '36 by Wm. Flummer, Elijah Collins, Richard Craw, John Flummer, Charles Royster, minor heir of Charles Royster, Sr., Daniel Cochran and George Comstock. Changes of title have taken place from time to time until at present section 20 is owned by D. Geyer, M. Craw, R. E. Craw, G. W. Collins, J. G. Delong, S. Barrick and M. A. Delong. Twenty is surrounded by good roads, and the Mississinewa crosses the northwest corner.

East of 20 is section 21, which was entered in 1832, to 1836, inclusive, by Wm. Cox, Isaac Cox, Samuel Wilson, Jacob Shideler, Jesse Lincomb and Peter Grimes. The owners of this section are now Wm. Cox, I. J. Hunt, Carrie Adsit, J. U. Studebaker and Joseph W. Younce. Twenty-one has a good supply of good roads, and is well drained by the Mississinewa, crossing the north half of the section.

We have already mentioned the fact that the two first entries of land made in Union township were both in section 22, by Nimrod Jester and Tristram Starbuck. These were both made in 1826. The balance of the section was entered in 1830, '31, '32, '33, '34 and '36, by John Essley, Abraham Zemar, Samuel Elliott, James Harter and James Galbreath.

The present land owners of section 22 are J. and R. Dragoo, J. L. Minnick, M. Highland, J. A. Thomas, A. Rench, J. Evans, J. S. Kirkwood and William Cox. This section has six miles of public road, there being one on each section line, and two passing through the section east and west, one on either side of the Mississinewa river, which crosses the section near the center in a north of west direction.

Section 23 was taken up in the years of 1833 and 1836, inclusive. The parties first purchasing the lands in this section were Abraham Shideler, Washington Heldren, John

Irvin, Absalom Edwards, Reuben Hampton, Isaac Edwards, Samuel Kite, Ochmig Bird, Benjamin Harris and James Harter. The present owners of land in section 23 outside of the corporation of the town of Eaton are E. N. Clouse, J. S. Clouse, J. Pixley and J. and R. Dragoo. However, as the amount of land owned by these parties and lying in section 23 is only 194 acres, it will be seen that the town of Eaton covers more than two-thirds of the section, and we have neither space nor data for giving the names of all the owners of realty in the thriving young city of Eaton. The Mississinewa river crosses the southwest portion of the section. School No. 1 is in the town of Eaton, and the German Baptist or Dunkard church is in the southwest quarter of the section.

Section 24 is the center of the township north and south, and in the east tier of sections. The lands of the section were entered in 1831, '32, '34 and '35, by William McCalister in 1831, by Junius McMillan in 1832, George and William Shearon in 1834, and Aaron Mote and James McMillan in 1835. The corporation of the town of Eaton now covers the southwest quarter of the section, while the other three-quarters are owned by D. A. Barley, M. Long, Wm. H. Propps, R. M Carter, M. Babb, Mississinewa Land and Improvement Co., and F. R. Foorman.

Section 25, lying south of 24, and joining Niles township on the east was entered by William Essley in 1830, Francis Harris in 1831, Reason Iams in 1832. Jacob Shideler, Roland Hughes and Mary James in 1833, and James B. Harter in 1836. About 28 acres, or that part of the section in the northwest quarter and lying north of the river, is also claimed by the town of Eaton, while the other lands of the section are owned by W. Peterson, H. Metcalf, G. W. Carter's heirs, William Bost and David Gump. The Mississinewa river enters this section a short distance north of the southeast corner and leaves it about the same distance south of the northwest corner, thus dividing the section into two almost equal right angle triangles. The Leard Cemetery is located in the southwest corner of the east half of the southeast quarter of the section.

Section 26, lying west of 25, was entered in 1833, '35 and 36, by Joseph Batreall, Jacob Gump, Joseph Snider, Hannah Studebaker, James Bowman, John Meek and William Mendenhall. About one-half of the northeast quarter of this section (the north part) is also within the corporate limits of Eaton. The other parts of the section are owned by the Eaton Land and Improvement Co., J. Pixley, S. Lamar, David Gump, S. and E. Smith, Mary Younce, S. R. Smith and R, Brandt et, al. The section is well supplied with public roads, and has the L. E. & W. railroad crossing it north

## UNION TOWNSHIP. 85

and south near the center. School No. 11 (also a church) is situated in the southwest corner of the section.

Section 27 was all entered in 1836 and 1837, except the east half of the northeast quarter (80 acres), which was entered by David Studebaker on the 27th day of October, 1835. The others entering land in the section were James Galbreath, Mary Ann McCormick, James Frazer, Philip Hedrick, Jesse Lincome, Emelie Galbreath and William Lewis. This section is owned at present (1899) by J. Garrard, H. Wittemyer, J. Evans, J. S. Kirkwood, J. H. Shoup, J. V. Studebaker, William Frazee, I Custer, W. and M. Gump et al., Robt. L. Brandt and C. T. Bartlett. The Studebaker pike is on the east line, and there are public roads on the north, south and west.

Section 28 was all entered by four entries, as follows: James Frazer entered the northeast quarter June 4, 1836, and on August 6 of the same year he entered the southeast quarter. The first of these entries is now owned by William Frazee and D. S. Rench, and the last, or southwest quarter, by John Evans. The northwest quarter of the section was entered on May 27, 1836, in the name of Virginia Royster, minor heir of Charles Royster, and on the same day the southwest quarter was entered in the name of Nancy, minor heir of Charles Royster. The present owners of that part of the section entered by the two heirs of Mr. Royster are G. R. Mansfield, F. Kiplinger and E. Younce. School No. 8 is located on the north side of this section at the half section line, and the section is surrounded by a public road on each line.

In 1834 James Love and Matthew Smith each entered 80 acres in section 29, and in the following year (1835) there were two 80-acre tracts entered by John Fipper. Then, in 1836, the remaining four 80-acre tracts were entered by Charles Royster, Jr., minor heir of Charles Royster, Sr., Johathan Jones two 80's, and James Love another 80. This section is now divided into small farms, owned by W. S. Isgrig, S. J. Duke, S. Duke, R. C. Wisehart, Union National Bank of Muntie, L. Miller. M. Rarrick, Snider and McKinley S. Rarrick, J. and A. Miller, N. A. Riggin and J. E. Smith. The seetion has a road on each section line, and Pike creek crosses it in a northwesterly course.

The northeast quarter of the northeast quarter of section 30 (40 acres) was entered on September 25, 1835, by Matthew Smith, and all the remainder of the section was entered during the following year (1836) by Matthew R. Smith, John J. Adsit, William Martin and Jonathan Jones.

The present land owners in section 30 are Union National Bank of Muncie, B. Studebaker, T. Hedgeland, Andrew

86   HISTORY OF DELAWARE COUNTY.

Johnson, A. J. Clifford, L. M. Hinton, C. Johnson, H. Wood and M. Williams. This section also has a public road on each section line. The west line is the township line between Union and Washington. School house No. 7 is in the southeast corner of the section.

Section 31 is the southwest corner of the township. The public lands in this section were purchased of the general government in the years of 1835 to 1838 by Stephen Dunlap, Eliza Wildy Wilson, William Adsit, William Daily, John W Stafford, Thomas Williams, and Joseph Wilson, Jr., and are now owned by A. Johnson, E. Shields, William Carroll, W. Fine, D. S. Rarrick, Eli Snider, F. A. Waller, S. F. Woodring, J. Wilhelm, G. Monroe, J. Rench and S. Rench. The section has a free gravel pike along the north line, and public roads on the east and south.

The west half of the northwest quarter of section 32 (80 acres) was entered on the 14th day of December, 1835, by Stephen Dunlap, and the balance of the section was entered in 1836 by the same man and Robert Huston, Willis Hance, Isaac Mendenhall, and John W. Stafford. The section is owned at present by C. F. Eiler, W. A. Brinson, D. M Shoemaker, D. M. Snider, J. B. Rench, Snider and McKinley, John Snider, and F. A. Waller. Thirty-two has a gravel road on both the east and north lines, and public roads on the west and south.

Aside from one 80 and one 30-acre tract that were entered in section 33 in 1835, the section was entered in 1836. The first owners of land in the section were William Mendenhall, John Houston, Vincent Martin, Samuel Martin, Abraham C. Culbertson, Nicholas Sherry, and Simeon Maxson. Section 33 is also a section of small farms, no one person owning more than 80 acres in the section. The owners of this section are A. Harkle, A. Russell, G. Russell, R. Hest, Snider et al., C. F. Eiler, F. Waller, I. H. Shideler, N. and R, Minnick, G. L. Calvert et al , John Snider and S. Studebaker. Good roads surround the section. There is a Baptist church located on the northwest quarter, and school house No. 9 on the southwest.

There were no entries of public lands in section 34 until 1836, in which year the entire section was entered, except two 40-acre tracts, both of these being entered the following year (1837). The original land owners in 34 were David Sherry (father of ex-Sheriff William Sherry), Eli H. Ross, Daniel Sherry, Thomas Ewell, James Egnew, Israel Martin, Elizabeth Martin, and Vincent Martin. None of the original owners' names are now found in the section, the present owners being A. Studebaker, J. A. Frazee, W. Snitzer, M.

Snitzer, A. C. Young, A. Miller, A. Snider, G. Cruea, W. H. Taylor, C. A. Manor and William Brown.

Section 35 was also settled in 1836 and 1837. Its lands were first purchased by John Gregory, Maitsell M. Cary, Harvey Millspaugh, George Pyke, David Sherry, Thomas McCormick, Joseph S. Austin, Sarah Simonton, Joseph Hance, Michael Thomas, Solomon McKee, and William Sleeth. Michael Thomas entered the northeast quarter of the southeast quarter (40 acres), lying just north of the present village of Shideler, on the 20th day of January, 1837. Mr. Thomas is at present a citizen of the village of Granville, in Niles township, where he is engaged in selling groceries. A man in his eighties, though hale and hearty still, a splendid entertainer, and one who loves a joke and knows how to tell one to get the most out of it. Section 35 is owned by J. Cunkle, T. Leard, Mary Younce, J. A. Frazee, W. Saunders, M. Cruea, M. Darton, A. L. Lewellen, A. Darton, L. Cruea, and E. M. Rairigh. The section has four miles of good road, the L. E. & W. railroad crosses it, and one-half of the village of Shideler is within its borders.

Section 36, the southeast section of the township, was entered in 1833, '34, '35, and '36 by William Gregory, Ephraim Laird, Peter R. Bradshaw, Samuel Payton, George Laird, Nancy Egnew and William Guthrey. The present owners are I. C. Goodrich, S. Laird, W. Peterson, J. R. Simonton, T. G. Gibson, S. and C. Deeter, J. Cunkle and M. Swearengen. The section is well provided with roads. School No. 10 is in the northwest corner. The section has two post-office towns within one and two-third miles of its borders.

We love to revisit the old cabin for-sooth,
And recall the days of our childhood and youth,
   When my sweetheart and I were young,
When she was a "lass" and I was a "lad,"
Oh, the good old-fashioned times we had,
   The good old songs we sung.

We smile when we look at the logs in the wall
Remembering the time when receiving a call,
   (Or, rather, "invite," we should say),
To "come to our raisin'," whatever you do;
Tell "Dick" to come also, and "Polly" and "Sue,"
   The "gals" have a "quiltin'" that day.

To the "raisin'" we went and cleared off the ground,
The cabin was raised to the very last round ;
   The quilt was quilted and done,
Then swung to the joists quite out of the way,
Just to give room for the sport and the play,
   And thus we enjoyed our fun.

And then we remember the old "huskin' bee,"
And "Oh, Sister Phoebe, how merry were we,"
   And other old plays of the kind ;
Oh, jolly old times! Oh, jolly old days!
And the jolly sweet kisses that come in the plays
   The cabin brings fresh to our mind.

No wonder that old folks love to come
To a place representing their childhood's home
   Of youthful, innocent joys,
It gives us pleasure to watch and trace
The smile steal over the care-worn face
   Of those dear old "girls" and "boys."
                            —Ellis.

# Hamilton Township.

Hamilton township is in the center tier of townships, or what is known as district No. 2, the county being laid off into three districts, each comprising a tier of townships (4) running north and south, and each district represented by one county commissioner. Hamilton in dimensions is five by six sections, or miles. It is bounded on the north by Union township, on the east by Liberty, on the south by Center, and on the west by Harrison. The surface of Hamilton is generally level, save in the southeast portion of the township, where it is slightly rolling. But about the only places in Hamilton township worthy of the name of hills, even in this level country, are in sections 24, 23, 22, 15 and 16. The soil is uniformly fertile, being composed of a rich admixture of clay and loam, well worthy the name of a good "mulatto" soil, and well adapted to the growing of the field crops and fruits of this latitude. Hamilton has no water course of any magnitude, yet the township is fairly well drained by small creeks, which various acts of legislature has permitted our enterprising citizens to ditch until all the land of Hamilton has become not only tillable, but very productive. The timber of this township was much the same as those heretofore mentioned, consisting of the several varieties of oak, ash, hickory, maple, beech and walnut, with sassafras on the high lands and undergrowth of prickley ash and spice brush on the more level lands.

As to the first settlers in this township we know very little, aside from what we may learn from the tract book of entries of public lands. The first entry of land in the township was made October 21, 1829, by Owen Russell, grandfather of Isaiah Russell, grocer, now of Muncie. Mr. Russell, coming to Hamilton at that time, found a settler on the land he entered by the name of Boggs, and traded him a yoke of oxen for the improvements he had made before going to the land office and proving his title, but we have no way of ascertaining when Mr. Boggs came to the township. The land he settled on was the southeast quarter of section 26, now owned by Milton Hamilton. The northwest corner of this quarter is crossed by the Muncie and Granville pike, about three miles out from Muncie. Prairie creek crosses this (southeast) corner of the towdship, draining sections 24, 25 and 26. Kilbuck also has its source in section 24, running entirely across the township in a north of west course. Mud creek also crosses the township almost parallel with Kilbuck, with which it forms a junction near the west line of the township. Jakes creek drains the southwest portion and Pikes creek has its

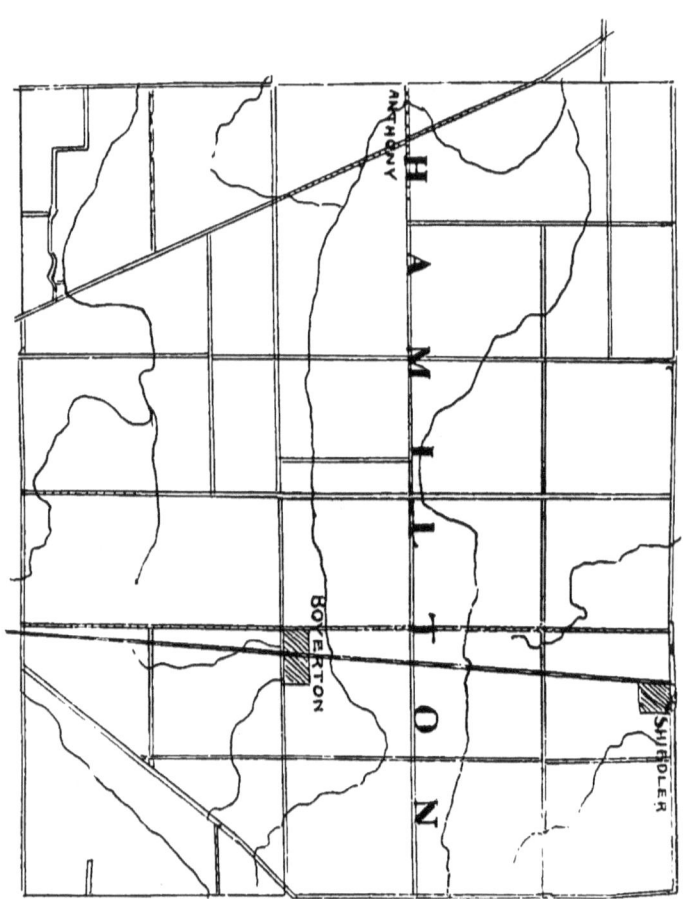

headquarters in the northern part of the township.  Every one of the thirty sections of land in Hamilton township is drained by some of these several creeks or their tributaries.

Hamilton township seems to have settled up rather slowly at first, as after Mr. Russell entered his land in section 26 it was almost a year until there was any other entries recorded, and then but two. This was on October 2, 1830, when Adam Shafer entered land in section 22 and Peter Williamson in section 25. These two pioneers were brothers-in-law, of the hardy, honest and industrious type, the kind of men who have made Delaware county to stand in the front rank among the counties of the Union. These two lived to raise large, respected families of children, and to enjoy the fruits of their early labor for many years, and their children and grandchildren still own and occupy the early home of their honored parents.

In 1831 there was only nine eighty acre tracts entered in the township, four of them being in section 24, one in 25 and four in 26. Thus far the settlements seems to have been entirely confined to the southeastern portion of the township.

As late as 1840 there were, according to the tax duplicate, but 118 freeholders in Hamilton township, and among these there were a number of non-residents who had purchased land for speculation. The heaviest tax-payer in the township in that year (1830, fifty-nine years ago) was Stephen R. Martin, whose total taxes were $24.11. The next was Stephen Davis, $15.72; then came Nathan Dean, $12.90; Joseph Gared $12.10. Then came Philip Leffler, (the father of Philip Leffler near Royerton and grandfather of the Hon. Joseph G. Leffler), whose taxes were $8.99. The lowest on the list was Robert Arnold, whose taxes were 60 cents. The total amount of taxes paid by citizens of Hamilton township in 1840 including real estate, personal and poll was $264.34.

"In a new settlement the occurrences of events that, until then, were without parallel, are marked by an unusual interest and live long in the memory of their witnesses, coming naturally to the surface in a review of the olden times by one of the surviving members of the pioneer community. And, although subsequent events transpiring in the same locality may be of much more consequence and fraught with more important results, they are some times suffered to perish from memory while the first of their kind live through many generations, handed down from father to son, from mother to daughter. This is true in the history of Hamilton township. The date of the first marriage, the first birth of a white child and the first death can be stated accurately. These were, of course, important, as illustrating the dawn of civilization in the wilderness and the introduction into the gloom of customs and events which had their counterparts in the older settled localities from which their participants had come. But equally important events, such as the first election, the officers chosen at that time and other questions affecting the civil existence of the township, seem to have passed out of the memory of the oldest inhabitant. However, the first elections which the writer has any knowledge of were held in the cabin on the southeast quarter of section 15. This land was entered by Archibald Smith in 1833, afterwards owned and occupied by William Wire, then owned by the widow and heirs of Samuel Collier, then Abraham Sheets, and now owned by R. W. Stradling. The cabin stood on the west shore of a rising ground near the foot of the hill or slope not far from a fine spring of water and about fifty rods north of the road running west from Royerton. Here the elections were held until Center school house was built (No. 5) of hewn logs by the settlers in 1850 or '51. And here at this cabin would also assemble the several candidates for the various county offices and discuss the political issues of the day, and get acquainted with the people.

In 1850 to 1853 the writer lived at this cabin with his parents, and he well remembers some of the political gatherings at a beech grove just west of the house.

During one campaign there were a dozen or more candidates for sheriff, and at an appointed day they came to Hamilton township to electioneer the inhabitants who might assemble. On this occasion there were, perhaps, a dozen farmers to hear the candidates talk. We remember the candidates, for they were looked on by us boys as the great men of the community. At this particular meeting we remember Clark McCauley, James Trimbell, Stephen Kennedy and Solomon Barrett as candidates for sheriff. And while some talked, others sat around on logs and listened or interrupted the speaker with questions as they were suggested to their minds. One of the candidates we remember as sitting on his horse during the meeting. He was in his shirt sleeves and bare-foot. He was not elected, the prize being carried off at the election by Clark McCauley.

At one of these meetings is the first time we ever remember seeing our fellow citizen, Mr. Marck C. Smith, who was then a young man and a candidate for member of the legislature.

The first apple orchard in Hamilton was set out by Owen Russell in 1830. This consisted of one hundred seedling trees purchased of a man in Wayne county. Stephen R. Martin and Joel Russell were the first to build brick dwellings in the township early in the forties.

In the year 1832 the dark pall of death was first thrown

PHILLIP LEFFLER,
Pioneer farmer, Royerton, Ind.

HON. JOSEPH G. LEFFLER,
Judge Delaware Circuit Court.

J. H. LEFFLER,
ıty Clerk Delaware Circuit Court.

LEONIDAS A. GUTHRIE,
Court Stenographer, Muncie, Ind.

## HAMILTON TOWNSHIP.

over the settlement by the demise of Charles Hopkins, who came here with the family of Owen Russell, in delicate health, his malady subsequently developing into consumption, from which he died. There being no cemetery then in the township, he was buried at Muncietown. For several years the deceased members of the community were buried on their own or their neighbors' farms. We remember several graves in different localities. There were several (as we now remember in 1850) in the southeast corner of section 15, adjoining the present village of Royerton. At that time these graves were covered with rails, and these were even then quite old and rotten, indicating that the graves had been there for several years. Another group of graves similarly protected were located on the northeast quarter of section 22, and near the northwest corner of that quarter. They were on the south side of where the road running west from Royerton now runs, and nearly a half mile west of that village. But the first cemetery (or grave yard) in the township was deeded to "the clerk of the court, and to his successors forever, for the use of the public as a burial ground" by Thomas Reeves. This deed was executed in 1840. The cemetery was on the southeast quarter of section 24, and a portion of the 80-acre tract now owned and occupied by John Cullen, and is still used for burial purposes. The act which constituted Hamilton a civil township was passed by the commissioners in 1838. However, all records of this first township meeting are lost (if ever made), as the trustee's office contains no records earlier than 1853 The constitution of the state, as revised two years previous, made the keeping of the records obligatory upon the township clerk, and these records have been preserved. The first entry in this volume is a record of a meeting held by the trustees April 11, 1853. The members present were: Stephen R. Martin, Aaron Moore and Jacob H. Slonaker, trustees, and A. J. Green, clerk. Stephen R. Martin was chosen president of the board for a term of three years, and Samuel Strohm (who had been previously elected) took his seat as a member of the board of trustees.

April 16, 1853, the board met pursuant to adjournment, and transacted no further business than to levy a tax of ten cents on each one hundred dollars of taxable property, for township purposes.

At the next meeting, May 20, 1853, we find the first record of money paid for school purposes. William N. Jackson was allowed $41.30 for services as teacher of school in district No. 5 (although other schools had been taught here previous to this. The first school here was taught by Dr. Boyd, then came William Sleeth, then Benjamin Halcomb).

94    HISTORY OF DELAWARE COUNTY.

Money was also disbursed as follows: To John Robinson for services as trustee, $2.00; to George Northcutt for services as township clerk, $9.00; to Jonathan Martin for teaching school in district No. 2, $23.70: to John Hatfield for teaching in district No. 1, $9.10; Jacob H. Slonaker for services as trustee, $1.75; Isaac Shideler, township trustee, $3.20; Isaac Freeman, receiver for Wilson F. Steen, teacher in district No. 4, $18.95: to Stacy A. Hains, teacher in district No. 7, $60; to Isaac Freeman for services as school trustee, $1.25; to John B. Armstrong, $6.00 for extra labor as supervisor: to Seth R. Martin, $1.00; Levi Beal, $4.25; Alexander Snyder, $5.25, and William McCormick, $2.25, for services as supervisors.

Presuming that our readers all know the condition of Hamilton township schools of today, and the cost of maintaining the same, that they may intelligently compare the early days with the present, we compend the following statement of the condition of the public schools of Hamilton township for the year ending on the first Monday of April, 1854, as rendered and filed with the county auditor. Total number of children between the ages of five and twenty-one years, 266: number of males, 140; number of females, 126: number of children who have attended school during the past year, 225; number of males attending school, 123; number of females attending school, 102; average daily attendance, 125.5: number of teachers, 5; number of schools, 5; male teachers, 4; female teachers, 1; average wages of male teachers per month, $19.44⅔; wages of female teacher, $15.33⅓ per month; length of term, 62 days. Amount of expense for instruction during the year, $279.36; amount of public funds appropriated to the township, $318.12; amount charged by township officers for managing the educational affairs, $33. Hamilton has but two villages, Royerton, founded in 1870 by John Royer, and Shideler, founded in 1871 by Isaac Shideler. so for many years Hamilton was a township without a town,

Beginning at the northeast corner of Hamilton township, we find that section No. 1 was all entered in the year 1836, by Jesse C. Dowden, John Gamble, John M. Thomas, William Free, Elizabet Martin, William Silvers, William Phagan, George Leard and George Baldridge. The present land owners of section 1 are M. E. Studebaker, J. R. Simonton, D. Simonton, L. K. Burt, E. M. Powell, M. A. Flinn, H. Williams and A. Cates. A public road surrounds the section on each section line.

Section No. 2 was entered in 1836 and 1837, five eighty acres tracts having been entered in the former of these years and three in the latter. The purchasers were Joseph Hamer, Jackson Green, Isaac Shideler, John Richeson, Willam Mar-

## HAMILTON TOWNSHIP. 95

tin, Rebecca Comer, William McCormick and William Silvers. Jackson Green entered the southwest quarter of the northeast quarter of this section on January 24, 1837, and here, in 1851, was born his son, Dr. George R. Green, now of Muncie. The doctor grew to manhood and began the practice of medicine in Hamliton township, and is, therefore, a purely Hamilton township production.

The lands of section 2 are now owned by Wm. H. Bosman, R. R Gibson, J. Cates, W. H. Mitchell, D. W. Wingate and J. G. Leffler. The south portion of the village of Shideler is in this section and school house No. 9 is also located here. Section 2 has public roads on the north, east and south and the Muncie and Studebaker gravel pike on the west line.

Section 3 was entered in 1837, except the northwest quarter, which was entered in 1836 by Thomas Erell. Those entering the lands in '37 were John Richeson, Samuel P. Anthony, Howard Mitchell, Samuel W. Mitchell and Samuel Cromer. Howard Mitchell, above mentioned, was the father of Joseph and James Q. Mitchell of Muncie. Mr. Mitchell never settled on his Indiana lands. However, his younger son, James Q., settled and improved the land entered by his father in section 9, where he resided several years, but finally sold out and purchased and buift the property where he now lives on South Monroe street, Muncie.

The present owners of section 3 are L. Beall, I. H. Shideler, J. M. Stafford, M. E. Pixley, S. Studebaker, J. R. Rench and S. Stafford. Section 3 has free gravel roads on the north and east, also a public road on the south and west.

Section 4 was entered, likewise, in 1836 and 1837, by four persons, each securing a quarter of a section. These persons were Thomas Erell, Alvin Sleeth, Joseph Hance and Howard Mitchetl.

Section 4 is now owned by A. J. Yohey, W. H. Yohey, A. White, J. Knox, J. F. Studebaker, H. Suber, H. and J. Gump and E. F. Lovett. Like most of the sections in Hamilton No 4 is surrounded by good roads.

Section 5 was all taken up in 1836 and, like No. 4, was entered by four parties. Those securing this section were James and Thos. Kennedy, Jos. Garrard and Thos. Stafford.

Section 5 is owned at present by J. Pierson, G. Snyder, William Love, J. Shoemaker, L. E. Spencer, Samuel Gerrard, W. L. Gerrard, L. Heffner and James McCormick. Section 5 has a road on each section line; also one east and west on the half section line.

Section 6 was entered in 1836 and 1837 by Joseph Gerrard, William Singler and William Arnold.

This section is now owned by J. B. Reiber, J. F. Shoemaker, Otto Holaday, M. A. Brown, S. Gerrard, M. L. Gerrard et. al., Orlo Halady, W. L. Gerrard, J. N. Cox, J. R. Cox, T. A. House, M. Moody, H. Bowen and M. Crampton. No. 6 has roads on the east and north and east and west through the center. School No. 3 is in the southeast corner of this section.

Among the early ministers of the gospel of Hamilton township were Abner Perdue, Henry Grist, Larken Mullen, Scott Richardson and Benjamin Halcomb. The meetings were generally held at the residence of some of the settlers, then later on, at the school houses. Among other settlers who opened their houses for worship were William Sleeth, Adam Shafer, William Gard and others. We remember attending religious meetings in a barn, on the farm of Nathan Dean, now owned by A. McCormick, on the Studebaker pike. This was early in the fifties, but even at that late date church buildings were very scarce. But to return to the first settling of the lands by sections we find that the land in section 7 was entered by George Stafford, Barnard F. Hook and John Roop in 1836, and Richard Chandler in 1837.

The present landlords are J. P. Baxla, F. E. Baxla, R E. Baxla, N. J. Baxla, J. S. Baxla, L. A. Baxla, M. D. Baxla, M. Langsdon, L. A. Bunyan, E. J. Crist, C. C. Crampton and W. and E. Bell. Section 7 has public roads on the east and south. The Muncie and Wheeling free gravel pike crosses the southwest corner of the section, Kilbuck creek crosses the pike in this section, running almost due east at this point, and here in early times the people would assemble to witness the ordinance of baptism by immersion. The creek afforded but little water, but this slight inconvenience was overcome by digging a hole in the creek and allowing it to fill with water to a sufficient depth to cover the candidate to the satisfaction of all concerned and the requirements of the creed.

The land in section 8 was entered in 1836 and '37 by Charles F. Willard, Jonathan Mason, Ralph Stafford, Cyrus Pence and Noah Tracy. This section is now owned by Jane North, C. C. Foster, D. Craw, O. E. Sherry, G. and J. Meeks, J. and A. Baxla, J. Dragstrom and R. A. Johnson. The section is surrounded by a public road on each section line, and Mud creek crosses the northeast corner.

Section 9 was all taken up in 1836 except two eighty acre tracts which was entered in 1837. The parties securing these lands were James Stafford, Cyrus Pence, Jacob Fortney, Noah Tracy and Howard Mitchell. The present owners of land in this section are H. Heaton, J. Heaton, S. C. Mansfield, D. Heffner, S. C. Main, J. North, T. H. Snider, P. Mansfield, R. and A. Monroe, N. North, R. W. Stradling and J. A. Snider. This section, like No. 8, has a road on

CHAS. A. VAN MATRE,
County Superintendent Public Schools.

## HAMILTON TOWNSHIP. 97

each section line and the south half is drained by Mud creek crossing it.

Section 10 was entered in 1835 and 1836 by four persons, each securing a quarter section (160 acres) they were Cyrus Pence, Henry Shafer, Stephen Davis and William Commons. The present owners of section 10 are A. McCormick, J. E. Pixley, D. Pixley, K. P. Shafer Rachael Mansfield, C. C. Mansfield, C. Mansfield and M. West. Mud creek drains the section by running through the central and southwest portions of it. Public roads run on the north, west and south, and the Studybaker pike on the east line. Eden church, belonging to the Christian (or New Light) denomination is situated in the northeast corner of the section.

Section 11 was also entered in the years of 1835 and '36 by James McCormick, Sr., William McCormick, Robins R. Wilson, Henry Shafer, Jonathan Johns and James McCormick, Jr. This section is owned by James McCnrmick (a portion of his farm is the tract entered by his father, Wm. McCormick on April 18, 1836.) J. M. Warfel, C. C. Mansfield, Mathew McCormick, C. and A. Mansfield, and D. Mansfield. This section is also drained by Mud creek passing through the south half, good roads surround the section with the Studybaker pike along the west line. The Muncie and Ft. Wayne R. R. crosses the west half. School No. 1 is located on the east side of the section just south of the half section line.

Section 12 lying east of 11, and adjoining Delaware township on the east, was entered in 1834-35 and '36 by J. Ashcraft, (for Catharine and Margret Chancy) Archibald Smith, Robert Kirkpatrick, Henry Shafer, Henry Huddleston, Barbara Huddleston, and James McCormicĸ. The parties now holding the title to the lands in section 12 are R. S. Cultice, D. E. Brammer, O. A. Stafford, E. and R. Witt, C. C. Mansfield, W. M. Corbley, S. A. Stafford, L. Mansfield and N. P. and E. Martin. Section 12 is also surrounded by a public road on each section line and drained by Mud creek passing in almost a due west course through the south half of the section.

Section 13 was all entered by two men, they being John D. Albin who entered the east half of the section on April 18, 1836, and Waitsell W. Cary who entered the west half on Sept. 9, of the same year. The northwest quarter of this section was know in early years as "Iowa" from the fact that William Thomas sold his home near Granville in Niles township with the avowed purpose of moving to the then new state of Iowa, but subsequently bought and located on this northwest quarter of section 13, and the neighbors gave it the name of "Iowa" by which the farm was generally known for miles around. J. Vint Abbott now owns and occupies this entire state of "Iowa."

The owners of section 13 are R. E. Baker, F. M. Pittenger, E. J. Pittenger, W. Campcell, J. V. Abbott and S. K. Thomas. The head waters of Kilbuck creek crosses the southwest portion of the section, and the section is surround with good public roads on each section line.

Section 14 was also entirely taken up of the government by two purchasers, Alexander Gilfllan entering the south half April 18, 1836, and Henry Shafer, the north half May 28, of the same year. The land in section 12 is now owned by J. Morgan, F. W. Heath, J. Miller, M. D. Baker, A. and M. Palmer, R. Hunt, D. Scott, Dick & Kirkwood and J. K. Reiff. The village of Royerton is located in the southwest corner of this section. The first settler, where Royerton stands, was William Sleeth, who purchased the land and built a cabin early in the forties. He was an intelligent and an industrious man, going to work with a will he soon had improved a quantity of his land, and early in the fifties, he burned a kiln of brick, and erected the brickhouse just north of the village, and near the site of his cabin, he afterwards sold out to John Royer who located the village, and for who it was named. Royerton is a railroad station on the Ft. Wayne branch of the L. E. & W. R. R. and a convenient trading point for a considerable scope of territory; 14 has public roads on the south, east and north, and the Studebaker pike on the west line.

Section 15 was entered by Henry Shafer, Stephen Davis, Daniel Smith and Archibald Smith in the years of 1834 and 1836. Daniel Smith entered the south half of the southwest quarter, and Archibald Smith the south half of the southeast quarter of this section in 1834, but could not have owned it very long, as John Parker and William Wire owned and improved these two tracts in an early day. The present owners of this section are N. J. White, D. Scott, M. U. Johnson, H. S. Mansfield, R. W. Stradling, L. F. Johnson, J. M. Johnsonbaugh, J. Labateaux, and Alexander Snider. Killbuck creek crosses the south half of the section, and public roads surround it, that on the east and also west being free graveled pikes.

Section 16 in Hamilton township, as in all other townships, was sold for school purposes. This sale occurred on January 19, 1838, and was made in 40-acre tracts. The purchasers were A. C. Custar, Robert Ismael, Jacob Hardesty, Samuel R. Collier, Jacob Holland, William Parker, and Alexander Hewitt, Mr. Parker getting seven of the tracts, Mr. Collier two, Mr. Ismael three, and each of the others one. The lowest any of this land sold for was $1.82¼ per

## HAMILTON TOWNSHIP.     99

acre, and the highest $4.06¼, the entire section aggregating the sum of $1,746.53.

The section is now owned by J. M. Snider, J. D. and S. Collins, G. Turner, C. Frye, T. F. Kirby, N. S. Tauberger, A. Pardine, E. E. Phillips, T. Parker, S. Parker, M. J. Cummings, J. A. Snider, and J. M. Laboyteaux. Sixteen has a public road on each section line, also a road north and south 80 rods west of the east line. Killbuck runs west through the south half of the section.

Section 17 was all purchased of the government by William Daily entering the southeast quarter October 31, 1835, and Samuel Snyder the other three quarters on May 17, 1836, only two men being the original owners of 17. The section is still owned by but three persons, D. Connell and Jeremiah Quinlan owning the north half and Prof. John M. Bloss the south half of the section. Killbuck also drains the south half of this section. There are public roads on the north, east and south.

Section 18 was all entered in 1836, except 80 acres, which was entered by Elijah Casteel in December, 1832. The other entries were made by Jeremiah Gard, Jacob Holiday, Solomon Ismael, Joseph Turner, Samuel Snyder, William Harlan, and Robert Ismael. The present owners of land in this section are L. L. Petre, F. G. Connell, John M. Bloss, G. R. Keller, J. Gassell, W. Sherry, and C. A. Moore. Eighteen has public roads on the north and south lines, and the Muncie and Wheeling pike angles through the section, and Killbuck crosses the northern part in a northwestern direction.

Section 19 in Hamilton township was entered in the years of 1836 and 1837, except the west half of the southwest quarter (67.16 acres) now owned by Geo. Luick, which, as shown by the records, was entered by Samuel P. Anthony as late as September 20, 1848.

The entries in 1836 and 1837 were made by John Meeks, Thos. Pritchard, Benjamin Campbell, John Weidman and Thos. Adams. The present owners of section 19 are T. Sullivan, A. Hammond, O. J. Newcomb, M. Thomas, L. Morris, J. W. Thomas, W. H. Snider, A. A. Hammond, M. W. M. and C. Smith, and George Luick. Nineteen has public roads on the north, south and west, and the Muncie and Wheeling pike crosses the northeast corner.

Section 20 was all entered on the same day (May 17, 1836) by John Weidner, Garrett Williamson, Jacob Weidner and Jeremiah Miller, each securing a quarter section (160 acres). This section is now owned by W. Pittenger, H. Cooley, Eliza Pittenger, S. E. Hayden, W. A. McClellan, E. McClellan, S. F. Kiser, D. M. Snider, C. Jetmore, M. A.

Smith and J. W. Thomas. The Muncie and Wheeling pike crosses tne southwest corner of the section and public roads are located on the east and north lines.

Section 21. On May 17, 1836, Samuel Wiedner entered the northeast quarter of this section, and on the same date John Snider entered the southeast quarter. Then on the fifth day of the following October, (1836) Mr. Snider entered the west half of the section, so this entire section originally belonged to two men.

The owners of Section 21 at present are R. C. Rarrick, J. W. Rarrick, A. Snider, T. R. Buffington, L. Waters, F. and R. Reiser, F. M. Hurt and John F. Shafer.

Center (or school No. 5) is located on the northeast corner of this section. It is one of the oldest schools in the township, having been located here in 1850, and a log school house built by the settlers in the woods where the present brick now stands. Twenty-one has a public road on the north, east and west, also east and west through the center. The headwaters of Jakes creek drain the south part of the section.

Section 22 is one of the old sections of the township, the first entry of land in it being by Adam Shafer in 1830. The other parties who entered this section were Archibald Smith, Stephen Kennedy, James H. Fitzpatrick, Thomas Pritchard and Thomas Brumfield.

Stephen Kennedy, who located on the northwest quarter of this section, was reputed one of the greatest hunters that lived in the county, and we doubt if any man ever killed as many deer in the county as did Mr. Kennedy. During the winter of 1851 and '52 he killed thirty-two deer, most, if not all, in Hamilton township. We can remember seeing him start out of mornings, in his hunting garb of light colored clothes, on his gray mare, the snow several inches deep, with his trusty rifle, his ever companion, a strap around his mare's neck, to which was attached a cow-bell. The game might just as well have made up its mind to come home with him, as he scarcely ever returned empty. If he secured but one deer during the day's hunt, he would probably throw it across "old gray" and bring it along, but, as was often the case, if he killed two or more during the day, he would hang them up in the woods, then return and hitch "old gray" to a small sled and gather up his game. The outside walls of his cabin were often nearly covered with skins of various wild animals, where they were stretched and left to dry. Mr. Kennedy was also an accomplished violinist (or as we called him, "a good fiddler), and was at one time a justice of the peace.

Section 23 was all entered in 1836, except the west half

## HAMILTON TOWNSHIP.

of the southwest quarter, which was entered by Adam Shafer in 1831.

The parties entering these lands in 1836 were Samuel Martin, Jr., Elijah Reeves, George Leiber, Peter Williamson and Owen Russell. The land owners of 23 are now W. W. Spangler, S. W. Williamson, J. Morgan, James Williamson, J. M. Williamson, Mary Martin, G. F. Shafer, and J. Roach.

Section 23 is surrounded by good roads, that on the west line being the Muncie and Stndebaker pike.

Section 24 was one among the first to be settled, one-half of it being entered as early as 1831, and the last of the government land in the section was taken up in 1835. The first purchasers of the section were Owen Russell, Mordecai Massey, Stephen R. Martin, Thomas Reeves, Isaac Massey, James Massey, and Joel Russell.

The present landlords of section 24 are E. Martin, T. B. McCulloch, John Cullen, M. Adams, W. W. Spangler, and W. H. Anderson. Section 24 joins Delaware township on the east, has public roads on the east, west and north, with the Muncie and Granville pike angling through the center.

The first land entered in section 25 was an eighty acre tract by Peter Williamson, and an eighty by his brother-in-law, Adam Shafer, both entriel being on Oct. 2, 1829. The other entries were made by Alexander Crawford, Stephen R. Martin, Joel Russell and Archibald Hamilton in 1831-32-33 and '35. This section is now owned by C. M. Kauffman, G. Payton, Wm. Reed L. O. Wilson, E. V. Palmer, J. M. Williamson, J. Keener and G. Green and E. G. Wilson. Twenty-five is the southeast section of the township. The Granville pike crosses the northwest corner of the section.

Section 26. The first land ever purchased of the government in the township, was the southeast quarter of this section. This purchase was made by Owen Russell on October 21, 1829, or nearly seventy years ago. The others who availed themselves of the government prices of land in this section were Morgan and William Conner, Joseph Williamson, Geo. Lieber, James D. Collier, Henry Slover and James Nottingham.

These lands are owned by J. M. Williamson, J. Keener and G. Green, Milton Hamilton, M. F. Hamilton, F. J. Settle and C. and A. Bartlett.

The Granville pike angles through the section and school No. 10 is located in the southwest quarter.

Section 27 was all entered in 1835 and '36 by Samuel R. Colier, Abraham Slover Jeremiah Miller, Wm. H. Brumfield, James P. Mathews, John Snider, Peter D. Green and James Bowman. The present owners of the land in the section are

M. F. Hamilton, F. J. Settle, Joseph Sheets, W. A. and C. B. Price, M. S. Harris, E. M. Weir, Adam Williamson and L. Morris. The section has free gravel pikes on the east and west, a public road on the south and school No 7 in the west center.

Section 28 was entered and settled in 1836 and 1837 by Naomi Powers, William Harlan, George Leiber, Stephen Norris, Mary Butcher and Thomas Brumfield.

The present owners of 28 are Carl Spilker, E. M. Weir, Adam Williamson, L. G. Cowlng, A. Cowing, E. Wilson and John Williams. This section has public roads on the south and west and a free gravel pike on the east line.

Section 29 was settled in the years of 1834-35 and '37. The purchasers of the land were Samuel Snyder, John Nottingham, Stanley L. Lobertson, Isaac Branson, Joshua Turner, Robert Ismael and Josiah Williams.

This section is owned at present by G. and A. Wissel, W. W. Scudder, E. Wilson, G. Cowing, L. Morris, L. C. Watson and Duncan Williams. The Wheeling pike (formerly the old state road) angles through the section and the head waters of Jakes creek furnishes drainage.

Section 30 is the southwest section of the township and was all entered in 1835 and '36 by Solomon Burris. Lewis Moore, William Moore, Samuel Moore, Isaac Freeman and Peter D. Green. (Perhaps if there had been any more Moores they would have come in for their share). This section is owned at present by William Ginn, L. Moore, F. and W. Minton, John Minton, A. Moore, W. R. Moore, F. F. Hartley, T. Freeman and J. Freeman. There is a public road on the north, also on the west, while another runs through the section at different angles. School No. 6 is situated an the northeast corner of the section.

As I walk the streets of the city gay,
I often think; and sometimes, say,
Is all this real, or is it a dream?
Are things and places what they seem?
Is this where 'neath the forest shade
The warrior courted the dark-eyed maid?
If so, then what has become of the race
Who lived and loved in the self-same palce
Where you and I in modern life
Enjoy the comforts of home and wife?
Who builded this church with tapering dome
To take the place of the Red Man's home?
Who built the city of mansions grand
On the Indians' home and the Indians' land?
Perhaps it is right, but then somehow
When at my couch I humbly bow
The thought comes to me as I pray,
Are we much better now than they?
What have we done for the human cause?
What are our lives, our morals, laws?
Can we believe that this, our race,
Was sent to take the Red Man's place?
And if so, why shall we remain
If we are sinful, cruel, vain?
Well, perhaps, in former years,
When first the sturdy pioneers
Came with rifle, axe and plow,
And earned their bread by sweat of brow,
Before the days of trading tricks,
Corruption, now called politics,
And other evils gained the sway;
Perhaps we were as good as they.
We love our country and her cause,
We love our liberties and laws,
We ought to love the world beside;
But none of those with boastful pride.
And may we ever bear in mind,
God will survive the fittest kind.

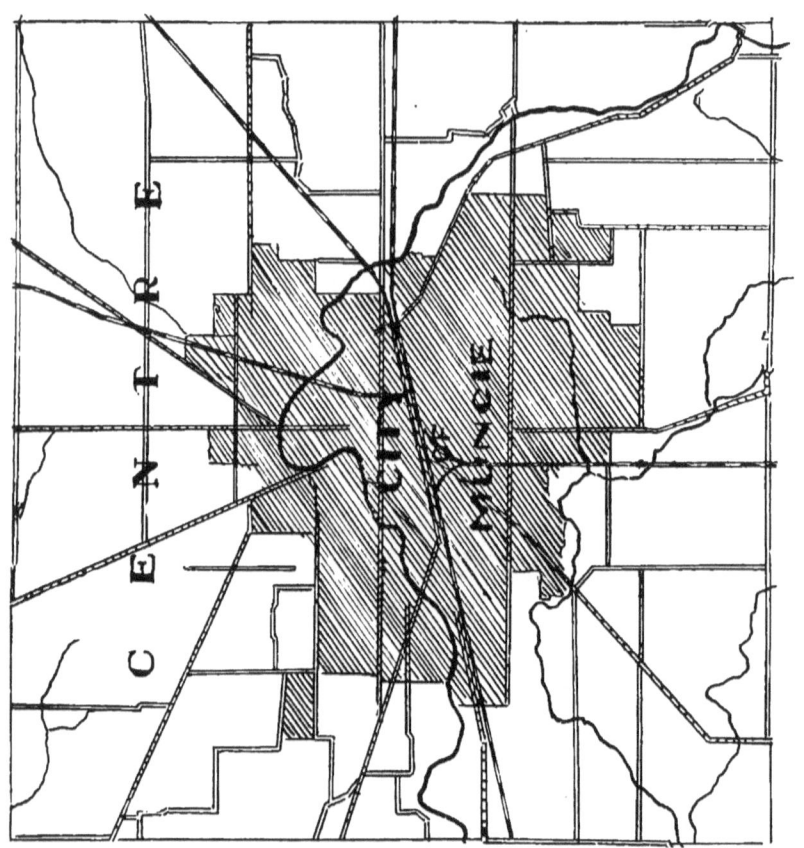

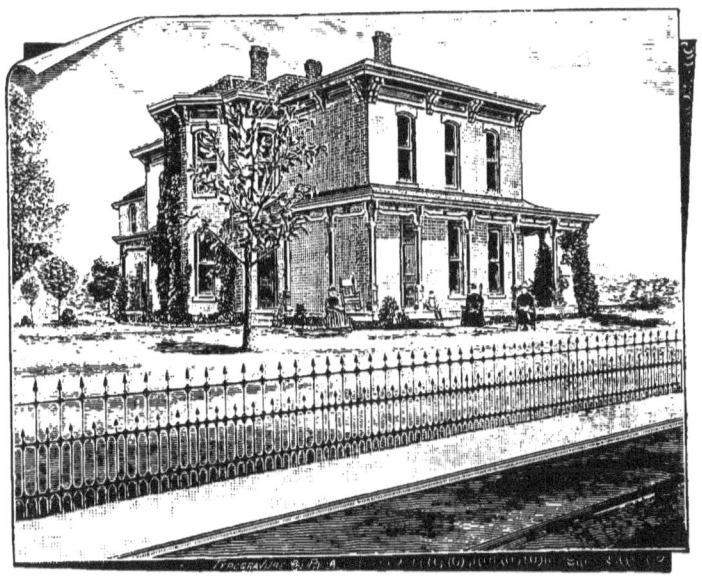

RESIDENCE OF MAYOR ED TUHEY,
South Walnut St., Muncie.

T. H. BARTON,
Treasurer, City of Muncie.

F. W. CLEVENGER,
Clerk, City of Muncie.

# Center Township.

In Center township, Delaware county, is located the county seat of government, the city of Muncie, the geographical center of the county, is in the center of section 33 of this township, where the lands of Stephen Hamilton, W. H. Harrison, C. R. Weaver and Mrs. A. A. Truitt corner, or at the northwest corner of Mrs. Truitt's land, or in other words 2½ miles north and one-half a mile west of the crossing of Walnut and Jackson streets. Center township is bounded north by Hamilton, east by Liberty, south by Monroe and west by Mt. Pleasant and a portion of Harrison township. The principal water way of the township is White river, which enters the township near the southeast corner in section 25, drains sections 25, 24, 13, 14, 11, 10, 9, 16, 17 and 18, from which section it enters Mt. Pleasant township. The south west part is drained by Buck creek, which finds its way to White river near Yorktown in Mt. Pleasant township. All of Center township is in Congressional township 20, except the north tier of sections which is in 21, and all in range 10 east. There was but one entry of land in the township under the treaty with the Delaware Indians of 1818, but our records do not show the date of this entry, it was made by Goldsmith, C. Gilbert and was the southeast quarter of section 18. White river, the Big Four railroad and Yorktown pike, all cross this quarter just west of the city of Muncie. A good portion, if not all, of this tract was subsequently owned and occupied by Thomas Bishop and was once known as the Bishop farm. But the first entry of land in Center township after the establishment of the government land office, was made by James Bryson on the 24th day of December, 1822. This tract was the east half of the southeast quarter of section 25, lying in the southeast corner of the township and now owned by the widow of John Fulhart and R. A. Johnson (assignee). Sometime subsequently to 1825, Goldsmith C. Gilbert bought the Hackley reserve of the widow Hackley, she being of the Delaware tribe of Indians, and having inherited the said tract of land. There was 672 acres in this reserve, the southeast corner being not far from the Boyce flax mill, the southwest corner is now in the river near the old dug road nearly north of the new Jefferson school building, the northeast and northwest corners being one mile north of the two corners mentioned, the tract being parts of sections 3, 4, 9 and 10. The south line of this reserve passes through the center of the Court house   Mr. Gilbert paid $960.00 for the tract which at that time was considered a very fair price. Here Mr. Gilbert erected two cabins, a residence and trading post, which were the foundation of the present prosperous city of Muncie. The name of Muncie seems to have been taken from one of the principal chiefs of the Delaware's (Little Munsee,) and for many years the place was known as Munseytown. Technically speaking, Delaware county was organized on April 1, 1827, at which time it became necessary to locate a seat of justice for the new county and a committee having been appointed by the Legislature for that purpose, after having examined the several sites proposed in conformity with the requirements of the law, selected the site owned by Mr. Gilbert, Samuel G, Jackson and William Brown. All three of these pioneers making liberal donations of land to the county, the donations centering in the middle of the public square, where the court house now stands. The donation of Mr. Gilbert coutained 20 acres and 9-100. That of Mr. Jackson 9 acres and 72-100, and that of Mr. Brown, 20 acres, so the entire tract contained in round numbers 50 acres of land, yet, it is said that at that time persons thought it was useless to include so much territory as it was thought it could never possibly be utilized for town purposes. The first term of the Delaware circuit court was held in a log house near where the jail now stands, and after hearing the evidence and the charge of the Judge, the jury retired out of doors to a big oak stump to deliberate, and the business of the sheriff was to keep intruders out of hearing. The first newspaper printed in Muncietown was the Muncietonian and we give here verbatum an article that appeared in one of its issues in 1837, believing that it will be of interest to many of our readers.

"Muncietown, the seat of justice of Delaware county, is situated on the south bank of White river, on an elevation of about thirty feet above the bed of the river. It was laid out in 1827, by three different proprietors, in the form of an oblong square. The four principal streets are sixty feet wide, the others forty-five, all crossing each other at right angles. It contains at present 320 inhabitants, a post office, a printing office, four physicians, six mercantile stores, three taverns, three groceries, one grist mill, one saw mill, one distillery, one carding machine, one cabinet maker's shop, two tailors, two hatters, one shoemaker, six house joiners, one brick layer and plasterer, two chairmakers, two tanners, two blacksmiths, one gunsmith, one wagon maker, one painter, one saddler's shop, four milliners, one school mistress, one sheriff, one clerk of the court, two magistrates, one school commissioner, one county surveyor and recorder. A superb court house, with cupola, etc., 45 feet square and 28 feet high, is to be built, and is now under contract. The contemplated central canal will pass through this place, and the connecting link, to be by railroad, between the Central and

White water canals will, in all probability, terminate at this point, as the Board of Canal Commissioners have reported favorable to such termination. The state road, from the Ohio state line to Indianapolis, passes through this place. A state road from Richmond to Logansport, a state road from New Castle, in Henry couuty, to Fort Wayne all pass through this town. There is also a state road leading to Pendleton and one to Delphi. Muncietown is about 61 miles northeast from Indianapolis; north latitude 40 and 7; west longitude 8 and 9."

The first court house in Delaware county was a frame building, erected on the west side of High street, between Main and Washington streets, about the year 1829 or 1830. This building did duty as a court house for some ten years and until its successor was built in 1838 or 1839, on the site of the present court house.

The first school in Muncietown, of which we can get anything like an accurate account, was taught in a log cabin that stood at or near the southwest corner of Main and Wal nut streets, during the winter of 1829 and '30 by Henry Tomlinson, a native of North Carolina, who had come here a short time previously from Preble county, Ohio. The families represented in this school were about eight in number, sending some twenty pupils. It was maintained by subscription, the patrons agreeing to pay and paying so much for each and every scholar. Such was the custom of those days. As a consequence the schools were not continuous, occupying about three months during the winter, with an occasional summer term.

Sections 31 to 36, inclusive in Center township is the north tier of sections and are in congressional township 21.

Beginning with 31, we find the first entry of public land in this section was made by John H. Collins on may 11, 1835 and was the east half of the southeast quarter, (80 acres) now owned by James McClellan. After Mr. Collins entry Bowen Rees entered two 80 acre tracts in the section the following November after which time (in 1836) John Miller entered the north (fractional) half and Daniel Jarrett the (fractionel) west half of the southwest quarter. We find the present owners of 31 to be W. Ginn, Jane Taylor, M. McGraw, James McClellan, Joseph Huffman, J. E. Smith and A. Justice. The section has about two and a half miles of public highway, half-mile of which is the Bethel pike which crosses the southwest corner.

John Isaac Jetmore was the first to procure a title to public land in section 32, which was the south half of the southwest quarter (80 acres). This entry was made on November 15, 1834, and is now owned with other lands by C.

M. Preston. The remainder of section 32 was entered by William P. Williams, Charles Francis Willard and John A. Gilbert in 1834 and by Charles Francis Willard, Daniel Jarrett. John Whiteside and George Leiber in 1836. The present owners in section 32 are E. H. Jones, S. E. Seitz, Wm. Tell Seitz, E. M. Everett, G. Eiler, P. Eiler, G. Eber, C. M. Preston, J. Eiler, M. A. Willis and Joseph Heaton. The section has some two miles of public road, a part of which is the Muncie and Wheeling free pike, which crosses the northeast corner of the section.

Section 33 was all entered in the years of 1835 and '36. In 1835 by William and David S. Collins in the southwest quarter and in 1836 by George Leiber, Joseph Dean and Mayor Powers. At present the section is owned by S. Hamilton, W. H. Harrison, Henry C. Marsh, Mrs. A. A. Truitt, John Williams, C. R. Weaver and John S. Petty's estate. The section is almost surrounded by public roads, that on the east line and across the southwest corner being free gravel pikes As before stated the geographical center of Delaware county is in the center of this section. The first purchase of government land in section 34 was made October 21, 1829, by Joseph Bennett and was the east half of the southeast quarter (80 acres) and now owned part by Abner Keplinger and part by Brice Powers. After this entries were made in 1831 by Jacob Holland, in 1835 by Ezekiel Bazzill, in 1830 by Mayor Powers, David Adams, George Leiber and a second entry by Jacob Holland. We find the present land owners in section 34 to be M. Mansfield, W. J. Cassady, Brice Powers, William Strandling, Abner Keplinger and John Williams. The section has four miles of public highway, one and a half miles of which is free pike. Ft. Wayne bradch of the L. E. & W. railroad crosses the east part of this section.

The first land entry in section 35 was made by Thomas Reeves on March 28, 1829, and was the east half of the northwest quarter of the section, a portion of the farm now owned by Milton Hamilton. After this entry our records show purchases by Joseph Bennett in 1829, Stephen Hamilton in 1830, Owen Russell and Jacob Holland in 1831, and Daniel Leiber in 1836. The present land owners in section 35 are Milton Hamilton, Mrs. Harriett Hamilton, B. Moore, A. A. Hamilton, Brice Powers and Abner Keplinger. The section has three miles of road, one-half mile of which is the Muncie and Granville free pike angling across the northwest corner.

Section 36 is the northeast section of the township, and consequently joins both Hamilton and Liberty townships. The first entry of public land in this section was made by

GLOBE CLOTHING HOUSE, C. L. BENDER & CO.
118 South Walnut, Muncie.

RESIDENCE AND OFFICE OF DR. H. A. COWING,
S. High Street, Muncie.

CONGRESSMAN GEO. W. CROMER,
A Delaware County Production.

## CENTER TOWNSHIP.

Stephen Hamilton November 11, 1830, and was the 80-acre tract now owned by Thomas Gibson, after which entries were made by John Guthrie and Archibald Dowden in 1835, Truman Conklin in 1836, and Thomas Albin in 1837. The section has a public road on the north and also on the south line. Section 36 is now owned by John McCormick, J. E. Reed, S. Holdt J. Cullen, C. Kauffman, Thomas Gibson, J. S. McGalliard, E. H. Holt, and T. Pacy.

All of section 1 in Center township remained unsold by the government until June 1, 1835, when Benjamin Goodin purchased two tracts, being the north fractional half of the section. The next purchaser was Penelope Anthony on May 12, 1836. The three remaining 80-acre tracts were entered by Dr. George W. Garst, for many years one of the best known citizens of the county. The doctor was at one time eminent in the practice of his profession, and was a natural humorist, all enjoying his jokes. A number of his family still reside in the community, and are among our oldest and respected citizens. This entry of land, above referred to, was made on June 18, 1836.

The present owners of land in section 1 are J. S. McGalliard, A. J. McGalliard, W. F. Holbert, S. A. Richison, J. Priest, E. Priest, L. Shirey and R. Jones. The section has public roads on the north, south and west lines, that on the south being the Centennial free gravel pike. The L. E. & W. railroad angles across this section.

Joseph Bennett was the first purchaser of public land in section 2. The date of his purchase was November 24, 1831, and his purchase was the fractional northwest quarter, containing 95 68-100 acres. William Helvie entered the east half of the section in 1835 and 1836, and James Sears the southwest quarter June 1, 1835.

The present owners of section 2 are W. Hibbitts, E. D. Keplinger, I. E. Crews estate, T. Wilson, W. S. Wilson, J. H. Smell, T. R. Buffington, and W. McMahan. Two has public roads on the north, south and east, that on the south line being the Centennial free pike, and school No. 1 is located on the southeast corner of the section.

The first entry in section 3 was made March 26, 1829, by Joseph Bennett, and was the fractional northeast quarter, 95 35-100 acres. Then followed the purchases of Owen Russell, December 7, 1829; James Howell, February 4, 1833; David Brooks Buckles, October 16, 1835, and William H. Brumfield, December 14, 1835.

A portion of this section is now platted and a part of the suburb of the city of Muncie, known as Northview, the balance or unplatted part being owned by E. D. Keplinger, Samuel U. Huffer, B. W. Bennett, John Williams, W. Carson, M. E. Streeter, H. W. Streeter, and S. R. Streeter. The Granville pike angles across this section, and the Central pike forms the west line.

Aaron Taff was the first party to enter land in section 4, which entry was dated November 16, 1832. This entry comprised the southeast quarter of the southwest quarter (40 acres). The next entry was that of Abraham Buckles, father of the late Judge Joseph S. Buckles, deceased. This entry was made June 14, 1833, and comprised the fractional southeast quarter, containing 136 12-100 acres. After this other entries were made by John Buckles and John Blackford in 1833; William Diltz and Thomas Gustin in 1834, and William Diltz again in 1835.

The section is owned at present by Simon Conn, Carson and Meeks, M. A. Marsh, C. H. Anthony, E. Lindsley, C. B. Campbell, L. Cowing, R. G. Anthony, Delaware County Fair Association, and William F. Watson. The Central pike is the east line. There is a public road on the greater part of both the north and south line, and the Wheeling pike angles through the section, while school No. 2 is located on the northeast corner.

The first entry of land in section 5 was made on February 4, 1833, by Pete Nolin. This was the south half of the southeast quarter (80 acres), and now owned by C H. Anthony and William F. Watson. After this entry by Mr. Nolin, others were made by Thomas Kirby, and Charles Francis Willard, jointly, in 1833; James Nottingham in 1834; John Collins, James Nottingham, John Buckles and Peter Shanks in 1835, and John Sutherland in 1836.

The land owners in section 5 are now William F. Watson, James McClellan, C. H. Anthony, James Huffman, A. Anderson, and S. A Pierce. The section has over two miles of public road, more than half of which is free pike. School No. 3 is located at the west center of the section.

The first land entered in section 6, in Center township, was a 40 acre tract in the northeast corner of the section and now in the name of A. Anderson. This entry was made on the 18th day of March, 1833, jointly by Thomas Kirby and Charles Francis Willard, two of Delaware county's best known citizens, both having lived and prospered in the town (afterward city of Muncie, for many years, and have left a respectable posterity who are still among our most enterprising citizens. After this, entries were made by William Beatty, Dec. 18, 1833, Peter Shanks, Thomas J. Collins and Nathan Stansberry, in 1835, and Thomas C. Anthony in 1836. The present owners of the section are A. Andrews, S. Hathaway, S. A. Pierce, E. A. McKinley, G. S. Wilson, E. O. Weir, Joseph S. Buckles heirs, and Thos. Weir, Jr. The section

## CENTER TOWNSHIP.

has about 2¼ miles of public road, one-half of which is the Bethel free gravel pike which crosses the northeast corner of the section.

Land in section 7 was first purchased on the 22nd day of April, 1831, by Isaiah E. Beck, being the east half of the northeast quarter, containing 80 acres. The second entry was made in 1832 by George Shafer, this was an 80 acre tract lying immediately south of the purchase of Mr. Beck, and still remains in the family, as the present owner, as shown by our latest map, is Mr. John W. Shafer. Following this, entries were made by Nathan Stansberry and William Nottingham in 1833, Isaac White and Thomas Collins in 1834 and by John Henderson Collins and Jeremiah Howell in 1835. The section is owned at present by S. A Pierce, J. W. McKinley, The Kimberlin Mfg. Co., Joseph S. Buckles' heirs, John W. Shafer, Joseph Stradling and James E. Eber. The section has nearly 3 miles of public road, much of it being free pike. The L. E. & W. railroad angles across the southern portion of the section. On the 24th day of July, 1830, Jacob Calvert purchased land of the government just west of White river, containing 160 acres, 80 acres of which was in section 8, and was the first entry made in the section, it being the east half of the southeast quarter and now being entirely in the town of Westside and lying on the north side of Jackson street pike. Here Mr. Calvert lived for many years, and here he reared a large family of children, some of whom still live in Muncie and are among our very best citizens. After Mr. Calvert's entry, the next in this section was that of John, William, James and Mayor Nottingham, Oct. 14, 1830, Joseph Williamson, Nov. 27, 1830, Isaac E. Beck, April 22, 1831, George Shafer, July 2, 1832, Joseph Emmerson, Nov. 3, 1832, Joseph Williamson again Nov. 30, 1832, Elijah Reeves, Oct. 18, 1833, and Joseph Williamson his third entry, Nov. 19th, 1835. At present the section outside of what has been platted is owned by J. Munsey, L. Shick, M. A. Mills and J. W. McKinley. Three-fourths of this section has been platted and is within the boundry of the new town of Normal City. The Normal College being located in this section, also the Westside school, and we predict that the south half of section 8 is soon to become an important adjunct to the city and county.

Almost three-eights of section 9 was included in the Hackley reserve before mentioned in these pages and purchased by Goldsmith C. Gilbert prior to the purchase of any government land in this section by individuals. The first entry made in the section was a part of the southeast quarter, (58 and 62-100 acres) by Elemuel Jackson, Feb. 13, 1827. Next was 36 and 43-100 acres in the northeast quarter by Conrad Mutter Oct. 12, 1829. Aside from these two purchases, all the balance of the east half of section 9 was included in the reserve. The west half of the section was entered by four parties each securing an 80-acre tract, as follows: Philip Mose, the east half of the southwest quarter (the Jackson street bridge over White river west of the city is located near the southwest corner of the tract) Jacob Calvert the west half of the southwest quarter July 24, 1830. John Nottingham the west half of the northwest quarter, now owned by L. Shick) Oct. 14, 1830, and Samuel Merrill the east half of the northwest quarter Dec. 16, 1831. With the exception of 77 acres owned by L. Shick and sixty-two acres by the heirs of Jacob Calvert (the original purchaser) section 9 is all platted as suburban additions to the city of Muncie. The Delaware county court house is in this section (9) near the southeast corner, which corner is at the crossing of Walnut and Jackson street.

All of section 10 was included in the Hackley reserve except 113 and 55-100 acres in the southeast quarter entered by William Blynk, Sr., Oct. 2, 1826, 27 and 64-100 acres in the southwest quarter by William Brown June 13, 1827, and 103 and 84-100 acres in the northeast quarter by James Howell June 1, 1833. The section lies entirely within the boundry of the city of Muncie, and the suburbs of Whitely and Northview. The first land entry in section 11, was made Oct. 8, 1827, by John Trimble. This purchase was the west half of the southwest quarter 80 acres. That our readers may be able to locate it more readily, we will state that the L. E. & W., railroad crosses White river east of the city on the southern part of this tract. Mr. Trimble spent a long and useful life in this community, and was identified with most of the enterprises for public good. One of his daughters is still a citizen of Muncie; we refer to Mrs. Jacob Dodson. The other original purchasers of government land in section 11, were Elijah Casteel in 1831, Elijah Walden in 1832, Moses Wilson in 1833, Thomas Kirby and Charles Francis Willard in 1834 and Moses Wilson, George Howell, Jesse Bracken and Elijah Walden in 1835. Aside from about one-hundred acres in the northwest part of the section, platted and within the boundary of Whitely, the section is now owned by T. Wilson, G. Haney. E. Austin, Austin B. Claypool, James Boyce, A. Patton, N. S, Smith et al and J. Maring. A number of important factories are located on this section and the suburb of Boycetown is in the southern portion.

Section 12 is on the east side of Center township, the third tier from the north, and joins Liberty and was all purchased of the government in the years 1835 and 1836. The first to avail himself of these lands was Jesse Bracken. Mr.

PARSONS' BLOCK,
Southwest corner Main and High (Old Hodge corner), Muncie.

## CENTER TOWNSHIP. 113

Bracken was a blacksmith by trade and lived many years at the village of Graville on the Mississinewa river. A number of his children still live in the county. His entry was a 40 acre tract in the southwest corner of the township, now a portion of the Claypool farm, and was dated January 9, 1835. After which entries were made by Michael Sills, Dan Sills and George Howell in 1835 and by Aesop Gilbert and Archibold Dowden in 1836. At present we find the land in 12 owned by C. W. Linsey, A. Rodgers, Thomas Wilson, J. M. Watt and Austin B. Claypool, Mr. Claypool owning the entire south half of the section and an 80-acre tract adjoining, in section 11 The section has over 3 miles of public road, the north line being the Centennial free pike. The public domain in section 13 was in the market nearly ten years, as the first entry was dated December 7, 1826. This entry was made by George Truitt; this was the west half of the northwest quarter, 80 acres. And the last entry was the southwest quarter (160 acres) made by Lewis Moore, August 14, 1839. Mr. Parker Moore's residence, at the point where the Muncie and Smithfield pike crosses White river, is on the tract above mentioned. Between these entries, purchases were made by John Moore in 1831, Lewis Moore and John Moore in 1833, James Blackford and Michael Sills in 1835, and James Blackford again in 1836. We find section 13, now owned by Catharine Meeker, L. F. Fender, M. Moore, S. E. L. Truitt, M. and E. Butterfield, Parker Moore and P. W. Franklin. White river crosses the southwest corner of the section, as also does the Muncie and Burlington free pike. The Smithfield free pike forms the south line and the Big Four railroad crosses the north end of the section. On June 23, 1827, John Brown purchased of the government the west half of the northwest quarter of section 14, (80 acres) after which entries were made by Solomon Hobaugh in 1828, George Truitt and Elijah Reeves in 1829, Littleton Dowty and James Franklin in 1831, James Barton Eastburn in 1832, and Joseph Walling in 1834. More than one-half of this section is now platted and sold in small parcels to various owners too numerous to be here mentioned. But the larger tracts are owned by S. E. L. Truitt, G. and V. Palmer, O. L. Meeks, John Luicks heirs and G. Hughes. School No. 5 is located at the east line of the section, one-fourth of a mile north of the southeast corner on the north side of the Muncie and Burlington pike. The city of Muncie water works company have their machinery and wells on the southeast quarter, near White river, which angles across the southeast, northeast and northwest quarter of this section.

The first land entry in section 15 was made by William Brown and was the west half of the northwest quarter (80 acres). The northwest corner of this tract is at the corner of Walnut and Jackson streets, where the Senate block is located, extending thence south along the line of Walnut street a half mile to what is now the north line of the ground occupied by the Anthony residence, or, Willard.street, thence east one-quarter of a mile to Madison street, thence north on the line of Madison street to Jackson and west on Jackson to Walnut, to the place of beginning. This entry was made on June 13, 1827. The next entry in section 15 was the east half of the northeast quarter on August 24, 1829, by James Murphy. Two days later, August 26, 1829, James Thompson entered the west half of the northeast quarter. June 11, 1830, Jonathan Reeder entered the east half of the northwest quarter, August 10, 1831. Samuel P. Anthony entered the west half of the southwest quarter, a portion of which tract is still owned by his heirs and where Mr. Anthony died some time in the seventies. More than forty years after his purchase. Mr. Anthony was a physician by profession, although he was frequently engaged in mercantile pursuits and was one of the best known men in the county for many years. Several of his grand-children and other relatives are among our best known and highly respected citizens of today.

September 13, 1831, James Franklin entered the east half of the southeast quarter, where he made his future home. He was the father of P. W. Franklin and the grandfather of C. P. Cary and Loan Franklin and also of Mrs. W. W. Shirk, all citizens of Muncie and highly respected by the community. June 9, 1832, Daniel Thompson purchased of the government the east half the southwest quarter; and January 5, 1833, William Clary entered the last of the government land in section 15, which was the west half of the southeast quarter. Fifteen is now all within the corporate limits of the city of Muncie.

Section 16, as in all other townships, was donated by the government to Center township for school purposes. This section lies south of Jackson and west of Walnut streets, having its northeast corner at the crossing of these streets. The commissioners who were empowered to do so, sold the section on April 12, 1830, to the highest bidders. David Gharkey was the largest purchaser, he buying one tract in the northwest quarter of 135 and 25-100 acres for $500.38. Samuel G. Jackson bought 28 and 50-100 acres in the same quarter for $116.56. Other parcels were sold as follows: Lots 14, 5 and 11-100 acres to David Gharkey for $51.15; lot 15, 9 and 45-100 to same for $94.59; lot 26, 12 and 54-100 acres to same for $28.34; lot 27, 21 and 56-100 acres to same for $40.53; lot 1, 39 and 24-100 acres to Thomas Galyon for $49.05; lot 2, 41 acres to James Jackson for $51.25; lot 3, 40 acres to Samuel

## CENTER TOWNSHIP.

Jackson for $50.00; lot 4, 40 and 25-100 acres to same for $50.31; lot 5, 40 and 75-100 acres to Peter Nolin for $107.17¼; lot 6, 40 acres to David Gharkey for $60.00; lot 7, 41 acres to same for $61.50; lot 8, 39 and 24-100 acres to M. Buck for $58.86; lot 16, 3 and 44-100 acres to James Hodge for $16.37½; lot 17, 3 and 33 1-3 acres to James Murphy for $13.48½; lot 28, 3 and 34-100 acres to same for $16.28½; lot 19, 3 and 54-100 acres to Ezekiel Jewell for $15.93; lot 20, 3 and 93-100 acres to William Fitzpatrick for $17.17¼; lot 21, 3 and 92-100 acres to Joseph A. Vestal for $23.52; lot 22, 9 and 71-100 acres to John Marshall for $38.84; lot 23, 6 and 82-100 acres to Abner Smith for $20.66½; lot 24, 6 and 82-100 acres to I. Edwards for $20.46; lot 25, 6 and 82-100 acres to James Hodge for $13.64; lot 28, 21 and 56-100 acres to David Gharkey for $53.12½; lot 29, 24 and 83-100 acres to William Fitzpatrick for $55.86¾. This left only the strip of land extending from Jackson to Adams streets and six blocks beginning at Walnut and running west to Gharkey street. This strip was laid out in six blocks, numbered from one to six consecutively, these were sub-divided into lots. eight to the block, making each lot 62½ by 125 feet.

Block No. 1 is that portion of ground surrounded by Walnut, Adams, High and Jackson streets. Lots 1, 2, 3 and 4 front on Jackson, beginning at Walnut, conseqnently lot 1 in block 1 is on the corner of Walnut and Jackson streets, 62½ feet on Jackson and 125 on Walnut. This lot was sold to Joel Russell for twenty dollars and was the highest priced lot in the block. Thomas C. Anthony bought lot No. 2, where Turner's saloon and Dr. Morin's barber shop is located for seven dollars. Lots No 5 and 6, the corner now owned and occupied by Dr. Kemper (one-fourth of the block) was sold to Samuel W. Harland for six dollars each $12 for two lots. The corner now owned and occupied by the Misses Calvert was sold to William VanMatre for nine dollars, while that part west of the alley now occupied by Mr. McNaughton and W. H. Moreland as residences was sold to Samuel W. Harland for seven dollars, and the corner lot owned by Mr. Kerwood to the same person for eight dollars. The quarter of this block now occupied by the High street M. E. church and parsonage was sold to William Van-Matre for eleven dollars, the one bringing five and the other six dollars. D. Thompson bought the two lots now owned by Henry Klein on the corner of Jackson and Liberty streets for fifteen dollars. D. W. Lyons purchased the lot where C. B. Templar's residence stands for eight dollars, and the one joining it on the west extending to the alley, for seven dollars. David Gharkey bought the west half of block six, extending from the corner of Jackson and Gharkey streets south to

Adams street and east to the first alley, for twelve dollars. And all this was only about sixty-nine years ago.

Section 16, like 15, is all inside the Muncie city limits. White river crosses the northwest corner of the section. April 25, 1829, Isaac Fielder entered the east half of the southeast quarter of section 17; (80 acres).

The next entry was made by Levi Bishop, March 20, 1830, when he entered the entire southwest quarter of the section (140 acres) during the same year (1830) entries were made by David Gharkey, John Collins, James and John McKee and in 1832 by George Calvert. Most of this section is now platted and within the limits of the city or suberbs. However there are still some outlying tracts; these are owned by H. C. Keesling, J. A. Umbarger and D. Kinney. Under article 7 of the treaty made with the Indians at St. Marys, O., October 5, 1818, Goldsmith C. Gilbert secured the fractional southwest quarter (149 and 59.100 acres) and the southeast quarter (160 acres) of section 18; this included the entire south half of the section. Entries were afterward made in 18 through the land office by Thomas Collins in 1829, John McKee in 1830, Levi Bishop in 1831, Thomas Collins again in 1834 and Morgan Johns in 1835. The section lies just west of the city of Muncie on both sides of White river which pretty evenly divides it, and is owned by J. A. Umbarger, Joseph Stradling, H. Stephens, A. Humes, J. J. Warfel, Consumers Paper Company, D. Kinney, J. B. Scott and T. J. Williamson. May 26, 1831, Jeremiah A. Wilson purchased of the government the fractional west half of the southwest quarter of section 19, containing 74 acres. This land, with others, is still in the Wilson family. After Mr. Wilson came William Briggs and John Tomlinson in 1832, Asher Storer in 1833, Abner Perdieu in 1834, Thomas Bishop, Absolem Perdieu and Joseph Yount in 1835. The present owners of section 19 are J. B. Ssott, T. J. Williamson, M. Perdieu, A. Yingling, S. and R. Martin, J. Perdieu, John Castle, William Y. Williams, M. and S. Martin, C. and M. Huffer and W. and B. Wilson. The section has three miles of public road and Buck creek crosses the southeast corner of the section in a southwest direction.

On October 25, 1831, William McConnell entered the ease half of the northeost quaater of section 20 (80 acres). Here Mr. McConnell lived for many years and raised his family. The old family residence stands a little west of the Middletown road (now pike) on the north bank of Buck creek. On the same day of this entry John McConnell, Jr., entered the west half of this quarter, making 160 acres in the two entries. John, the eldest son of Wm. McConnell, still

## CENTER TOWNSHIP. 117

owns the north part of this tract. A portion of it, however, has been platted as a suburb of the city.

Near the southeast corner of this northeast quarter of section 20 a saw mill was built in the early days, and power furnished by the water of Buck creek. Subsequently, early in the fifties, Mr. Samuel Hurst, a gentleman of English nativity, purchased this mill site and erected a woolen mill, which he operated successfully for a long time. After his death his son, William, continued the business for a number of years, when the machinery was taken out and the whole converted into a flouring mill; but those old land marks have all disappeared. Other settlers followed Mr. McConnell, and entries of land were made in section 20 by William Y. Williams, in 1832; Samuel and Asher Storer in 1833; Daniel Wilson and John McConnell in 1834; William McConnell again in 1835, and Charles Storer in 1836.

Aside from the portion of section 20 above mentioned as being platted, we find the land now owned by John McConnell, J. A. Miller, H. C. Keesling, C. Witt, John W. Wilson, M. West and F. Hines. The section has over four miles of public road, including the Muncie and Middletown free pike, which crosses the southeast portion of the section, and school number 10 is located on this pike in the northwest part of the southeast quarter. Buck creek crosses the north half of the section in a generally west course.

The first entry of public land in section 21 was made by Job Garner on November 5, 1831. This was the east half of the southeast quarter, (80 acres.) The south half of this tract is now owned by ex-Sheriff John W. Dungan. The next entries on record were these of Benjamin Irwin Blythe, James Garner, Daniel Cline and Asher Storer in 1832 and William Clary, Samuel Storer and David Storer in 1833. The north part of the section is platted and much of it improved, being a portion of Avondale, a suberb of Muncie. Other lands in the section are owned by the Muncie Land Company, J. Stewart, S. Campbell, G. Bowers, M. D. Witt, John Dungan, John W. Wilson and The Muncie Pulp Company, who have their extensive mills in the south-eastern portion of the section. Another large manufacturing interest carried on in section 21 is that of the Muncie Steel Works which is located near the half section line on the east side of the section and west side of Walnut street, which forms the east line of the section. Isaac Tilden was the first purchaser of land in section 22 his entry bears the date of July 8, 1830, and was the west half of the northwest quarter having its northwest corner at the present crossing of Homer avenue and Walnut street. After this enteries were made in 22 by Pairpoint Blowers in 1830, Daniel Thompson in 1831, Anderson Redman in 1832 and by Oliver H. Smith and George Thompson in 1835. The section with the exception of 60 acres in the southeast corner belonging to George Luick is all platted and mostly in the suberb of Congerville.

Section 23 was all purchased of the government during the years of 1835 and '36. The first of these entries was made by Thomas Kirby on July 21, 1835. This was the west half of the northwest quarter, following the purchase of Mr. Kirby were those of Joseph Jackson, Oliver H. Smith, Stewart Boltin and George Thompson in 1835· and Joseph Johnson, Henry Henkle and Oliver H. Smith in 1836. The present owners (others than those owning in the northwest quarter which is all in the town platt) are P. W. Feanklin Muncie Land Company, M. Kurp, W. H. Luick, C. Luick, L. Detrick, C. Heath, J. Heation, J. Mock and George Luick.

Section 24 is on the east side of the township, and joins Liberty. The first entry of land in this section was made on the 3rd of October 1827 by Charles Stout. It was tne east half of the northwest quarter 80 acres. White river runs through this tract near the center in almost a due nort direction James Jackson entered an 80 in the section Dec. 7 of the same year. In 1830 (Jan. 21) Johnson King entered the east half of the southwest quarter of the section. White river runs in a north course through this tract also, and along the river the banks are high and bluffy. Here among these hills was the famous "Old town," and here near the south line of section 24, is the place where legent says was planted the stake where the Indians executed their prisoners by burning them at this stake. It is said the stake was afterwards cut down and made into canes or walking sticks, but be this as it may, when we were boys there were many stories told of the ghosts that were seen hovering about the "old town" hills, supposed to be the spirits of the departed Indians and their victims, and many bloodless battles were fought over again by these specters for the especial delectation of the gullible and the superstitious, and at one time the excitement ran so high that persons came from many miles around to witness the uncanny ghost dances at "old town" hills, but after a certain painter, (who by the way still lives in Muncie) with other associates had played ghost, until they were about to be captured, or at least feared so, they desisted, which broke up the ghost business, and nothing has been heard of them for many years. Near the northwest corner of 14 is an old residence on the west side of the Burlington pike owned by Mr. P. W. Franklin, which is one of the old landmarks. The house stands a short distance south of where the Smithfield pike leaves the Burlington pike. It was built early in the forties, has been occupied by thirty-one families and,

## CENTER TOWNSHIP.

strange to say, there never was a death in the house. After the entry above mentioned of Mr. King in 1830, the next was that of John Moore, in February, 1821, then that of Lloyd Wilcoxon in November, 1831, and Joseph Dungan, James Jackson and Littleton Dowty in 1833. Section 24 is now owned by W. Ribble, William Walling's heirs, M. Leonard, W. H. Luick, P. W. Franklin, D. H. Simmons, J. L. Simmons, John Inlow, E. C. Ribble and M. V. Warner.

The first land that was ever entered in the government land office and lying in Center township was the east half of the southeast quarter of section 25, lying in the southeast corner of the township. The 80-acre tract was entered on December 24, 1822, by James Bryson. After this, purchases in 25 were made by Henry Massburg in 1831, Samuel Simmons and Samuel Cecil, Jr., in 1832, Samuel Simmons, Samuel Cecil and Johnson King in 1834, and Littleton Dowty in 1835. The present land owners in section 25 are John Inlow, Wm. Driscoll, S. Cecil, W. H. Luick, C. Fullhart, R. A. Johnson, (assignee) O. Lenon, H. Morris, J. Reynolds, J. Hopping and C. Hopping.

Section 26 was all taken up in 1834, '35 and '36, by Wm. Heaton in 1834, Littleton Dowty, Henry Massburg and Samuel Moore in 1835, and William Fowler, James Homan, Arthur Morrison, Henry Keys, Thomas C. Anthony, Samuel Heaton, Robert Gibson and Daniel Heaton in 1836. Twenty-six is owned at present by W. H. Luick, J. H. Huffman, R. Walburn, W. Heaton, Cox & Brown, Lewis Rees, H. C. Parkison, F. W. Ross, A. Whitney and L. Ross and heirs. The section has 3½ miles of public road, one mile being free pike, and school No. 6 is located on the northwest quarter of the section. Pairpoint Blowers and Thomas Goble were the pioneer land owners in section 27, their entries dating back to 1830. In 1832, Charles Mansfield entered two 80-acre tracts. In 1833 there were two entries made by James Mansfield, in 1834 one by Anda Gibson and in 1836 the remainder of the public lands were taken up by Wm. Kiger and Thomas C. Anthony. The section is now owned by Lewis Rees, G. W. Carmichael, B. A. Rees, E. Postal, E. and L. Postal, O. A. McConnell and S. and A. Postal. The section has three miles of public road, one mile of which is the Walnut street free pike. The southwest and west part of the section is drained by Buck Creek.

In section 28 entries of public lands were made as follows: In 1831 by John Brown; in 1832 by Charles Mansfield; in 1833 by James Mansfield, and in 1835 by Wm. H. Brumfield, Wm. Chipman, Oliver H Smith and Elizabeth Brumfield. The present owners of this section are W. A. Haymond, John R. Hines, John W. Wilson, John McConnell, Thomas J. Fuson, A. McKinney, J. N. Shaw and J. F. Carpenter. The Cincinnati Division of the L. E. & W. Railroad crosses the east part of the section.

Section 29 was taken up in 1835 and '36 by Oliver H. Smith and Arnold, Naudine, Edward, Tatuall and Merritt Canby (in 1835 and 1836) and William Y. Williams in 1835, and by Thomas Brumfield, John Brooks and David Storer in 1836. At present the land owners in section 29 are John W. Wilson, I. B. Barrett, G. L. Lenon, C. E. Armintage, W. A. Reynolds, A. Clark, R. Carmin, O. Clark, W. Clark and William Clark.

Section 30 is the southwest corner of Center township. The first land entries of this section were in 1831 by William Finley, Jeremiah A. Wilson and Jesse McKinney. One entry in 1834 by Abner Perdieu, two in 1835 by Asher Storer and Patrick Justice, and three in 1836 by Daniel Wilson, Warren Stewart and Joseph Thomas. Section 30 is now owned by C. E. Armintage, W. Wilson, J. A. Wilson, N. F. Pittenger, E. J. Pence, Farrer & Fudge, C. Coffman, E. & M. Storer, C. M. Perdieu and A. C. Perdieu.

Old time slips away
'Til it seems but a day
(Yet 'tis seventy-odd years, we know),
Since the fiast cabin stood
In the dark, gloomy wood—
The pioneer home of Monroe.

Old earth for the floor,
Split puncheons the door,
But the latch-string hung outward, you know ;
Warm welcome and rest
Awaited the guest
Of the first pioneers of Monroe.

But the old pioneer
Is no longer here,
Yet his influence continues to grow.
Golden fields now appear
Where roamed the wild deer
When the pioneers came to Monroe.

Modern mansions are found
On the same spot of ground
Where log cabins stood years ago,
And mud roads at last
Are things of the past
Since the pioneers came to Monroe.

The old corduroys,
When we were beys,
Were bumpy, rough and slow,
But the pikes of today
Have chased them away
Since the pioneers came to Monroe.

But the old pioneer,
With the bear and the deer.
Have gone, like the melting of snow.
Yet still we may find
Many men of their kind—
Warm-hearted, brave men of Monroe.

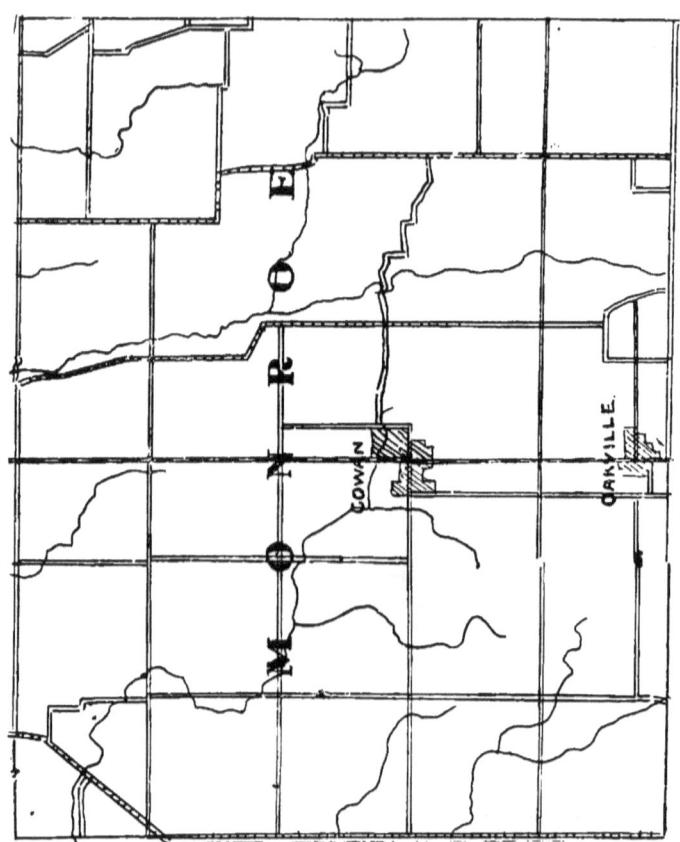

# Monroe Township.

Monroe is the most southern of the middle tier of townships. It is bounded on the north by Center, east by Perry and west by Salem township, while its southern line is the north line of Henry County.

In size Monroe is fine by six miles, containing thirty sections, and, in round numbers, 19,200 acres. In this, as in most of our civil townships, the congeessional townships ran over the border lines, and we find all of Monroe in Range 10 east, but only four-fifths—or Sections 1 to 24, inclusive—in Township 19 north, while Sections 31 to 36. inclusive—they being the north tier—are in Township 20 north. Monroe is generally level land, the only notable exceptions being along the southern line, and in the southeastern part of the township, where the land is more rolling.

The township is well drained by Buck creek, Flat Spring creek and Juda branch in the eastern half of the township, while "No name" and other tributaries of Bell creek drain the western portion of the township. Most of these creeks and branches have been straightened by being ditched, thus reclaiming many acres of land, which have become very productive and proportionately valuable.

Monroe was originally covered by dense forests of valuable timber, which has almost entirely disappeared. The natural law of supply and demand regulating values is very evident in the advance prices of timber from the pioneer days of our county to the present. Where the timber at one time was considered of no value, would, if we had it today, be of many times the value of the land on which it grew.

As to the first settler in Monroe township, there seems no doubt of his being Mr. Jonathan Mills, who came with his family from Wayne county to Monroe township in Delaware. This was in the fall of 1821. Mr. Mills was related by marriage to the Gibson family, also pioneers of Monroe and Perry, and a name as familiar in the southern part of the county as is that of Black and Stafford in the northern part. Mr. Mills seems to have been a perfect type of the woodsman and hunter, never clearing more land than was needed for raising grain and vegetables for home consumption, depending on the chase for his exchangeable commodities. It is said of him that whenever he could hear a neighbor's chickens crow the neighborhood was too crowded for him, and he at once broke camp and went in search of more retired territory, And so in the case of his Monroe township home, as he remained here but a few years (about 1830), when he moved on to the westward, locating near Anderson. Mr. Mills never entered land in the township, but, it would seem, just squatted and remained until the settlers began to get thick and game scarce.

The first entry of land ever made in Monroe township was on January 15, 1827, by Amaziah Beeson. The tract purchased was the east half of the northeast quarter of section 10 (80 acres). This tract of land lies on the east side of the Muncie and Newcastle pike, five miles south of Muncie, and is owned by W. F. Anderson, M. Losh and James Watson.

The next entry in the township was the east half of the southeast quarter of section 3 (80 acres), and was entered on March 31, 1827, by Benjamin Antrim. This tract lies adjoining the entry made by Mr. Beeson, on the north, so all the lands entered in Monroe township prior to 1828 was this strip of land, one mile long by one-fourth of a mile wide. During the year 1828 Valentine Gibson entered the west half of the southeast quarter of section 2; Robert Gibson the west half of the northeast quarter of section 12, and Zenas Beeson the east half of the northeast quarter of section 23. Thus it will be seen that in the space of two years five settlers only had taken up their abode within a territory of about two and a half miles each way, and this was about the time that Mr. Jonathan Mills concluded that the neighborhood was becoming entirely too thickly settled for him. During the year 1829 there were five entries in the township. They were Peter Simmons, in section 10; Willliam Gibson, in section 12; Rebecca Gable, in section 15, and Lauvel Brown and James Mansfield, in section 23. Thus in three years from the time of the first purchase of public lands in Monroe township there were but ten entries of about 800 acres. However, it should not be presumed that there were only ten families living in the township at this time, for we find many settlers lived on and improved their land extensively before making their purchase. This was, perhaps, in many instances on account of financial inability, and, perhaps, sometimes neglect. Be that as it may, it is a matter of history that these delays very frequently caused neighborhood troubles and feuds that required years to heal, as sometimes one man would improve land that some one would enter and dispossess the original squatter.

During the year 1830 there were ten entries of public land recorded for Monroe township, and the following year (1831) the purchases numbered nineteen. In 1832 there were twenty-two. But here we note a decrease in the settling up of the township, as in 1833 there were but ten entries recorded. However, in the next year, 1834, the number had

HOME AND NURSERY OF WILLARD FULLHART,
Four miles southeast of Muncie on Burlington pike, Monroe township.

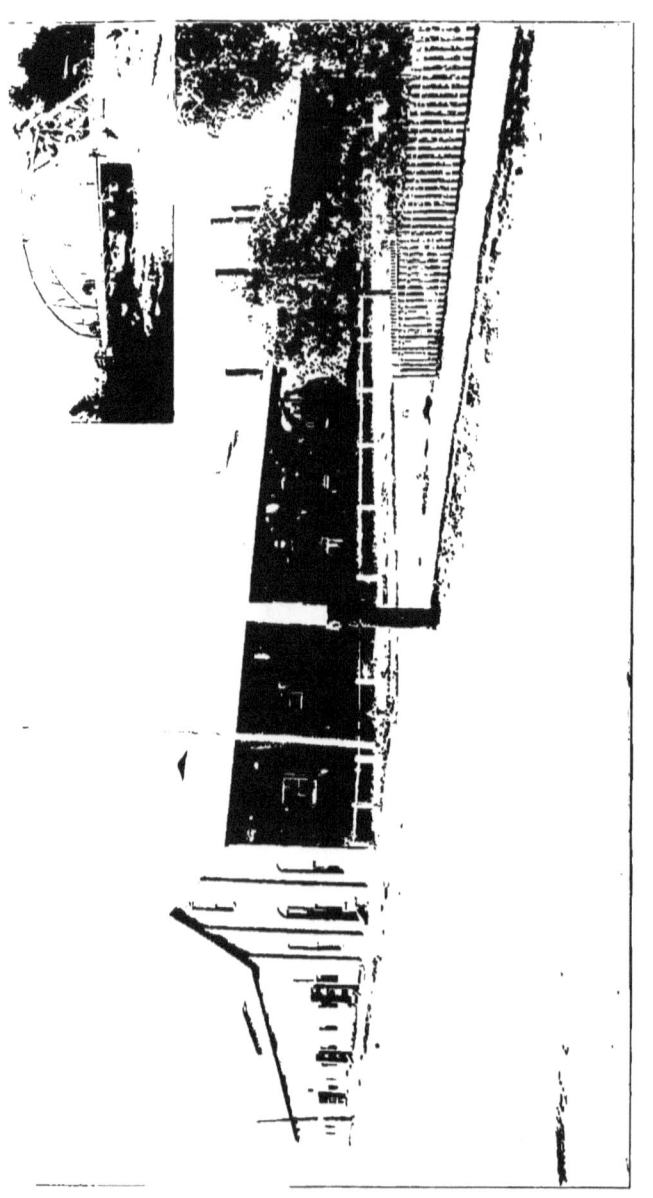

## INDIANA BRIDGE CO.

Showing 200-foot span of their North Walnut street bridge, Muncie. Manufacturers of Steel Bridges, Substructures, Viaducts, Roof Trusses and Steel Buildings. Established in 1886. Annual capacity, 5,000 tons.
C. W. Kimbrough, Pres. and Gen. Mgr.    Geo. F. McCulloch, Vice-Pres.    John R. Marsh, Sec. and Chief Engineer.

## MONROE TOWNSHIP.

again increased to the maximum up to this time, there being twenty-two entries made again this year. In 1835 the number of entries reached thirty-four. However, during the following year (1836) the rush at the land office was correspondingly great for Monroe lands, as in other townships, and the choice lands in all parts of the county seem to have been taken up by the close of this year. The number of entries of Monroe lands during the year of 1836 were ninety-seven, or more than in any three years before or afterwards, as during 1837 there were but ten entries, and in 1838 there were but three. The last of these were two 40-acre tracts, entered on December 6, 1838, by William M. Clarke, they being the southeast quarter of the southwest quarter of section 1, now owned by E. Carmichael, and the northwest quarter of the southwest quarter of section 17, now owned by E. and R. Nixon, the two tracts being some five and a half miles apart, and the last of the public lands in Monroe township, except school section No. 16, which was sold in July and August, 1847.

In this chapter we propose giving the history of that portion of Monroe township lying in township 20, north, being the north tier of sections and numbered 31 to 36 inclusive.

The public lands of section 31 (the northwest section of the township) were entered by Ralph Heath in 1830; Edmond Aldredge, Enoch Tomlinson and Jesse McKinney in 1831; Enoch Tomlinson in 1835 and William Hutton and Arnold, Nadine, Edward, Tatuall and Merritt Canby in 1836.

This section is now owned by B. Reynolds, A. W. Ross, C. Gibson, J. A. Tomlinson, E. Miller, J. W. Driscoll's heirs and J. A. Ross. Section 31 has a public road on its south line, and the Muncie and Middletown pike angles through the section.

The public land in section 32 was all entered in the year 1836, from January 6 to October 17, by Abner McCartney, William Hutton, Arnold Nadine, Edward Tatuall and Merritt Canby, Mary St. Clair, John Rupe and Jeptha Johnson.

The present land owners in section 32 are G. F. Heath, J. and J. Peacock, B. Reynolds, A. W. Ross, Samuel Drumm, B. Bartling, C. Gibson and the heirs of J. W. Driscoll. Public roads are located on the north, south and east lines, also along the south half of the west line, and school No. 10 is in the northeast corner of the section.

During the year 1835 Isaac Branson, Oliver H. Smith and Patrick Carmichael entered land in section 33, on January 1, 1836, Wm. H. Brumfield entered an 80 acre tract, and on the 27th of the month Mary St. Clair entered a quarter section which was the last of the public land in the section. The present landlords of 33 are T. J. Fuson, L. Fuson, D.

Shaw, Samuel Davis, M. Beemer, A. E. Pugh, J. N. Shaw, E. R. Clark, W. T. Clark, C. L. Pence, N. J. Ogle and N. Ogle.

This section has a public road on the north, south and west line. The Cincinnati division of the L. E. & W. railroad runs across the section one quarter of a mile west of the east line.

Land was entered in section 35 by Charles Mansfield, Wm. Clark, John Mansfield and Samuel Andrews in 1832, by Jacob Whitinger in 1833; by "Anda" Gibson and Amos Harrold in 1834, and by Samuel Heaton, Henry Whitinger and James Mansfield in 1836.

The present owners are V. G. Carmichael, L. Carmichael, Charles Cooley, J. Stiffler, N. McKinney, O. and L. Williams, O. Williams, A. P. Reed, T. Fuson, Anda Gibson estate and L. Humbarger. The section has public roads on the north and south lines while the Muncie and New Castle pike crosses the sction on and near the center, tne section is crossed near the center by Buck Creek in a west of north direction.

In 1833 James Allison, Christian Acker and John Acker purchased public land in section 35. In 1835 Garret Gibson and Samuel Heaton entered 40 acres each. In 1836 the remainder of the section was entered by William Heaton and William Abrams. These lands are now owned by William W. Ross, J. Drumm, J. W. Abrell, S. Carmichael, V. G. Carmichael, Catherine Gibson and I. Lenox. The section has two miles of public roads besides the Macedonia pike crosses the section north and south through the center. School No. 1 is in the south center, of section and a M. E. church in the northeast corner.

Lewis Rees entered two 80 acre tracts of land in section 36 in the year of 1830 and one 80 acre tract in 1831. In 1832 Thomas Hacket (a step-son of Cornelius Vanasdol, the first settler of Perry township) entered 40 acres. In 1833 Lewis Rees and Stewart Boltin each entered a 40 acre tract. In 1835 Samuel Cecil entered 40 acres. In 1835 Lewis Rees entered two 80's and a 40; leaving a 40 acre tract which was entered by Samuel Cecil June 6, 1836. Mr. Rees' entries in cludeded three-fourtes of the section or 480 acres. The section is owned at this time by W. Fullhart, W. Moore, A. Conner, J. Rees and J. Reynolds, A. G. Kiger, David Rees, G. and L. Hughes, O. M. Bell and G. W. Fullhart. The section has two and a quarter miles of public road, and a half mile of free gravel pike. White river crosses the northeast corner of the section cutting off about 30 acres on the east side.

Section 1 in Monroe township is the most eastern section

## MONROE TOWNSHIP.

of the most northern tier in Congressional township No. 19 North. In 1830 Bowater Gibson and Rebecca Keasling each entered an 80-acre tract of land. In 1831 Mr. Gibson entered another 80-acre tract. In 2832 Daniel Keasling entered an 80 and a 40-acre tract. In 1833 John William Rhoades entered 80 acres. In 1836 Valentine Gibson entered 80 acres and Jacob Keasling 40, which was the last of the public land in the section. The land owners in section 1 at this time are G. and L. Hughes, R. Rees, C. A. Fullhart, M. Bell, P. Walburn, E. Rees, C. Cunningham, E. Carmichael and J. W. Walburn. Section 1 has no public roads on its section lines, although one crosses the section east and west through the center, and another three-fourths of a mile, near the east line.

In section 2 Valentine Gibson was the first purchaser of the public domain. His entry was made on January 19, 1831; following his entry was that of Elisha Gibson, in 1832; William Clark, in 1833; John Gibson, David Beard, Otho Williams and Elisha Gibson, in 1836, and Boyd Linville in 1837. The present owners of these lands are W. W. Ross, P. Walburn, Catharine Gibson, G. and M. Ross, M. J. Clark, J. W. Walburn, E. Carmichael, M. E. Anderson and W. F. Anderson. This section has two miles of good roads, more than half of which are free gravel pike.

The first purchase of public land in section 3 was Oct. 25, 1831, by Isaac Branson. Then came the purchases of Abe Williams in 1832, Jacob Whitinger, Jr., in 1833, French Triplett, John Crum and Homer Brooks in 1834, Arnold, Naudine, Edward, Tatuall and Merritt Canby and Absalom Gibson in 1836, followed by the last entry in the section by Benjamin Antrim, on March 31, 1837.

The title to the lands in section 3 is now held by L. Humbarger, M. J. Clark, W. E. Driscoll, M. Oard, J. A. Stewart, C. Gibson, W. B. Kline, R. J. Henley, W. F. Anderson, W. F. Watson, and William Snider. School No. 2 is located at the north center of the northwest quarter of this section. The section has one and three-fourth miles of public road, besides one mile of the Walnut street pike. The east half of the section is well drained by Buck creek crossing it from south to north.

The first public land taken up in section 4 was on November 4, 1835, this entry being made by John Rudolph Palmer, and is a 40-acre tract now owned by W. B. Kline.

The balance of the public land in this section was all entered the next year (1836) by Arnold Naudine, Edward Tatuall and Merritt Canby, John Rudolph Palmer and Mary St. Clair.

Section 4 is owned at this time by C. Gibson, W. B.

Kline, G. Nichols, John Nichols, W. S. Finley, William Snider, M. Gibson, W. H. Peacock, R. Cheesman, and J. and M. Heaton. The section has public roads on the north, south and west, and the L. E. & W. railroad crosses north and south through the section.

In section 5 the first entry was made by William Owen on March 17, 1834, and another by George Washington Finley in the following month (April) of the same year. In 1835 Robert Heath, Jr., entered a 40-acre tract, a portion of the land now owned by R. Cheesman. Then the balance of the public land was taken up in 1836 by Mary St. Clair and Abner McCarty.

Section 5 is now owned by M. D. Witt, A. McConnell, W. W. Ross, E. A. Funkhouser, R. Cheesman, William Miller, W. Cheesmsn, and F. and C. Clevenger. This section has a public road on each section line.

On the 25th day of July, 1831, Aaron Ross purchased the first land in section 6, Monroe township, of the government. This was the north half of the northwest quarter of the section, and is still owned by a member of the family, Mr. J. A. Ross. James McKinney entered a tract in 1832, the Canbys in 1834; Abner McCarty, the Canbys and Harvey Heath in 1836. This was the last of the public lands in section 6.

The present owners of these lands are D. R. Armentage estate, J. A. Ross, S. Acker, F. M. Mercer, J. T. Heath, E. Dewitt, Harvey Heath and W. W. Ross. The section has a public road on the north, south and east lines, a free gravel pike on the west line, with the Middletown pike crossing the northwest corner of the section.

On the 19th day of February, 1836, Harvey Heath entered the northeast quarter of the northwest quarter (40 acres) of section 7, and the following May he entered 40 acres just north of this tract in section 6 (before mentioned.) Here Mr. Heath built his cabin and brought his wife, and here the two have lived continuously ever since, and still live, one of the few instances of where a Delaware county pioneer can be found occupying his original home that he purchased of the government, and the only case we have yet found where the husband and wife are still enjoying that first home together. Mr. Heath is in his 86th year, and his wife is his senior by a few years. They have accumulated a competency and are prepared for the other home at the 'Master's call. The others entering land in section 7 during this year (1836) were William Drumm, John Losh, Sr., William Tamsett, Ephraim Bundy, Richard S. Taylor and Thomas Fleming. These purchases included all the land in the section, except a

## AFTER FIFTY YEARS.

Fifty years ago there was a firm doing a furniture and undertaking business on the north side of Main street, opposite the old Anthony "Tavern." The old "Tavern" has been superseded by the Kirby House, and on the opposite side of the street is the magnificent establishment of Potter & Moffitt, Undertakers and dealers in Furniture, showing as great improvement as does the modern university over the old log school house.

## MONROE TOWNSHIP.

47-acre tract, which was entered on February 13, 1837, by Buford Jones.

The owners of the land in section 7 now are S. Pitzer, Harvey Heath, E. T. Sharp, J. H. Heaton, D. M. Hays, W. H. Sweigart, J. H. Clevenger, and J. McLain. School No. 4 is located in the east center of this section, and public roads surround the entire section, that on the west line being a free pike.

Mary St. Clair, who entered several tracts of land in the township, purchased the first public land in section 8 on December 18, 1834. This purchase was the east half of the northeast quarter, now in the name of A. Tuttle, L. Trowbridge, and G. W. Kabrick. All the remaining land in the section was entered during the next year (1836) by Mary Moore, Mary St. Clair, and John S. Resler.

The land in this section is owned at this time by A. Tuttle, L. Trowbridge, G. W. Kabrick, S. Davis, N. J. Clark, J. Houck, I. Turner, U. and C. Springer, C. Goodwin, P. Oxley, and A. Acker. Public roads surround the section on each section line.

One-half of section 9 was entered in 1835 and the other half in 1836. The first entries were made by John Gibson and Enos Strawn, both on November 19, 1835, Mary St. Clair making the other entry of that year December 18.

In 1836 the balance of the section was entered by John Beard, John Gibson and Thomas Strawn, Jr., and now, some sixty-two years since these first purchases, we find none of the original names among the free-holders of the section, but in their stead we have Mrs. W. Snider, Wm. Snider, W. and E. Quick et. al., John H. Reynolds, A. Peacock, S. Drumm, J. Hill, J. A. Flemming, C. Houck, S. Houck, M. Houck, B. C. Bowman, J. Houck, U. and C. Springer and I. Turner. The section has public roads on each section line. The village of Cowan is situated in the southeast part of the section in which is school No. 5, and through which passes the Cincinnati division of the L. E. & W. railroad.

Section 10 can justly lay claim to the first entry of land in Monroe township, this was the entry made by Amaziah Beeson on January 15, 1827, being the east half of the northeast quarter of the section. The next entry in the section was made January 17, 1829 by Peter Simmons; in 1830 there were two entries made, one by John Mansfield and the other by Samuel Merrill; one in 1832 by Andrew Carmichael, four in 1836 by Miles Harrold, Samuel Underhill, John Branson and Allen Beeson. At present we have as the freeholders in section 10, M. Losh, James Watson, O. P. West, W. H. Neff, A. Quick, H. West, T. Hiatt and C. H. and C. Harris, 10 has 3¾ miles of good road and is in a high state of cultivation. In section 11 the entries were made as follows: Garrett Gibson and John Lenox in 1831, Daniel DeWitt and John Lenox in 1834, Henry Taylor in 1835, Ezekiel T. Hickman, Otto Wilson, John Lenox, Wm. Culberson, Samuel M. West and Henry Taylor in 1836. The present owners of this section are G. and M. Ross, M. J. Simpson, T. Lenox, M. Losh, James Watson. R. and S. Gibson and M. E. Casper. 11 has a public road crossing the southwest part of the section and the Macedonia pike on and near the east line. School No. 6 is located in the east part of the section.

Robert Gibson entered an 80 in section 12 in 1828, Wm. Gibson entered an 80 acre tract in 1829 and another 80 in 1831, after which time there were no more entries untin 1835, when Alexander Cheesman took up an 80 acre tract. In 1836 entries were made by John H. Payton and Wm. Townsend, and the last entry made by Robert Maples April 11, 1837.

The present land owners of section 12 are John Driscoll, M. Gibson, M. and V. Gibson, G. B. Gibson, P. Gibson, J. W. Keesling, N. Gibson, C. E. Turner, Vol. Shockley and F. Shockley. The section has two miles of public road, Flat Spring Creek drains the section passing through it from southeast to northwest.

On the 17th day of March, 1830, Daniel Ribble entered the first land in section 13, Monroe township, it being the northeast quarter of the section, and now owned by J. W. Keesling and J. and N. Chalfant. On September 14 of the same year, Daniel Yandes and John Johnson jointly entered an 80-acre tract in the southwest quarter of the section, after which time entries were made by William Cheesman in 1831, by Jonathan Beeson in 1832; Joseph Cheesman in 1834, and Isiah Lee, Elisha Ogle, Alexander Cheesman and William Cheesman in 1836.

In the list of land owners in section 13 we now find the names J. W. Keesling, J. and N. Chalfant, Vol Shockley, M. Oliphant, P. P. Turner, J. A. Welch, R. Foster and J. W. Nelson.

The section has a public road on the south line, another through the center, east and west, and the Macedonia free gravel pike on the west line.

In 1830, Jonathan Beeson and Jonathan Harrold each entered an 80-acre tract in section 14. After this came the entries of Homer Brooks, John Mansfield and Abel Williams in 1832; Henry Bower in 1834; Joseph Brown in 1835; and William Hickman and John Mansfield in 1836.

The owners of these lands sixty years after the last public land in the section was entered, was U. Springer and T. Turner, W. A. Reynolds, W. Reynolds, et al., L. Benbow, T. Fierce, R. Brown, J. and H. Priddy, S. A. Hiatt, et al., and I. L. Nichols. This section has public roads on the

## MONROE TOWNSHIP.    131

south line and across the northeast corner, also the Macedonia pike on the east line. The section has three church buildings, two in the northeast and one in the southeast corner; also School No. 7 in the southeast part.

One of the early entries of the township was made in section 15, being the east half of the southeast quarter, on July 14, 1827, by John Crum, then Rebecca Gable in 1829, Homer Brooks and William Mansfield in 1831, Andrew Carmichael and David Williams in 1832, David Williams again 1834 secured the last of the public lands in the section. The present owners of 15 are James Watson, F. Nottingham, M. S. Ulrich, J. B. Hupp, J. E. Harrold, M. Harrold, W. B. Harbaugh and D. W. Hickman.

Section 15 has a public road on the south line, also one north and south eighty rods west of the east line. (School) Section 16 was sold as follows: On July 17, 1847 80 acres to Allen C. Perdue for $131; on same date 40 acres to Walter Gibson for $100; on same day, 40 acres to same, $71; same day, 80 acres to Joseph Clevenger, $125.50; same day, 40 acres to Enoch Nation, $71; same day, 40 acres to Walter Gibson, $99; Aug. 13, 1847, 40 acres to Isaac McLain, $71; Aug. 13, 1847, 40 acres to Isaac McLean, $61; July 17, 1847, 40 acres to Enoch Nation, $51; July 17, 1847, 46 acres to Enoch Nation, $61; July 17, 1847, 47 acres to Enoch Nation, $81; July 17, 1847, 40 acres to Wm. J. Hightower, $91; July 17, 1847, 40 acres to Enoch Nation, $61; July 17, 1847, 40 acres to Enoch Nation, $112.

This was sold in lots as here given from one to fourteen inclusive, to the highest bidder, and as will be seen the entire section (640 acres) brought the sum of $1,186.50 or something less than two dollars per acre. This may seem like a very low price for this valuable land, but when we calculate the coast of clearing, ditching, fencing and otherwise improving the land, and compound the interest for fifty-two years, we will perhaps conclude that it cost about as much then as now, yet this would hardly be a reasonable comparison, as the land has yielded some returns to its owners for many years past.

The village of Cowan is partly in this section, the land of the section, the land of the section is now owned by R. and A. Marshall, J. Rinker, D. M. Tuttle, S. H. Reynolds, O. A. Shaw, A. Marshall, J. and E. Kern, J. W. Kern, R. A. Johnson, A. M. Comstock and J. J. Jefferson and E. M Crandell. Sixteen has public roads on the north and south lines, also through the center north and south. The L. E & W. R. R. passes through the section one-quarter of a mile west of the east line.

There was no entries of land recorded in section 17,

until October 1, 1835, when Jacob Bowers entered the west half of the southwest quarter. School house No. 9 is now located on the southwest corner of this eighty acre tract. On the 17th of the same month Samuel Fessler entered the east half of the southeast quarter, now owned by J. A. Bates. In 1836 entries were made by Peter Shiveley, Samuel Fessler, Philip Shiveley, John S. Ressler and Edward Jones, then the last of section 17 was entered by William M. Clark on December 6, 1838. Sixty years later we find the land in section 16 owned by M. Himes, N. J. Ralston, R. E. Chalfant, Priddy et al H. L. Petterson, M. J. Ball, J. A. Bates, E. Nixon and E. and R. Nixon. Seventeen has public roads on its north, south and west lines.

The southwest quarter of section 18 containing 173 and 96-100 acres, was entered by John Swope November 8, 1832. The next entry in the section was that of William Haines in 1834. The next, that of Jacob Bowers in 1835. and the remainder of the public land in the section was taken up by Henry Richman, Wm. Andes, John Tuttle and Adam Banks in 1836. After sixty years we find the owners of land in section 18 to be Joseph Mann, A. Andes, J. J. Clevenger, W. J. Painter, C. Ball, M. Ball, C. Burcaw, S. R. Burcaw, A. D. Welsh, J. W. McKinney and R. M. McKinney. 18 has a public road on each section line, that on the west being a free gravel pike.

The first entry of land in section 19 was made by Wm. Clevenger who entered the east half of the section on November 22, 1832. Michael Thompson entered the east half of the northwest quarter in 1834, and John Fessler and Eleakin Wilson the remainder of the section in 1835. The present owners of land in section 19 are J. W. Jones, S. Davis, N. J. Fleming, N. R. Fleming; G. Fleming and R. C. Ball. Public roads extend along the east, north and west lines of the section. 19 is the southwest corner of the township and consequently the west section of the south tier, and borders on Henry county,

Section 20 was all taken up of the government in 1835, '36 and '37, by James Jones, John Dusthimer, Jesse Raider, John J. Bulingall and George Hivecker in 1835, A. Rhoton in 1836 and John Howell in 1837. The list of landlords in section 20 at this time are N. and H. Swain, C. D. Hale, M and E. Drumm, J. L. Rinker, W. P. Bowers, D. H. Jones and N. R. Fleming. 20 has public roads on the north and west lines, also through the south from east to west.

Section 21 was all taken up by four persons, each securing a quarter section as follows. David Williams the northeast quarter June 4, 1832, Abel Williams southeast quarter October 17, 1831. James Orr the northwest quarter and John

## MONROE TOWNSHIP. 133

Dusthimer the southwest quarter, both on October 16, 1835. The village of Oakville is in the southeast quarter of this section, being near the Henry county line. The section outside of the village is now owned by R. Hickman, C. A. Hickman, L. D. Williams, E. Peckenpaugh, Charles Hill, J. Kern, J. Metzker, T. H. Johnson, M. Veach, A. D. Ball and J. Ball. The section has three miles of public road and the Cincinnati branch of the L. E. & W. R. R. passes through it.

The first entries of land in section 22 were made in 1830 by Michael Bonner, John Howell and John Rutledge. Then in 1831, by Abel Williams in 1833, by Temple Smith, and the last in 1834 by David Williams. This section is now owned by J. B. Yost, D. L. Wright, S. Fleming, J. and W. Yost, L. J. Hickman, J. V. Koons, John Robe, John Rutledge, J. J. Rutledge, J. Metzker and T. Robe.

Section 22 has about 4½ miles of public road, the south half of the section is perhaps entitled to the name of hilly, if any part of the county is worthy of the title. School No. 11 is located in this section at the east end of the village of Oakville.

In 1828, September 10, the first entry of public land was made in section 23. This was an 80-acre tract in the northeast corner of the section, and the entry was made by Zenas Beeson. In 1829, Lauvel Brown, James Mansfield and John Howell entered an 80-acre tract each, after which time we find purchases made by Aaron Stout in 1831, John Mansfield and Abel Williams in 1832, James Orr in 1835, Wm. Underhill and Sarah Davis in 1836. This land is now owned by C. Benbow, A. Nelson, P. Turner, H. Howell, Walter Gibson, T. H Nelson, J. W. Kern, A. West, J. and W. Yost, D. L. Wright, John Robe and Stephen Fleming. Section 23 has roads along the north and south lines and a pike on the east. Buck Creek drains the west part, and since being dredged and ditched has proven that some very valuable land lay hidden along its banks for many years.

Section 24, the southeast section of Monroe township, was entered in small tracts, there being fourteen entries of 40 accres each and one of 80. The entries were made in the following order: David Ogle in 1832, James Ogle and Samuel Shockley in 1834, Valentine Gibson in 1835, David Ogle, Jonas Turner, John Brown, Jonathan Turner and Elisha Ogle in 1836, David C. Martin, William Morris, Gilbert C. Millspaugh, Robert Morris (2 entries) and Jonas Turner in 1837. And now after a lapse of some sixty years we find these lands owned and generally occupied by eight land owners, to-wit: James A. Reynolds, P. Turner, William West, H. Howell, G. L. Holbert, M. B. Preston, M. Gibson and J. Gibson.

Section 24 has public roads on the north and south lines, also a free gravel pike on the west line.

## SETTLEMENT OF SALEM.

The pioneer of Salem,
  As all must agree,
Was Joshua Baxter
  In the year twenty-three.
Then in twenty-six,
  (Some three years later)
Came Robert Williams,
  John and David VanMatre.

During the year twenty-seven,
  (For so goes the tale)
Came Johnson and Marsh,
  Suman, Huston and Dale.
The name of the latter
  Remains with us still,
But to the name Dale
  We have added the "ville."

In the year twenty-eight,
  One eighty acre lot
Was the only entry made,
  And that by Powell Scott,
In the year twenty-nine
  There came many others
Fosnot and Tomlinson,
  The two Nichols brothers.

Daniel Shawhan, Ralph Heath,
  John Lain and Perdue,
George Michael came also,
  And a Carpenter too.
Then in eighteen-thirty
  As by record appears
There were ten names added
  To Salem's pioneers.

In the year thirty-one
  Twenty-seven more came,
After that they become
  Too numerous to name,
But as its more easy,
  As all may suppose,
I shall give you the rest
  Of this history in prose.

## Salem Township.

From the circumstances that Salem township lies in two congressinal townships and also in two ranges, we find two sections No. 1; two No. 2; two No. 13; two No. 24, and two No. 36. The west tier of sections (all bordering on Madison county) is is range 8, east, while all the sections of the town ship east of that tier are in range 9, east.

The north tier of sections, bordering on Mt. Pleasant township, is in congressional township 20, north, while all south of this tier are in township 19, north.

Salem township is five miles north and south, by seven miles east and west, containing thirty-five sections or (in round numbers) 22,400 acres of land. It is the southwest corner township of Delaware couty, and is bounded north by Mt. Pleasant township, east by Monroe township, south by Henry county, and west by Madison county. The surface of the land is generally rolling. This is more observable in the proximity of the streams, but sufficiently so in all portions of the township to make drainage easy and complete. The soil in Salem township is perhaps not excelled in fertility by any body of land of the same extent in the state, and equalled by but few. Originally the face of the country was covered by heavy forests of the variety of timber common to this section of the country, but the immense growth of black walnut timber in section 21, the west half of section 22, the east half of section 20, and the south half of section 16 gave to this neighborhood the name of the "Rich Woods," by which name it has been known for many years. The name has been often more generally applied to a much greater scope of the township than that mentioned above, but we think we are correct in our statement that the term was applied originally to the above described territory, but today the name would seem a misnomer, as the "woods" are nearly all gone, while the "Rich" only remains, and that richness of soil extends generally through the township.

The township is well drained by numerous creeks and branches (now ditches) passing through almost every section of land in the township. White river is the only stream in the township of much size, and it has but two and a half or three miles of its course within the boundaries of Salem, entering the township about one and a fourth miles east of the northwest corner, flows nearly south one mile, thence southwest, and leaves the township two miles south of the northwest corner, thus merely crossing the corner of the

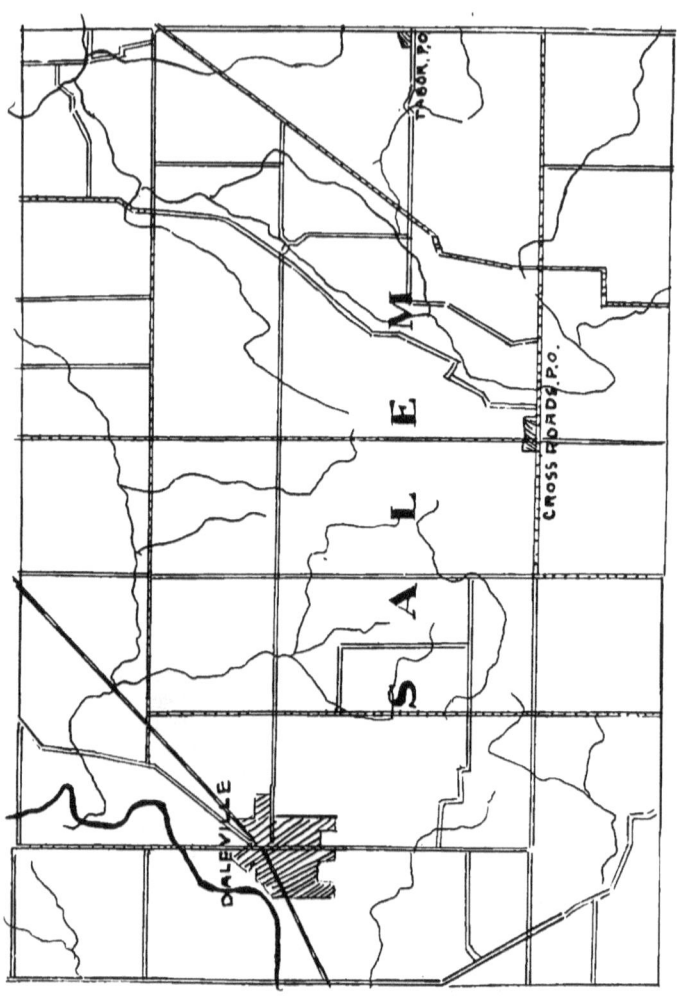

GEORGE E. DUNGAN,
Recorder Delaware County.

LARHUE M. DUNGAN,
Deputy Recorder Delaware County.

ARTHUR H. DUNGAN,
Deputy Recorder Delaware County.

## SALEM TOWNSHIP.

township. Other parts of the township are drained by Bell creek, Sly Fork, Williams creek, Prairie ditch and others.

It is said that William Dilts was the first white man who ever became a permanent resident of the township, although the first person to enter land in the township was Joshua Baxter, who entered the west half of the northeast quarter of section 31 on May 15, 1823. This 80-acre tract lies about one and a half miles northeast of Daleville, on the Yorktown road, and is owned by C. and R. Helvie and L Hoover. Mr. Baxter entered this land about the time Mr. Dilts came to the township. There were evidences of former residents in the township, as huts, built apparently for habitations, were found in different localities, but as they were vacant when the first settlers came, it is fair to suppose they were built as temporary residences for parties who were hunting or trapping in the vicinity, and who, after supplying themselves with meat and furs, sought their former or new homes. Mr. Dilts became a citizen of the township, and resided here a number of years, but later moved to Chesterfield, a few miles west in Madison county, where he spent the remainder of his life, and near where many of his descendants still live.

After the entry of Mr. Baxter in 1823 we have no other land entries on record until November 1, 1826, when John Van Matre entered an 80-acre tract in section 20, and also the northwest quarter of section 21, and on the same day (November 1, 1826) David Van Matre entered the southwest quarter of section 21. Fourteen days later Robert Williams entered an 80-acre tract in section 22. So we see that from 1823, the year of the first purchase of public land in the township, until the close of the year 1826, we have but four purchases of land within the boundary of Salem township. After this the settlers began to arrive and take up the land in increased numbers, until in 1835, during which year there were eighty entries of public lands recorded. The year following (1836) there were but forty-five entries made. However, in this year section 16 (being a school section) was sold in six lots, so that we might consider the purchases in 1836 equal to fifty-one entries, but the years of 1835 and 1836 seem to have about consumed the public lands of Salem township, as at the close of the last mentioned year there were but forty acres of public land remaining unsold in the township. This was the southwest quarter of the southwest quarter of section 24, township 19, north, range 9, east, the southeast section of the township.

This 40-acre tract was entered by Christian Sauerwine on March 22, 1837. This tract is owned at present by O. and L. Pence, and was the last of the Congress land in Salem Among the early settlers of Salem there were many who afterward became prominent characters in the community and who left living monuments to their memory in their posterity, many of whom are still residents of the county. Among such we might mention the names of Dale, Williams, Nation, Witt, Perdue, Summers, Van Matre, Sharp, Pitser, Makepeace, Kilgore, Shoemaker, Stewart, Sunderland, Campbell, Jones, Suman, Fenwick, Fosnot, McAlester, Oliver H. Smith and others.

The first effort at merchandising in Salem was that made by John C. Gustin at what is now Cross Roads, in the year 1832, but for the want of sufficient custom, Mr. Gustin very soon quit the business and returned to Madison county. However, after the lapse of several years, about 1838, William and Erasmus Moffitt opened a stock of goods at the same place (Cross Roads) and continued the business for several years. About the same time of the opening of the Moffitt store at Cross Roads, Abraham Depboye "hung out" the first general store sign at the village of Daleville. Mr. Depboye seems to have met with sufficient success to hold out for some two years, when he, too, closed out his business. And so it seems that for many years merchandising was almost as uncertain in Daleville as is the gold crop in Alaska.

The first school house in Salem was in the "rich woods." The building was on the land of David Van Matre, in section 21, and we find a school taught here as early as 1828-29, by Elza Watkins, a man of superior culture and attainments, and feel it is no disparagement to other townships in the county when we say Salem has ever kept up her reputation for good schools and competent teachers.

As has been heretofore stated, Salem township is in congressional townships 19 and 20 Also in Ranges 8 and 9. Now, in giving its history by sections, we will first take up the tier of sections bordering on Madison county, commencing at the northwest corner of the township we have Section 36. This section is in Township 20 north and Range 8 east. The first to enter land in this section was Oliver H. Smith, father of Hon. M.C. Smith, of Muncie, on May 30, 1831. He entered the northwest quarter of the northeast quarter of this section, 40 acres, and a portion of the land now owned by H. C. Schlegel. On October 15 of the same year Wm C. Van Matre entered the east half of the southeast quarter, now owned by G. Goodpasture.

In 1893 there was but one entry, that of Aaron Brewer, 40 acres, on October 31, 40 acres in 1833 by Samnel Brown, a 40-acre tract by James M. Chambers and an 80 by William Nelson in 1834. In 1835 there were entries made by Jesse Dearth, Frederlck Bronenberg, Jr., and James Miller Chambers, which included all the land of Section 36, except a 40-

## SALEM TOWNSHIP.

acre tract which was entered by John McClanahan on January 27, 1836.

Our records show the present owners of lands in Section 36 to be: H. C. Schlegel, G. Goodpasture, M. and J. Walters, J. J. Schlegel, G. Chambers, J. Rinker and C Thomas. The section has public roads on the north, south and west lines, also a free pike on the east. School No. 3 is located in the southeast corner of this section.

South of Section 36 is Section 1. The earliest purchase of government land in this section was made on March 20, 1827, by Campbell Dale, although Mr. Dale had made purchases in the section south of this some two months prior to this date. The tract entered by him in section 1 was the east half of the southeast quarter, the south part of which is now occupied by the village of Daleville, and the north part owned by M. E. Bronenberg. In May following Chamberlain Hutson entereh the west half of this quarter. In 1831 purchases were made by Jason Hudson and William Caldwell Van Matre. In 1834 by John Bronenberg, and the last of the public land of the section was entered by John and Frederick Bronenberg in 1833.

The section is owned at the present time by J. Beck, J. Rickers' heirs et al., J. Bronenberg, H. Bronenberg, Peter Bronenberg, John Bronenberg and M. E. Bronenberg. There are roads on the north, east and west lines. The village of Daleville occupies the southeast corner, with the Big Four railroad crossing throngh the village.

On January 10, 1827, Campbell Dale purchased one half of section 12 of the government, including the northeast quarter (three-fourths of which is now within the corporate limits of Daleville) the east half of the southeast quarter and the east half of the northwest quarter. In May and June 1829 entries were made in the section by Isaac Carpenter and Thomas Fostnaugh. In 1844 by Allen Makepeace and in 1835 by Allen Makepeace and Joel Copher. The present owners of the land of this section other than town lots in Daleville, are J. Beck, J. Bronenberg, Jos. Dale, A. T. Stewart, J. J. Hurley, J. R. Shoemaker, W. Rozelle, R. I. Frazee, J. G. Hupp and B. F. Lefter. There is a public road on the east and also one on the west of the section, White river enters the section about one-third of a mile west of the northeast corner, then turning almost west, flows out into Madison county a few rods south of the northwest corner of the section.

The first land entry in section 13 was made in 1833, in which year Robert Lindsey Bartlett entered two 40 acre tracts. In 1834 Joshua Hurley entered 80 acres. In 1835 Robert L. Bartlett entered 40, and Joseph Dipboye 240 acres. In 1836 the last of the public lands were purchased by Lewis Rogers and Arbena Doubt. Section 13 is now owned by J. G. Hupp, James H. Walsh, A. C. Ellison, D Yount, S. F. Lanley, M. A. Moffett and R. I. Frazee. The section has about three and a half miles of public roads and school No. 12 is located on the south side of the section. As early as May 5, 1831, John Fleming and Peter Miller entered the southeast quarter of section 24. Mr Fleming taking the east and Mr. Miller the west half of the quarter. However, prior to this (Oct. 23, 1829) the east half of the southwest quarter of the section had been entered by B. F. and Joseph Nichols, after these entries others were made as follows; In 1832 by Jonas Gallahan; in 1833 by Joshua Hurley, in 1835 by William Fleming, Benjamin Bartlett, William O'Briant, Joshua Hurley and Abraham Dipboye, leaving a tract of 40 acres in the northeast corner of the section which was entered by Abraham Dipboye on November 14, 1836. This is the southwest corner of both the township and county, and the section is now owned by F. and E. Cooper, J. Huffman, R. Witt, J. J. Hurley, D. O'Bryant, C. Hurley, C. C. Hurley and C. Dipboye. The section has about three miles of public road on section and half section lines except one road which angles through the section, running from southeast to northwest.

In section 31, township 20, north, range 9, east, is where the first land in Salem ever purchased of the government is located, and as we have before stated, was entered by Joshua Baxter, on May 15, 1823, it being the west half of the northeast quarter of the section. The road running from Yorktown to Daleville enters this tract of land about two miles out from Daleville, and the traveler is on this first entered 80-acre tract when he crosses the little stream near the old Peter Helvie residence. The next entry of land in this section was the west half of the northwest quarter, and was made by John Suman on November 6, 1827. Then came George Michael in 1829, Francis Pugsley in 1832, John Suman, Joseph Van Matre and William Nelson in 1834. Then William Nelson and Jonathan Sheff entered the last of the public land in the section in 1835. The section is now owned by F. Kilgore, L. Hoover, C. and R. Helvie, G. Goodpasture, R. N. Cannon, H. Richman and William Pugsley.

The Yorktown and Daleville public road crosses the east half of the section, and White river the west half in a nearly south course.

The first purchase of public land in section 32 was an 80-acre tract, being the east half of the northwest quarter of the section. The purchaser was Powell Scott, and the entry was dated June 18, 1828. This tract is now owned by J. P. Shoemaker. The Big Four Railroad crosses the southeast

MUNCIE PULP COMPANY'S WORKS.

F. S. HEATH,
President Muncie News Co.

F. J. CLAYPOOL,
Sec. and Treas. Muncie News Co

C. R. HEATH,
Vice-Pres. Muncie News Co.

## SALEM TOWNSHIP. 141

corner of this land about midway between Yorktown and Daleville.

There were no other entries of land in section 32 for almost six years, when in 1834 entries were made by John Knopp, David Kilgore and James Washington Brown, in 1835 by Benjamin Franklin Hancock and Oliver H. Smith, and in 1836 by Oliver H. Smith and David Kilgore.

The present owners of section 32 are W. K. Helvie, F. Kilgore, J. P. Shoemaker, W. R. Moore, J. Miller, J. and M. Miller, Henry Helvie, W. M. Helvie, V. Sullivan and J. F. Cummings. The Big Four Railroad crosses the section from northeast to southwest. The section has free gravel pike on the east and south line, and Prairie ditch drains the south half.

In section 33 John Stewart entered an 80-acre tract on August 22, 1831. This was in the northeast corner of the section. In 1832 two entries were made by Willis Hardwick and William Antrim. In 1834 two entries were made by Jacob Saunders, in 1835 two by Theodore Lewis, and in 1836 two (they being the last of the public lands in the section) by Oliver H. Smith.

This section is now owned by Jeff H. Claypool, W. K. Helvie, Daniel Richman, J. Miller, J. and M. Miller and Henry Helvie. The south half of this section is also drained by Prairie ditch, and has gravel pikes on the east.

Section 34 was all entered by Oliver H. Smith on August 10, 1835. Mr. Smith was an eminent jurist in the broadest sense of the term, as well as an author and historian of some note. He became extensively interested in the early part of our county settlement and his only son, Hon. M. C. Smith, who has represented Delaware county in both branches of the state legislature, as well as having served the city of Muncie several terms as mayor, with distinction and honor, is still one of our respected citizens, hale and hearty, although seventy four years of age, most of these years having been spent in this community.

We now find this section (34) owned by J. Jernegan, M. Jernegan, E. Coffman, M. and C. Paulin, M. Paulin, R. G. Paulin, J. Bennett, E. R. Stewart, and W. Wiseheart. Section 34 has pike on the south and west lines, also a public road on the east line, and north and south through the center.

Warren Stewart entered the east half of the northeast quarter of Section 35, on Nov. 10, 1832. In 1833 Daniel Prilaman entered two eighty-acre tracts. During 1834 there were no entries made but in 1835 Thomas Brumfield, Sr., and Oliver H. Smith each made two entries. In 1836 Thomas Pierce and Joseph Prilaman secured the title to the balance of the public land in this section. These lands are now owned by J. H. Jones, E. L. Athey, J. and A. Wiggerly, W. J. Painter, Daniel W. Rees, J. Richman and S. McNairy. The section has some three and one-half miles of public road, about one-half of which is free gravel pike. School No. 1 is located on the north half of the southeast quarter of this section.

The first landlord in section 36, township 20, north, range 9, east, wast Ralph Heath, who on June 18, 1829 after prospecting in differant parts of the county, and while he had choice of almost all the land in the county, located on the southeast quarter of this section, securing the government title to the entire quarter section, 160 acres. He was the father of Jacob Heath, who is still with us now (1899) and it might seem to my readers like presumption on my part, were I to attempt giving a history of the Heath family in the southern part of Delaware county. Suffice to say they become a numerous family. Some of them have filled, and are still filling high positions of trust and profit in our county, state and nation, and always with credit to themselves and honor to the served.

After Mr. Heath came Samuel Stewart in 1830, Jesse McKinney and James Moffett in 1831, James Moffett again in 1832, James Knott in 1834, and James Goff in 1836. This section of land is now owned by Elijah Miller, S. Coffman, S. and G. Stewart, J. H. Jones, A. W. Ross, T. W. Tuttle, S. McNairy, M. Shirk and S. P. Heath. The section has some three miles of public road, and is well drained by Bell creek and its taibutaries.

We now come to notice that portion of Salem township in Township 19, north, and Range 9, east. Section 1 was first settled for a home by John Lane, a relative of Mr. Heath, who first settled in the adjoining section (36). Mr. Lane entered his land on the same day with Mr. Heath, (June 18, 1829), entering the northeast quarter of the section, so that his future home joined that of his kinsman. In 1832 entries were made in this section by James McKimmey and Asa Bishop. In 1835 by James Knott, and in 1836 by Thomas Perdue, William Simpson and John Jones.

We find the present owners of this valuable land to be John Sunderland, W. Hill, E. Sunderland, S. McNairy, W. Sharp, C. Sunderland and J. Richman. Section 1 has public highways on the east, north and west line, a portion of the south line, and the Muncie and Middletown pike crossing the southeast part of the section.

Robert Heath entered the northeast quarter of Section 2 on New Year's day 1830. In 1831 John Adams, Jr., entered an 80 acre tract, after which time entries were made by Adam Campbell in 1832, Robert Heath, Samuel Grimes Sunderland

## SALEM TOWNSHIP.

and Adam Campbell in 1834, by Eben Pitser, Francis McNairy and William McAlister in 1836.

Section 2 is now owned by J. A. Neese, S. McNairy, A. and L. May, S. Kendell, et. al., I. Pitser, S. Sunderland and William Sunderland. The section has four miles of public road and is well watered and drained by Bell creek and its branches.

The first entry of public land in section 3 was made by Abner McCartney on December 1, 1835. This was the northeast quarter of the section, but Mr. McCartney was not left long without neighbors, as all the land in the section was taken up during the following year (1836) by Griffith Thompson, William McAlister, Theodore Lewis and John Stewart. The present owners of section 3 are E. R. Stewart, Daniel Richman, S. E. Richman, A. H. Bronenburg, D. Richman, J. Moreland and G. Mingle. The section has public highways on the north, south and west lines, those on the north and west being free gravel pikes.

Section 4 was purchased of the government as follows: Southwest quarter by John Marsh June 1, 1831; southeast quarter by John Kennedy May 17, 1834; northeast quarter by James Leviston December 1, 1835, and the northwest quarter by Oliver H. Smith January 1, 1836.

Section 4 is now owned by D. and M. Dillman, J. Fenwick, G. M. Richman, Daniel Richman, W. and J. Coffman, G. Mingle, G. W. Richman and W. A. Shoemaker. Section 4 is a fine section of land, in a high state of cultivation, and the only section in Salem township entirely surrounded with free gravel pikes.

Section 5 in Salem township was somewhat late in getting her lands into market, as the first to avail himself of these lands was Haden Makepeace, who entered the north half of the northwest quarter (now owned by M. E. Helvie), on October 9, 1834. During 1835 purchases of public land were made by John Knoop, William Stewart, John Stewart, Jacob Saunders and Tandy Reynolds, leaving three 40 acre tracts not entered, which were taken up, two by Jonas Shoemaker and one by Wm. Fenwick, in 1836.

Section 5 is now owned by Henry Helvie, Daniel Richman, M. E. Helvie, T. Campbell, J. M. Hancock, J. Shoemaker, W. N. Reynolds, W. A. Shoemaker and Jonathan Shepp. The section has a public road on each of its section lines, those on the north, south and east being free gravel pikes.

School No. 6 is located near the southwest corner of the section, on the pike running east from the village of Daleville.

On the 6th day of November, 1827, when but few white

settlers had located in Salem township, John Suman entered the north half of the northwest quarter of section 6. White river, in a meandering course, divides this tract in almost aqual parts, the tract contains 81 and 17-100 acres, and lies just north of the village of Daleville. Mr. Suman had no landed neighbors in his section until 1831, or four years after his locating, in which year Ransom Makepeace entered the tract adjoing him on the south. On September 1, 1832, Justin Steele entered the southwest quarter of the section, in the corner of which is located a part of the village of Daleville. In 1833 entries were made by Ransom Makepeace and Samuel Rogers; in 1835 by Thomas Fosnot and James Griffith, leaving one 40 acre tract, which was purchased in 1836 by Oliver H. Smith.

Section 6 is now owned by H. Richman, F. W. Heath, William Pugsley, P. Bronenberg, M. Campbell. D. Rinker, J. Harkey and W. Ketchum. The section has about four and a half miles of public road. The C., C., C. & I. Railroad crosses the section from northeast to southwest. White river crosses the northwest corner of the section, and the southwest corner of the section is in the business center of Daleville.

Section 7, having its northwest corner in the village of Daleville, was entered in 1833, '34 and '35, by James Fenwick, in 1833; Michael Gronendyke, in 1834; John Simpson, Stephen Rogers, Henry Rogers and Abraham Pugsley, in 1835. The real estate of this section is now owned by Cary Fenwick, C. Goodpasture, W. Rinker, J. Rinker, E. Chrisman, A. and W. Rinker, M. Herman, J. G. Hupp, A. Rinker, John Davis and D. N. Minnick. The section has public roads on the east, west and north lines, those on the north and west being free gravel pikes.

On the 22nd day of September, 1832, Morgan Van Matre purchased of the government the northeast quarter of the southeast quarter of section 8. This first entered land in this section is now owned, with other lands, by H. Moreland. Following this entry of Mr. Van Matre, the entries in the section were made by James Fenwick, in 1833; Mathias Furrow, David Strickler and John Fesler, in 1834, and Henry Richman and Jesse Windsor, in 1835.

The real estate owners of section 8 are now S Coffman, J. N. Coffman, A. H. Pugsley, Jonathan Shepp, H. Moreland, S. E. Huffman, A. W. Huffman and D. M. Strickler. The section has public roads on the east, west and south to the center of the section on the half section lines.

The west half of the northwest quarter of section 9 was entered by Thomas Windsor on the 10th day of May, 1830. Thomas Pierce made an entry in this section in 1832, Lawrence Wilson in 1834, Thos. Pierce, Wm. Curry Windsor and

## SALEM TOWNSHIP.

David Van Matre in 1835, and William Price and David Strickler in 1836. At the present time we find the title to the lands in section 9 in the name of the following persons: W. R. Landry, George McWilliams, J. R. Shoemaker, M. Richman, W. Swanger and J. P. Huff. Section 9 has free gravel pikes on the north and east sides; also a public road along the west line.

The first entry of land in section 10 in Salem township was made in 1832, in which year there were four entries recorded by two persons, two by Obadiah Meeker, on August 16, and two by Adam Campbell, on August 27, after which there were no further entries made until 1835, when titles were secured by John Davis, David Strickler, Asa French and William Tomlinson. In 1836 William McAlister and Samuel Dusang secured the two remaining 40-acre tracts.

We find the land owners of this section at present to be A. and J. Corwin, H. H. Taylor, D. M. Yingling, M. Makepeace, W. R. Landry, J. M. Fisher, and M. Richman. The section has a free gravel pike on the west line, a public road on the north side and another crossing the southeast corner. School No. 7 is situated in the northeast corner of the section.

The east half of the southeast quarter (now owned by S. J. Moffett and J. Moffett) was the first land purchased of the government in section 11. The purchaser was Evan Pitser, and the date of the purchase September 26, 1831, after which the purchasers of the public lands of this section were as follows: Adam Campbell and William Summers in 1832; Lambert Moffett in 1833; Samuel Grimes Sunderland in 1834 and also in 1835, and David Stickler and John T. Vardeman in 1836.

The land in section 11 is now owned by M. E. Stewart, S. K. Sunderland, Perry V. Stewart, H. H. Taylor, I. Moffett, S. J. Moffett, and W. N. Summers. The section has public roads on the north and south sides, north and south through the center, another crossing the northwest corner, and the Muncie and Middletown pike crossing the southeast corner.

Bailes E. Jones entered the east half of the northwest quarter of section 12, on November 5, 1830. This 80-acre tract is still in the name of Jones, being owned by J. and W. Jones. John Braden Finley and Abner Perdue made entries in 1832; William Scruggs, Lambert Moffett and John B. Finley in 1835; and Abraham Hall, Edward Sharp and Daniel Miller in 1836.

The present owners of section 12 are S. I. Sharp, S. S. Stewart, J. and W. Jones, J. Moffett, J. A. Stewart, R. Bowers, M. E. Bowers, M. Bowers, and W. N. Summers.

The section has gravel pike along the east side and across the northwest corner, a public road along the south and a part of the north line. School house No. 8 is located on the west side at the half section line, and Tabor post office is in the southeast corner of this section.

Joining section 12 on the south is section 13. The public land in this section was entered by John H. Taylor March 11, 1830; Thomas Kidd January 3, 1831; Samuel Clevenger May 24, and Reece Carter June 19, 1833; and William Miller January 7, 1834.

Section 13 is now owned by O. E. Clevenger, Samuel Davis, A. F. Andes, S. C. Bowers, N. J. Fleming, and S. Ball. The section has free gravel pike on the east, and also on the south, and a public road on the north line.

On June 10, 1829, John Tomlinson entered the northwest quarter of section 14. In 1831 entries were made in the section by John Pitser and Aquilla Davis; in 1832 by Asa Bado Watkins and Christian Pence; in 1833 by Lambert Moffett and David McNutt. Present owners are A. F. Andes, Samuel Davis, Joseph F. Bowers, E. Abshire, J. G. Bowers, and M. S. Bowers.

Section 15, in Salem township, is in the south central part of the township, and that our readers may the more readily understand its location, we will state that Cross Roads, Post Office and Village, is situated in the southwest corner of the section. As this section borders on the Richwoods neighborhood, the land has been held at a high value, but whether or not the facts sustain the values, is a matter to be determined by those more directly interested, as it is the duty of the historian to state facts, and then let others search for the reasons. More than two years before any other purchases of public land in this section (July 30, 1829) Daniel Shawhan entered the east half of the southwest quarter of this section, an 80-acre tract, now owned by G. Young, after which entries were made by John Tomlinson in 1831, Christian Wall and Isaac Pitser in 1833, John Tomlinson in 1834 and William Parent and Christian Wall in 1835.

As owners of land in 15, we now find E. Abshire, M. West, W. S. Swanger, J. L. Mowery, Josiah Cromer and G. Young. The section has pike on the west and south, with other public roads through the section, but at such short unreasonable angles that it would almost require a cross-eyed and pigeon-toed person to follow them with any degree of certainty. The school section of Salem (16) was sold by the commissioners in the year 1836, as follows:

April 9th, 80 acres to Samuel McCulloch for $750.
May 21st, 160 acres to David Strickler for $1,500.
June 4th, 160 acres to James Windsor for $1,000.

## SALEM TOWNSHIP.

June 6th, 160 acres to John Fesler for $1,000.
June 7th, 80 acres to William Windsor for $750.
Thus the section, 640 acres, bringing the sum of five thousand dollars, or an average of $7.81¼ per acre. This price in 1836, when there was any amount of public land even in Delaware county to be had at the government price of $1.25 per acre, should be sufficient proof of the high estimation in which this land is held.

Section 16 is now owned by, A. Swanger, Fred Cromer, L. Sayford and S. VanMatre, M. E. Sayford, M. S. Graves and S. J. Strickler. The section has two miles of gravel pike and one mile of other public highway.

The first to avail himself of the public domain in section 17 was Homer Brooks, who entered the east half of the southwest quarter October 29, 1831, after which entries were made in 1833 by John Simpson, in 1834 by David Crist, Ephraim Cole, William Schofield and Samuel Stephens and in 1835 by David Strickler and John Fesler. We now find the land in 17 owned by R. Richman, W. H. Huffman, W. Rader, J. Rader, D. and A. Getts M. Richman and N. V. Franklin. Seventeen has 4½ miles of public hignway, one mile of which is gravel pike, school No. 11 is located on the southwest quarter of this section.

On May 23, 1833, Lemuel Fleming entered the first land in section 18, Salem township, this was a 40 acre tract, being the southeast quarter of the southwest quarter. This 40 acre tract still retains its individuality, and is now owned in its entirety by Mr. George W. Davis. The next entry in the section was an 80 acre tract in the northeast quarter by Evan Stephens, Oct. 17th, 1834.

In 1835 entries were made by Francis Lonsdale and John Graham. Then the last of the public land by John Graham, March 26th, 1836. This section is now owned by A. Van Matre, C. Van Matre, G. W. Brandon, L. Lambert, M. Woodward, A. Johnson, J. T. Brandon, H. C. Brandon, J. and A. Brandon, Geo. W. Davis and C. C. Shedron. Eighteen has over four miles of public highway, one mile of which is free pike.

On the 21st day of January, 1831, John Groves purchased of the government the west half of the southwest quarter of Section 19. After this entry by Mr. Groves we find the next entry by Zachariah Clevenger in Oct. 1832, and James Marsh in November of the same year. In 1833 entries were made by James Marsh and Lemuel Fleming. In 1835 by James Marsh, Abraham Dipboye and Wm. Fleming, and in 1836 by William Roberts and Arbena Doubt. The present land owners of 19 are: C. A. Brock, Geo. W. Davis, W. Wiseheart, E. C. Snider, et al., S. Lindemond, J. P. Prigg and J.

Graves. Nineteen has a public road on the north line, also a gravel pike along the east side and a road across the southwest corner.

On the first day of November, 1826, John Van Matre came into the wilderness and selected the east half of the northeast quarter of Section 20 for his future home. He afterwards, in 1833 and 1834, secured the title to the balance of the quarter section. In 1827 James Marsh entered the quarter section adjoining Mr. Van Matre on the south. The west half of the section was entered by William Summers in 1831, Joseph Chapman in 1834, Van Matre Stewart in 1835, and William Roberts and John Rinker in 1836. A portion of this section is in the original Richwoods, and at one time was literally covered with fine black walnut forests. The section is owned at present by Margaret Snoemaker, Henry Van Matre's estate and W. Wisehart. The section has three miles of highway, two of which is free pike.

On November 1, 1826, John and David Van Matre each entered a quarter section of land in section 21, John taking the northwest quarter and David the southwest quarter of the section. After this entries were made by Samuel Johnson in 1827; Naomi Van Matre in 1830, and Alexander McAllister and Mathias Pitser in 1831. So all the land in section 21 was entered by September 22, 1831, making it one among the oldest sections in Delaware county. This section is all in the original Richwoods, and is now owned by Enoch Witt, E. E. Pittenger, D. A. Funkhouser, R. H. Cromer, Josiah Cromer, Van Matre and Pianter, and C. Van Matre. Twenty-one has a public road on the east line, and free pikes on the north and west. The Cross Roads post office is at the northeast corner of thr section.

The first purchase of public land in section 22 was the east half of the southeast quarter, entered on November 14, 1826 by Robert Williams, and now owned by A. White, after which the entries were made in 1829 by John Perdue; in 1830 by Francis Colburn; in 1831 by Edward Sharp, Rufus Perdue and Mathias Pitser, and in 1832 by William Summers.

This section is now owned by J. G. and J. B. Bowers, Josiah Cromer, B. C. Bowman, A. White, and James Groendyke.

Twenty-two has two and one-half miles of highway, one and one-half miles of which is free pike.

On November 14, 1826, Robert Williams made two entries of land in section 23, being the northwest quarter and the west half of the southwest quarter. In 1830, four years later, the next entries were made by John Myers, William Sharp and Enoch Nation. Abraham and Samuel Davis entered 80 acres in 1831, and Enoch Nation in 1833 and again in 1834. At this time we find the titles to the land in section 23 in the name of J. Van Matre, N. Runyan, J. G. and J. F. Bowers, W. F. Painter, and John S. Moore. Twenty-three has two and a fourth miles of free pike, also one mile of other public road.

Section 24 is the southeast corner section of Salem township, and although Edward Davis entered an 80-acre tract of land in this section as early as November 14, 1831, yet the last piece of public land in Salem township to be sold was the southwest quarter of the southwest quarter of this section and was entered by Christian Sourwine on the 22d day of March, 1837. This tract is now owned by O. and L. Pence. Other entries were made in this section by Timothy Ives in 1832, and Enoch Witt, Eleakim Wilson, and Christian Sourwine in 1835.

The lands of section 24 are now in the name of Jesse Clevenger, Jacob Clevenger, Samuel Davis, L. Davis, N. Swain, D. Cooper, O. and L. Pence, and A. M. Pence. Twenty-four has three miles of public highway, one of which is a free gravel pike.

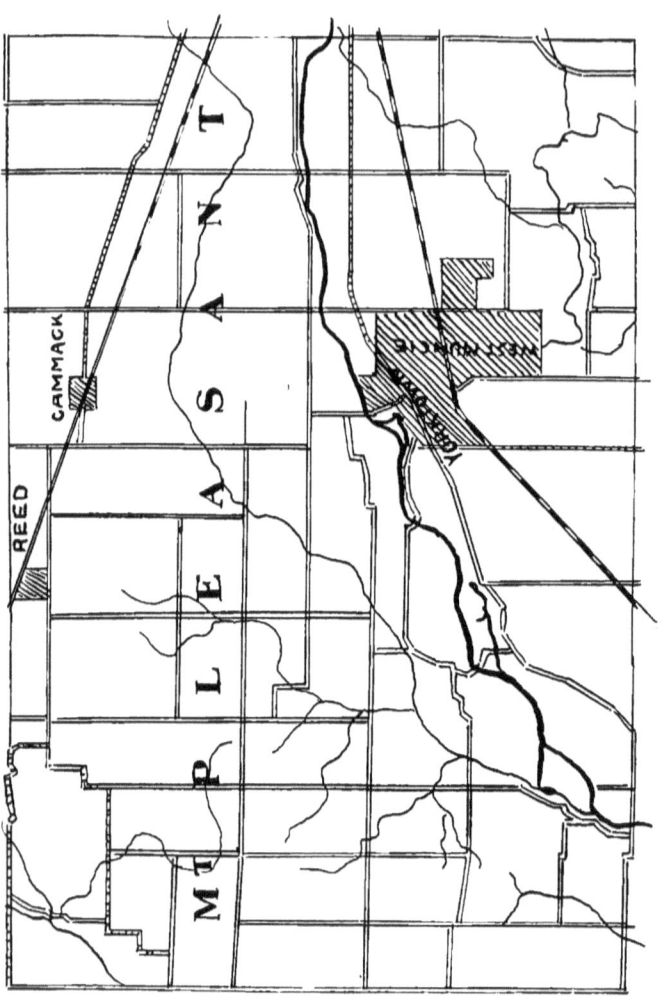

Mt. Pleasant, where the waters of White river run,
Where the pioneer came with his ax and his gun,
And drank of thy waters at gloaming and dawn,
Where the mother deer came with her young spotted fawn.

Where the red man roamed over valley and hill,
And was soothed to sleep by the sad whipoorwill,
Where the dark forests shaded the loamy rich soil
Which promised reward for the pioneer's toil,

Where the howl of the wolf or the growl of the bear,
Brought to the father both courage and care,
While the mother sat and her vigil kept,
By the trundle-bed where her babies slept.

But the pioneer came with his magic wand,
Preparing the way to a prosperous beyond,
The howl and the growl have ceased to alarm,
And the babies sleep on without fear of harm.

The ponds and slashes have melted away,
And the woods disappeared as if in a day,
The mansion now stands where the cabin once stood,
And the people are happy because they are good.

# Mt. Pleasant Township.

Mt Pleasant township lies in the west part of the county, in the west ties of townships and the second township from the south, or Henry county line. It is 4¾ miles north and south and seven miles east and west, is bounded north by Harrison township, east by Center township, south by Salem township, and west by Madison county. The north tier of sections in Mt. Plersant township is but three-fourths of a mile wide, and this shortage extends also through Center and Liberty townships east of Mt. Pleasant. This township, like Salem, has one tier of sections (on the west border) in range 8 east, all the balance of the township being in township 20 north, and range 9 east.

The general surface of the township presents a pleasing variety of hill and vale, being rolling in places, especially in the neigeborhood of the streams and more level as we leave the water courses. In some localities, along the streams, the hills terminate in precipitous bluffs, at the foot of which stretch level plains of rich bottom lands. The principle waterway of the township is White river, although Buck creek southeast and Mud creek north of White river, drain an extensive tract of valuable land. White river enters the township in section 13 crossing from Center township at the middle of the east line of Mt Pleasant, directly draining sections 13, 14, 15, 22, 21, 20, 29 and 30 on the southwest quarter of which section the river leaves the township, passing into Salem. Mt. Pleasant was originally heavily timbered with oak, walnut, poplar, ash, hickory, maple, beech, sycamore, etc., which in many instances grew to enormous size.

The first school taught in Mt. Pleasant township was by Judge David Kilgore in a deserted cabin. This was in 1831, and the teacher afterwards became one of the most prominent men in Delaware county history, leaving behind him a numerous posterity, many of whom are still prominent citizens of our county.

During the next year (1832) the first house was erected especially for school purposes. This was built of hewed logs. It was located near where school house No. 6 now stands in section 16, and the first teacher in this first school house was Mr. Sargent. This house, at that time and for years after, was known as the "Reed School House." The next school houses erected in the township were, Mt. Pleasant school house in 1841, Antioch, Yorktown and Nebo in 1842, and the Shepherd, (since known as the Lincoln School House) in 1844. These were all of the pioneer style of architecture, and presented a striking contrast to the neat and substantial school buildings in every school district of the township today.

School section 16 was sold in the year 1832, and the revenue thus obtained was in after years applied in payment of school expenses, partially relieving the strain on private purses entailed by the "subscription system" under which, until that time, the schools had been conducted, but this fund was insufficient to pay the expenses of a full term, and, when it became exhausted, the deficiency was made up by private subscriptions, as was the common practice in all parts of our then new country. The provisions of the public school law of 1851-52 became operative in Mt. Pleasant township in 1854, when the proper officers received the proportion of the public fund allotted to the township, and the old buildings were converted into free schools. A revised and improved course of study, better equipped teachers, and a consequent advance in the general intelligence of the community, were among the results following the adoption of the new system.

On October 3, 1818, a treaty was entered into with the Delaware Indians at St. Mary's, Ohio, the seventh article of which provided for the sale of government land within certain territory, including Delaware county, Indiana. Under the provisions of this article there were two purchases made in what is now Mt. Pleasant township. The first of these (as

## MT. PLEASANT TOWNSHIP. 153

well as the first purchase in the township) was that of Samuel Casman—usually pronounced Cossum by the pioneers. This was the north half of section 22, at present nearly all of which is within the corproate limits of the village of Yorktown and West Muncie.

The date of this purchase was September 16, 1820. Casman subsequently sold his land to Hon. Oliver H. Smith, who platted the village of Yorktown. The only other entry we find on record as being made under the provisions of the St. Mary's treaty is that of Samuel Tindall, being the southeast quarter of section 15, and joining the Casman entry on the north. Although other entries were made of public lands during the time intervening between these purchases, there is no mention on our records of their having been made under the treaty above referred to. The second purchase ever made in the township, according to the records, was that of Uriah Bulla, in section 20, and David Hillis, in section 29, both of which bear date of October 24, 1822.

Our record next shows the entries made by Joseph and William Van Matre, on July 22, 1823, when Joseph purchased the east and William the west half of the southwest quarter of section 20. As nearly as can be ascertained in the absence of records bearing on the subject, the date of organization of this township is the year 1831, at which time it embraced not only the present territory, but also that of what is now Salem and Harrison, making the township some seven miles east and west by sixteen miles north and south.

The first election of officers within the territory then embraced in the township of Mt. Pleasant was held in what is now Salem township, at the residence of Solomon Eisnagle, in the spring of 1831. The election was held shortly after the passage of the act creating a civil division of this territory and its erection into a township, as was usual in such cases, and establishes with a fair certainty the date of organization by the county commissioners. At this election William Jones was elected Justice of the Peace, in which capacity he served for a period of some twenty years, entitling him assuredly to the title of "Squire Jones," by which at one time almost every person in Delaware county knew him.

In writing the history of Mt. Pleasant, we shall first take up the tier of sections bordering on Madison county, as this tier is in range 8, east, and numbered accordingly, the numbers of these sections being identical with those in the eastern tier of sections. We will, therefore, commence with section number 1, it being the northwest section of the township. This is one of the fractional sections and containing but 485 and 13-100 acres. This section was entered entirely by John Groenendyke on the 25th day of May, 1832.

The present land owners in this section are L. Delph, O. P. Jones, J. and H. Black, T. G. Neely, J. R. Wellington, F. W. Younce, H. C. Brown, and J. A. J. Brunt. Killbuck creek enters this section from the north, near the center of the north line, thence running in a southwest course, thus draining much of the section very completely. The section has a free gravel pike along the north line, and public roads on the west, through the center and a portion of the south line. The section joins Harrison township on the north and Madison county on the west.

Section 12, lying just south of 1, and also in range 8, was entered in small tracts, there being but one entry recorded of a quarter section, that of Robert Griffis, who purchased the southwest quarter August 26, 1835. In the northeast quarter we find the entries made by James Groenendyke October 7, 1834; Aaron Adamson November 15, 1854, and William Jones June 28, 1838, and this was the last piece of public land sold in Mt. Pleasant township. It is the southeast quarter of the northeast quarter of the section (40 acres) and now owned by J. S. Aldredge. In the southeast quarter of this section the purchasers of public land were Robert Griffis August 25, 1835, and Purnell F. Peters, March 8, 1836. The northwest quarter was entered by Harlan Stone, October 26, 1833, Robert Swan Jones, and Bethene F. Morris, February 11, 1836. These with the entry of Mr. Griffis, first mentioned, comprised all the land in the section.

We now find the section owned by J. S. Aldredge, J. W. Mahoney, J. M. Hancock, Job Mahoney, J. P. Curtis, R. C. Curtis, G. Simpson, H. M. Childs, and John L. Hancock. The section has over five miles of public roads along or through its territory. Killbuck creek crosses the northwest corner, and school No. 4, or Sycamore school house, is in the southeast corner of the section.

In section 13, range 8, the northeast quarter was secured of the government by Robert Griffis and Thomas H. Sharpe in 1835 and 1836. The southeast quarter by Thomas H. Sharpe, February 12, 1836. The northwest quarter was entered by Thomas Fife in 1834, and Robert Griffis in 1835, and the southwest quarter by Thomas Fife, October 18, 1834, and Abner Ratcliff, October 31, 1835. The section is now owned by A. G. Ellison R. G. Van Matre, S. R. Childs, John L. Hancock, W. W. Hensley, and James W. Hensley.

This section has a public road on each section line and another crossing it north and south through the center.

Section 24, range eight south of section 13, was entered by Zimri Moon in 1830, Joseph and Johathan Dillon in 1835.

## MT. PLEASANT TOWNSHIP.

Oliver H. Smith, Flemming Reed and Daniel R. Moon in e836.

The present land owners of this section are J. Shields, M. S. Walker, S. R. Watson, F. Bonner, W. Haney, and J. and E. Vermillian. This section has nearly five miles of public highway.

In the southwest corner of Mt. Pleasant, is section 25, range 8, east. This section was all entered during the years of 1835 and 1836 by Absolem Van Matre, Oliver H. Smith, John Walters and Daniel R. Moon in 1836. Section 25 is now owned by C. H. Lennington, William Pittser, Mattie Flowers, et al, S. F. Martin, M. Watters and W. A. Watters. The section has three and a half miles of public roads.

That part of Mt. Pleasant township lying in congressional township 20, north, and in range 9, east, comprises all the civil township, except the west tier of sactions as before stated, and are sections numbered from one to thirty inclusive. No. 1 is the northeast corner of the township, its east line joining Centre, and its north line Harrison township. This section is also in the fractional tier and consequently only contains about 490 acres. The northeast quarter of the section was purchased by Thomas C. Anthony November 17, 1836. The southeast quarter by John Hayhurst April 4, 1835. The northwest quarter by Thomas C. Anthony November 21, 1836 and the southwest quarter of Sarah Swisher on October 24, 1834.

The section is now owned by M. A. Eber, J. Eber's heirs. Squire Fimple, Joseph S. Buckles' heirs and H. W. Wier The section has a public road on the west line, north and south through the centre and half way along the north line from the northeast corner.

Section 2 was all purchased of the government in the year 1836, except the east half of the northeast quarter (41 and 47-100 acres) which had been secured by Martin Williamson on December 19, 1835. The names of the parties entering land in this section in 1836 were John VanBuskirk, Oliver H. Smith and John T. Drummond.

The present owners of the land in section 2 are William Bennett, J. Weaver, S. Russell, B. S. Dragoo and S. C. Dragoo. This section has a public road on both the east and west line, and the Jackson street pike crosses the southwestern corner of the section. The L. E. & W., railroad touches the southwest corner.

In section 3, Oliver H. Smith purchased the northeast quarter on December 1, 1836, Stacia Haines the southeast quarter May 27, 1836, Jesse Coil the northwest quarter December

16, 1836, and Andrew Danner the southwest quarter September 23, 1835.

This section is now owned by S. B. Bradbury, D. P. Howell, Charles Fuson, Thomas Darbyshire, B. Dragoo, E. Dragoo, G. Dragoo and the village of Cammack, which covers some forty acres of land. The village was laid out, and named for Mr. David Cammack, who operated a saw-mill at this point for a number of years, but which was destroyed by fire several years ago and has never been rebuilt. The section has a public road on the east line and also on the west, a portion of which is free gravel pike. The L. E. & W. railroad crosses the section in a north of west direction, and the Jackson street pike crossses the south half.

In 1835 entries of public land in section 4 were made by John Danner, William Reed and James Cummings. The following year (1836) the balance of the section was entered by Samuel Danner, William Palmer and Willirm Norris Stewart.

The present landlords of the section are D. B. Snodgrass, F. W. Heath, H. and S. Darter, G. B. Snodgrass, S. Danner, W. Danner, H. Humbert, J. and N. McKinley, T. C. Stewart, J. Fullhart and M. L. Snodgrass. A portion of the village of Reed, a station on the L. E. & W. Railroad, lies in the northwest part of the section. The section has two and a half miles of public road, most of which is free gravel pike.

Entries of the public domain were made in section 5 in 1834 by Thomas Palmer and Thomas Draper; in 1835 by James Cummings; in 1836 by Robert Antrim, James Justice, Israel H. Shepherd and James Wiley; in 1837 Robert Antrim, Beltshazer Dragoo and Samuel Proud.

At present this section is divided up into small farms, there being no one person in the section holding more than an 80-acre tract. The owners of land in section 5 are M. Reed, H. Camp, M. Smelser, Samuel Stout, J. H. Snodgrass, W. L. Snodgrass, S. Darter, R. Curtis et al., B. D. Snodgrass and J. A. Jester. This section has three miles of public road, one mile of which is pike. A portion of the village of Reed is in the northeast, and School No. 3, or Lincoln school house, in the northwest quarter of the section.

Section 6 had a purchaser of public land as early as November 22, 1832, in the person of John D. Jones, who entered the northwest quarter of the section (93 and 9-100 acres). The next to enter land in this section was Thomas Draper in 1834, then Peter Shepherd in 1835, and James Wiley, Nathan Williams, Solomon McLaughlin, John McLaughlin and Mark Martin in 1836.

Section 6 is now owned by J. K. Snodgrass, R. M.

RL A. SPILKER, Pres.     EDW. OLCOTT, Cash.     J. C. ABBOTT, Asst. Cash.
Corner Walnut and Jackson Streets.

ARCHITECTURAL IRON WORKS, C. HANIKA & SONS,
South Walnut Street, Muncie.

# EVERYTHING IN MUSIC

## PIANOS and ORGANS,
10 of the standard makes.

MANDOLINS,    GUITARS,
 BANJOS,         VIOLINS.
All small instruments.

The Leading Talking Machines, Records and Supplies.

**THE MUNCIE MUSIC COMPANY,**
DENNIS & DETERLING, Props.
307 East Main Street,              Muncie, Ind.

## MT. PLEASANT TOWNSHIP.

Snodgrass, C. Wright, M. A. Jester, O. P. Jones, G. G. Curtis, M. Pence, J. Wellington, J. Stout, E. F. Aldredge and W. and M. Shoemaker. Section 6 has some three miles of public highway, much of which is graveled pike.

Section 7, in Mt. Pleasant township, was secured of the government in 3835, 1836 and 1837 by the following entries: Thomas Draper, the west half of the northwest quarter (74.44 acres), January 15, 1835; William Carman Parks, northeast quarter of the northeast quarter (40 acres), January 8, 1836; east half of the northwest quarter (80 acres) by John Greer, February 15, 1836; the southwest quarter (154.40 acres) by John Hutson Moore, June 6, 1836; west half and southwest quarter of the northeast quarter (120 acres) by William Palmer, June 23, 1836; west half of the southeast quarter (80 acres) by Joel Clem, July 1, 1836, and the east half of the southeast quarter (80 acres) by Isaac Darter, January 23, 1837.

This section is now owned by G. W. Dipple, K. A. Jones, J. Stout, E. J. Harmon, E. Dipple, H. J. Dipple, M. L. Kirkpatrick, J. Doyle, M. Brown B. Curtis and C. Curtis. This section has public roads on the east, west and south lines, also on the west half of the north line, and north and south through the center of the section.

There were no entries of public land in section 8 until January 8, 1836, and the last entry in the section was made on January 23, 1837. So it will be seen that the land in section 8 was only in the market one year and fifteen days after the first sale. The purchasers of these lands were Thomas Danner, Phineas B. Kennedy, Samuel Parker, William Carman Parks, and Stephen Reed in 1836, and Samuel Proud and Wesley Oliver in 1837.

The land owners in this section are now: Thomas Allen, W. S. Reed, E. Dipple, P. J. Hofherr, D. Cook, M. C. Ratcliff, W. J. Hunter, H. C. Dipple, S. Reed, S. and W. Hayden, and M. Reed. The section has four miles of public road, either through or along its borders.

The first entry of land in section 9 was made by Robert Gordon on November 2, 1832, when he purchased the west half of the southeast quarter (80 acres), now owned by P. J. Hofherr. After this, entries were made in 1833 by Andrew Cummings; in 1835 by Samuel Danner, Thomas Morris Gordon and William McKinley. Then the remainder of the public lands were purchased in 1836 by William McKinley, Robert Gordon and Samuel Danner.

Section 9 is now owned by Joseph McKinley, George McKinley, J. and N. Childs, G. Reed, S. and A. Summers, M. Miller, M. Summers, J. W. Black, J. Swift, Jr., C. Jones, S. Childs, P. J. Hofherr, and M. Hofherr. This section has public roads on the east and south lines, also through the center, north and south.

Section 10 was parchased of the government in small tracts, there being thirteen separate purchases, although two of the purchasers made two entries each, but at different times. The first of the these lands were taken up in 1833. The north half of the southeast quarter by Washington Reed, November 4, and the northwest quarter of the northwest quarter by John Antrim, December 5. In 1834 entries were made by Jefferson Reed and Samuel McKinley; in 1835 by William McKinley, John Reed, and Robert Antrim, and in 1836 by Christopher Terrell, Christopher Wilson and John Antrim.

The lands in Section 10 are now owned by Thomas Darbyshire, James McKinley, William Bennett, John McKinley, George McKinley, B & S. Dragoo, S. H. Dragoo and W. D. Dragoo and W. D. Childs. There is a public road on both the east and west line of this section and the L. E. & W. railroad touches the northeast corner.

The first entry of public land in Section 11 was that of James Williamson who purchased the southwest qnarter and the southwest quarter of the northwest quarter (in all 200 acres), on July 25, 1833. In 1834 but one entry was recorded in this section; that of the southeast section, by Samuel McKinley. That of James Williamson in the northwest qnarter again was the only entry in 1835. Benjamin Owen entered the remaining public land of the section in 1836, it being the northeast quarter (160 acres), and the northwest quarter of the northwest quarter (40 acres).

This section is now owned by William Bennett, S. R. O'Day, C. O'Day, M. J. Rhoades, M. T. Keys, B. Dragoo. J. L. McKinley, S. J. Isnogle, S. C. Dragoo, M. Williamson and Robert McKinley. This section has public roads on the east and also west lines, and another passing through the center of the section east and west. The Lake Erie & Western railroad crosses the north half, and Mud Creek ditch drains the south half of the section.

James Williamson was the first purchaser of the land in Section 12, his purchase being the southwest quarter of the section and dated November 30, 1832. Other entries in this section were made by Martin Johnson Williamson in 1834, John Howell, Martin J. Williamson and Henry Merritt, in 1835, and Samuel W. Harland and Jonathan T. Merauda in 1836. These lands are now owned by Joseph S. Buckles' heirs, C. Johnson, L. Johnson, A. A. Condit, S. Rowland T. S. Guthrie, T. C. McAlister, E. R. Miller, E. Williamson and S. Williamson.

Section 12 has some two and a half miles of highway, a

## MT. PLEASANT TOWNSHIP. 159

part of which is the Jackson street free pike, which angles through the north half of the section. The L. E. & W. railroad crosses diagonally through the center, and Mud Creek drains the southern part and School No. 1, better known as "Nebo," is located in the west center of the section.

Public land was entered in Section 13 as early as April 1, 1830, by Joseph Emersom after which entries were made by Isaac Norris and James Williamson in 1833, and John Fuller, John Howell and James Williamson in 1834. These lands are now in the name of J. J. Warfel, J. E. Eber, S. A. Williamson, E. R. Miller, S. Williamson, M. A. Stevens, J. W. Crawford, heirs of D. Proctor et al, and Otto Williamson. This section )13) is in the middle tier, and its east line joins Center township. White river crosses the section near the center, in a generally west course. The section has a public road on the west line, another through the section north of and near the river, while the Muncie and Yorktown free pike crosses the section east and west about sixty rods north of the south line.

Our records show that the south half of Section 14 was reserved for the use of the heirs of Isaac Wobby, whose representatives afterwarcs disposed of it to other and different parties. The first regular entry of land in Section 14 was that of Lemuel Green Jackson, on July 23, 1832. The next was Wm. Daughery February 26, 1834. In 1839 entries were made in the section by Sophia Prince, William T. Scott and William Daugherty, and in 1836 by Oliver H. Smith and Christopher Wilson. We find the present land owners of 14 to be Otto Williamson, J. Gilbert, T. J. Williamson, J. Gilbert and T. B. Parkison. The section has a public road along both the east and west lines, another through or near the center, east and west, and the Yorktown free pike across the southern part. White river crosses the section in a west course, near the center. The southwest corner of the section joins the the northeast corner of the corporation of West Muncie, in Section 22.

Section 15 was entered first by Robert Gordon on September 16, 1829, who secured 80 acres. John Gordon then entered 80 acres on May 17, 1830; William Daugherty, Sr., 80 acres, and Jonas Cummings, 240 acres in 1835. But prior to any of these regular entries, Solomon Tindal had been granted the southeast quarter of this section by the treaty of October 3, 1818, at St. Mary's The grant was dated on the 25th day of February, 1824, some five and a half years prior to any regular entry The William Daugherty, Sr., above mentioned, was a soldier of the revolution, and his son William (who was the stepfather of Hon. J. Harvey Koontz, of Yorktown) fought in the war of 1812.

Section 15 is now owned by James McKinley, E. V. Myers, M. E. Warfel, M. Warfel, H. C. Warfel, J. Warfel, I. Humphries, A. L. Reynolds, C. Jones, M. C. Parkison, P. A. Gilbert, T. Allen, George W. Parkison, M. Rice and A. Cornelius. The section lies immediately north of and adjoining the village of Yorktown and West Muncie. It has some four miles of public road, and the southeast part of the section is crossed by White river.

Section 16, the township school section, was sold by the commissioners for school purposes on October 27, 1832, to James Reed, William Antrim and Willis Hardwick. The minimum price was $1.25 and the maximum $1.51 per acre, the section bringing the total sum of $832. This section is now in the names of T. G. Coil, P. J. Hofher, M. L. Jones, S. O. Hawk, J. A. Ward, J. A. Ward et al., N. and G. Richie, J. E. Cook, George W. Parkison, A. Cornelius, J. M. Williamson, Ellen Reed, G. Cook, M. McCristie and R. J. Stout. The section has three and a half miles of public road. Mud Creek drains the west half, and School No. 6, or "Liberty" school house, is located near the center of the section.

Section 17 was all entered in small tracts, there being four entries of 80 acres each, the balance of the section being all taken in 40-acre tracts. The first entry made was by Peter Smelser in 1834. Then followed those of Beltshazer Dragoo, Stephen Brewer, Oliver H. Smith and Benjamin Franklin Laing, in 1835; William Antrim, James Clark and Zadoc Stewart, in 1836, and John Reed and Robert Watkins in 1837.

The title to the lands of section 17 are now held by J. R. Antrim, S. Hardwick, G. Reynolds, H. Stout, H. Stout et. al., J. and E. Jones, R. H. Curtis, E. J. Jester, R. J. Stout, A. F. Jones, F. J. McAlister and P. Miller. The section has five and one-fourth miles of public road, and is well drained by Mud creek and its tributary branches.

Section 18 was also purchased of the government in small tracts, there being some ten different entries, the first of which was that of Peter Smelser, in 1834; then Edward Redington (2), Oliver H. Smith (2), Phylonzo Redington and Joseph Danner in 1835, Joseph Danner in 1836 and James H. Jones and William H. Stewart in 1837.

This section is now owned by R. H. Curtis, W. Pugh, N. Yingling, Charles Brown, C. Brown et. al., J. G. Donavan, J. Jester, J. Overman and W. W. Hensley. This section has a public road on each section line, also one crossing the section north and south on the half section line.

The first public land purchased in section 19, Mt. Pleasant township, was the southeast quarter of the southwest quarter (40 acres). The purchaser was Amos Dillon Ken-

T. G. NEELY,

Merchant and postmaster at Gilman, Ind., with farm land in Harrison and Mt. Pleasant townships.

JAMES M'KINLEY

was born in Pickaway county, Ohio, Nov. 25, 1828. Departed this life April 5, 1897, aged 68 years, 4 months and 10 days. He moved with his parents to Delaware county, Ind., when a small boy, where he spent the remainder of his days. On Jan. 10, 1850, he was married to Nancy A. Landry. He was an ardent Democrat all his life.

MRS. NANCY A. LANDRY M'KINLEY

was born one mile west of Yorktown, Dec. 8, 1833. Was married to James McKinley, Jan. 10, 1850, and has lived at her present home for about fifty years. Mr. and Mrs. McKinley have always been active workers in the M. E. Church.

## MT. PLEASANT TOWNSHIP.

nard, and the date of purchase October 7, 1833. This entry was followed on the 16th of the same month by James Thomas Watson entering the west half of the southeast quarter (80 acres), and William VanMatre the northeast quarter of the southeast quarter on November 28 of the same year. In 1834 but one purchase was made, that of the east half of the northeast quarter by Peter Smelser, on August 18.

In 1835 entries were recorded in the name of Oliver H. Smith, Wm. VanMatre, Fleming Reed and Adam Antrim. No entries were made in 1836, but in 1837 the last of the public land in the section was purchased by Timothy Stewart on the 28th day of January. These lands in section 19 are now in the names of P. Miler, J. Harmon, Jr., T. C. Stewart, S. R. Watson, N. E. Burke, C. Harmon, M. C. Pool and J. E. Walker. The section has nearly four miles of public highway, and School No. 5 (or Walker school house) is located in the southwest quarter of the section.

One of the earliest entries of public land in the county was that of the east half of the southeast quarter of section 20. The entry was made by Uriah Bulla on October 24, 1822. This tract is owned at present by Margaret Reed and C. P. Keys. In fact, the entire section was settled at an early date by Joseph and Wm. VanMatre, in 1822; Stafford and Madison Hunt, in 1830; William Miller, in 1832; Joseph Landry and Thomas Hardwick, in 1833, and by William Daugherty, Sr., and Peter Smelser, in 1934.

This section is divided into small farms, the owners being: J. W. Black, Margaret Reed, S. Landry, S. O. Hawk, W. R. Landry, J. Reed, M. Taylor, C. P. Keys, R. M. McKinley, L. McKinley, M. G. Davis, P. F. Knight and C. Priest. The section has between three and four miles of public road, but much of it is so crooked that it would require a pretty good knowledge of geometry to get a very correct measurement of it. White river crosses the southeast and Mud creek the northwest portion of the section.

The first of the public domain in section 21 was purchased by Joseph Bell on June 28, 1825, being the west half of the northeast quarter (80 acres), and Joseph VanMatre entered the west half of the southwest quarter the same year, September 16. After this the land in section 21 was purchased as follows: 80 acres by William Hardwick, December 12, 1827; 80 acres by Absalom Daugherty, October 20, 1828; 80 acres each by Timothy and William Jones, in 1829; 80 acres by William Jones in 1832, and 40 acres by Samuel Parkison in 1835.

Section 21 is now owned by J. M. Williams, George W. Parkison, T. Allen, David Campbell, Ellen Reed, G. S. Slack et. al., R. J. Stout, Margaret Reed, A. Crawford, J. Hardwick, B. Hardwick, C. P. Keys and J. VanMatre. The section has some three miles of public road. White river crosses the northern part, and the Big Four railroad the southeast corner.

Section 22 has the honor of being the first settled section in the township, if not in the county, if we can call it settlement, as the most done in that direction was the purchase of land on September 16, 1820, by the half-breed, Samuel Casman, under the provisions of the St. Mary's treaty. This was the north half of the section, containing 320 acres, with White river crossing the northwest part and Buck creek the center, in a northwesterly course, furnishing excellent water power for mill sites, which were in later years utilized. It is said of this first land owner (Casman) that in the purchase of land and his love of "fire-water" were found his only traits of the white man. His first wife was a negro woman, who died here at their home. He married again, sold his land to Hon. Oliver H. Smith, moved to the Indian reserve on the Missinewa, near Peru, and was finally found dead in a hollow log somewhere in Madison county.

The remainder of section 22 was purchased regularly of the government, at its land office at Indianapolis, by William Hardwick in 1827, and Abner McCartney, Theodore R. Lewis and Charles Jones in 1835

The villages of Yorktown and West Muncie cover this section, with the exception of a small portion in the northwest corner, owned by the Muncie Strawboard Company and J. M. Williams, and some 68 acres in the sounthwest part of the section, owned by David Campbell.

Although Yorktown would strike the stranger passing that way now as a staid and steady-going old town, yet I can assure my readrs that Yorktown was at one time a dashing, jolly place, a kind of "rounding-up" town for hunters, horse racers, etc., where it was supposed one could find about as much "fun" and "frolic" as any other place of its size in the country. Yet Yorktown always had her steady-going, law-abiding citizens.

Section 23 was all entered in qaarter section tracts. The first of these was secured by Benoni Tindal, under the St. Mary's treaty, of 1818, on the 25th day of February, 1824, and was the northwest quarter of the section, now owned by S. and J. E. Andrews. The northeast quarter was entered by Thomas Bromfield, November 16, 1835, the southeast quarter by David Yount, November 6, 1835, and the southwest quarter by Oliver H. Smith, December 24, 1835.

Section 23 is now owned by G. Lenon, H. C. Brindel, J. R. Applegate, S. Andrews, J. E. Andrews, Thomas Port's heirs, J. R. Campbell, J. P. Stagg, J. Myers, and H. A.

Goings. Besides these owners there is about one-half of the southwest quarter of the section occupied by the village of West Muncie. There is a public road on the east and south lines, and the Big Four railroad crosses the north half of the section.

Section 24 was entered in the years 1831 to 1834 by John Beeth, William Templeton, Jeremiah Wilson, John Braden Finley, Thomas Bromfield, James stewart and Oliver H. Smith. Those now owning it are: W. G. Huffer, E. F. Huffer, J. S. Huffer, I. J. Williams, W. and J. Landry, N. F. Pittenger, W. N. Williams, M. Hoechst, and M. G. Brindel. The section has three miles of public road, the Big Four railroad crosses the north half, and school No. 7, or Center school house, is located in the west center of the section.

In Section 25 there were two entries in 1830, one by John B. Brown, the other by James Tomlinson. In 1831 entries were recorded in the name of Parnell Tomlinson and Edward Aldredge, leaving one 80-acre tract, which was taken up by Kezia Keasby May 13th, 1833.

Section 25 is now owned by P. W. Williams, N. P. Williams, I. J. Williams, A. C. Perdieu, J. Harmon and J. H. Koontz. The section has only one mile of public road—that on and near the east line. Buck Creek drains the section by running in a west course through the central part.

The first purchase of public land in Section 26 was by John B. Brown, in the year 1830. The next was by Keiza Keasby and Isaac Norris in 1833 and the last purchases in the section were by Thomas Bromfield and Oliver H. Smith in 1835 The land owners in 26, at this time (1899) are J. Harmon, J. J. Hoferr, J. R. Antrim, J. H. Koontz, W. J. Painter, J. Griesheimer, P. J. Hufherr and W. J. and A. Wiggerly. The section has three miles of highway and is drained by Buck Creek passing through the center in a west course.

The first entry of land in section 27 was by Samuel Bell in 1827, then followed that of Timothy Stewart in 1828, from that time five years intervened between the entries, or until 1833, when purchases were made by Thomas and Robert Hasket and Henry Enilseizer, and the last purchase in the section by Oliver H. Smith, August 10, 1835. Twenty-seven is now owned by A. S. Cooley, D. R. Warfel, S. Grice, M.E Bowers, O. Stewart, W. A. O'Day, G. Lenon (trustee) J. Paulin and C. Paulin. The section has nearly three miles of public road, that along the west line (one mile) being free gravel pike. The north part of the northeast quarter of this section lies in the village of West Muncie.

Section 28 in Mt. Pleasant township was all entered in 1835, save a 40 acre tract in the northwest quarter that had been purchased in 1833 by Timothy Stewart. Those securing these lands in 1835 were Thomas Hardwick, Theodore R. Lewis, Willis Hardwick and Joseph Stewart. Twenty-eight is now owned by J. S. Aldredge, Jeff H. Claypool, C. P. Keys, John Aldredge, J. S. Huffer and C. F. Warfel. The section has a pike along the east line, a public road on the west line and the Big Four R. R., angling through the section in a northeast to southwest course.

In section 29 we find another early entry of land that of David Hillis, October 24, 1822, being the northwest quarter of the section. No other entries were made in the section until that by Line Newland in 1829. The next after this was that by Joseph Van Matre in 1830, then David Kilgore in 1834, followed in 1835 by the purchase of Jefferson Reed and David Kilgore in two other entries.

As the landlords of this section, we now find C. P. Keys, D. Kilgore, Jr., J. S. Huffer, W. K. Helvie, J. P. Shoemaker, F. Kilgore, M. G. Davis, P. F. Knight, C. Priest and W. R. Moore.

The section has some two miles of public road, White river crosses the northwest corner and School No. 9, or Kilgore school house, is located in the north center of the section on the Yorktown and Daleville, or old state, road.

The land entries in section 30, Mt. Pleasant township, extend over a period of eleven years, from 1824 to 1835, the first of which was that of James Madison Van Matre in 1824, Isaac Jones, John Neely, Amos Dillon Kennard in 1833, Morgan Van Matre in 1834, and Oliver H. Smith and Jacob Redington in 1835. The section is now owned by N. E. Burke, J. Burke, A. Miller, W. R. Moore, J. C. Darst (trustee), L. and S. Donovan, C. H. Lenington, L. Harmon, S. F. Martin and L. E. Kilgore. White river crossing this section in a southwest course, divides itself in the northeast quarter, forming a junction again in the southwest quarter, thus forming an island in the center of the section of some 75 acres in extent.

## HARRISON TOWNSHIP.

Harrison, the largest, the latest, the last,
   The biggest, and one of the best,
Why, oh why did you linger so long?
   Why did you not start with the rest?

The wild roses grew as rich and as rare,
   Your trees grew tapering and tall,
Your forests were filled with turkey and bear
   That came at the rifle's call.

Thy forests stood stately for many long years,
   Awaiting the ax and the maul,
Which came in tne hands of the old pioneers,
   Making music from spring until fall,

And now, where once the dark forest grew,
   The fields are waiving and brown,
For labor's reward is pronounced by the Lord,
   So Harrison; take up thy crown,

# Harrison Township.

   Harrison is the largest of the civil townships in Delaware county, being six by seven miles in entent. It is all in congressional township 21, and all except the west tier of sections in range 9 east.

   Harrison therefore has 42 sections of land, aggregating 26,880 acres. It is bounded north by Washington township, east by Hamilton and Center, south by Mt. Pleasant and west by a portion of Madison county. The soil of this township can be said as a whole to consist of a clay with an admixture of sand, which condition prevails generally throughout the entire township. Big Kill Buck creek is the principal stream in the township, entering near the northeast corner and passing out near the southwest corner, it drains sections 1, 12, 16, 21, 20, 29, 30, 31 and 32. Jakes creek enters the east end of the township in section 25 and running in an almost direct west course, empties its waters into Kill Buck in section 29. The general lay of the land in Harrison is level, although sufficiently rolling for drainage. The township was origionally covered with a heavy growth of timber, of the varieties common to this latitude.

   As has heretofore been stated in these pages, the early settlers seemed to choose their homes in the neighborhood of the water stream, as we find all the earlier settlements made along the White and Missisinewa rivers, and thus account for

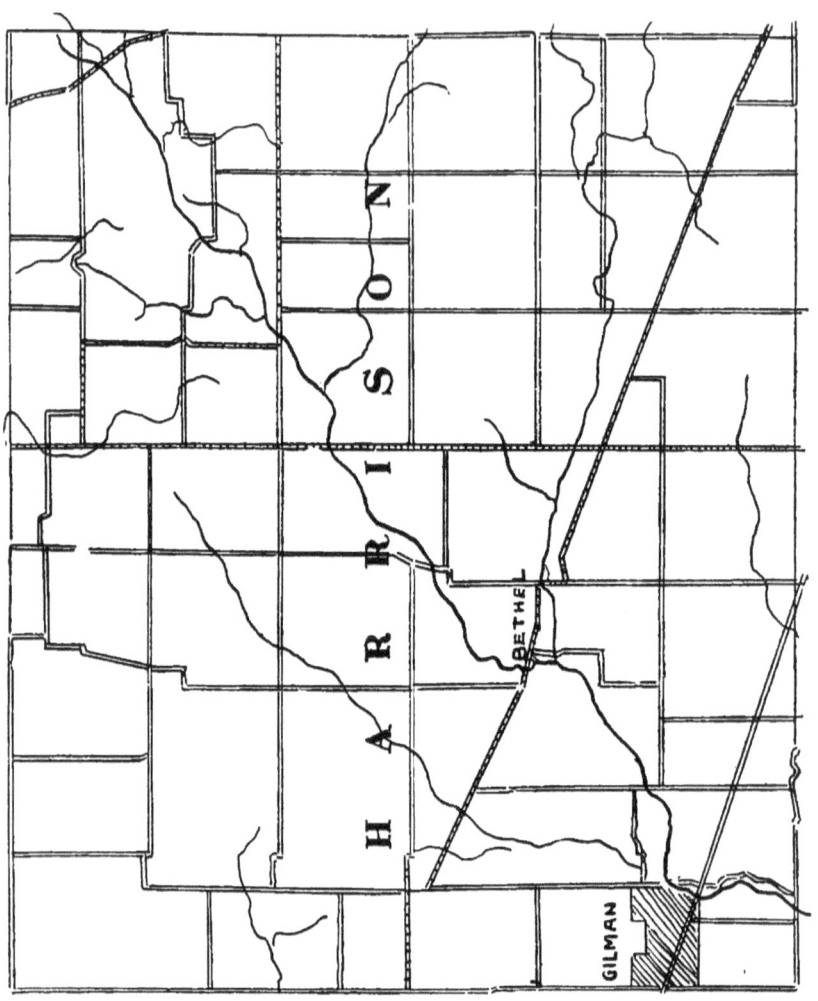

## HARRISON TOWNSHIP. 167

the seeming lateness in the settling up of Harrison township, and although Big Killbuck creek passes through the township and furnishes drainage outlet to much of the territory, yet it was never considered sufficient for water mill power, although Joshua Howell erected a mill for grinding corn, on Big Killbuck about one and a half miles below Bethel in 1842. This was one of the primitive contrivances so often found in the pioneer settlement, and was soon dispensed with, as mills of large capacity were erected on neighboring streams, and as roads were constructed whereby the settlers could get to them. Jesse Stout, a Baptist minister, erected a distillery on the west half of the southwest quarter of section 29, in 1842. Mr. Stout had entered the land in 1836, and seeing the demand for whisky concluded he could make a financial success of his enterprise and at the same time accommodate his neighbors. However, as the capacity of his still was but about three gallons per day the demand, and subseqnent legislatures, interferred somewhat with his business, he abandoned the enterprise, which gave him more time to devote to preaching.

Perhaps the first school in Harrison township was taught in the winter of 1834 and 1835 in a log school house built for school purposes on the land entered by John Garner, being the east half of the southeast quarter of section 29, and southeast of where school house No. 6 now stands and on the same section. Schools in these early days were very uncertain, as a teacher and an empty cabin could not always be obtained, but our early pioneers seemed to have had high appreciation of education as demonstrated in their early efforts to establish schools and which has culminated in our present healthful school system of which every Indianaian may feel justly proud.

The first merchant of Harrison township was Jacob Miller, who erected a store room adjoining his residence in the southeast part of section 20, in 1851, then in September of that year went to Cincinnati, Ohio, and bought three wagon loads of dry goods, groceries, etc., and hauling them home was prepared to accommodate his customers with many of the necessaries of life.

Harrison has never been noted for her towns and villages, but is entirely rural in her pretentions, her entire territory being given up to agricultural interests. Bethel (or Stout) is the only village in the township, although Gilman is geographicaly in Harrison township, yet, in fact, in Madison county. In other words, the paper town is in Delaware county while the buildings are in Madison. Job Garner at one time laid out a village on his farm in the southeast part of section 20 and named it Harrison, but after the land was sold to Jacob Miller he converted the town into farm land, as others might be converted to advantage.

In giving the history of this township by sections we shall commence at the northwest corner of the township, giving the west tier of sections, or those adjoining Madison county, and being in range 8' east, then commencing at section 1, take the sections alternately as they are numbered.

Section 1 in Harrison township, in range 8, is in the northwest part of the township. The first land entry in this section was made on October 17, 1836, when Otis Preble entered the west half of the southeast quarter (80 acres), and John Robb on the same day entered the southwest quarter (160 acres). In 1836 entries were made by Milton Lawrence and John Perdue; in 1838 by Almon B. Brand and Milton Lawrence, leaving the south half of the northeast quarter, now owned by A. J. Corwin, which found no purchaser until 1852, when it was finally entered by Allen Makepeace. The section is now sub-divided into small farms and owned by J. T. Broyles, O. Broyles, J. Broyles, A. J. Corwin, James B. Barwick, S. Dilty, E. Poindexter, R. Stiltz, L. Thomas, A. Woodring, W. Thomas, T. C. Day, E. E. Cramer and T. C. Archer. The section has three and one-fourth miles of public road.

South of section 1 is section 12, also bordering on Madison county. The first purchase in this section was also made by Otis Preble at the same time of his entry in section 1, it being the west half of the northeast quarter, 80 acres, now owned by W. H. Carter; and James F. Robb entered an 80-acre tract, joining him on the west, the same day. Then followed the purchases of John Perdue, John Hodson and Richard Justice in 1837, and that of Harrison H. Deal and Michael Null in 1839. Section 12 is now owned by W. Thomas, A. Jackson, W. H. Carter, G B. Finley, B. and E. Kline, M. and E. Myers, B. Kline, J. O. Kirkman, J. D. Kirkman, E. Leeson, and W. B. Leeson. The section has three and one-fourth miles of public road, and school No. 4 is located in the northeast corner.

Section 13, range 8, was all entered in 1837 by Enoch Garner, George Turner, Joseph Cook, Adam C. Lewis, and Miles Marshall, in the order named, and all made their entries from February 25 to March 14. The section is owned at present by C. Thomas, L. M. Jackson, W. Zimmerman, V. E. Garner's heirs, G. W. Clevenger, O. Garner, N. Shaw, L. B. Sayer, J. H. Smith, C. L. Nesbit, M. J. Stafford, C. King and T. C. Day. This section has four miles of public road, three-quarters of a mile of which is free gravel pike.

Section 24 was purchased of the government in the years of 1836, '37 and '39 by Tobias Benner, Jonathan Langley,

HOME.
Northeast corner High and Jackson Streets, Muncie, Ind. Built by John F. Sanders, deceased, 1874.

and Joseph Cox in 1836; Jesse H. Healey in 1837, and James Marshall, Thomas Worley, and Curtis Langley in 1839 The present landlords of this section are J. A. Hiatt, R. Brown, C. King, S. Hiatt, G .C. Stephenson, Draper and Miller, M. Hutson, Enos Hutson, T. Hutson, I. Hutson, M. Ferguson, and J. Wellington. The section has something over one mile of pike and three miles of other public road. School No. 5 is located on the east line, one-third of a mile south of the northeast corner.

Section 25 had a purchaser as early as July 10, 1834, in the person of Robert Swift, who on that date entered the east half of the southeast quarter. After this the entries were made by Jonathan Langley, Joseph Cox, Samuel Langley, John Starr and Francis Davis in 1836, and Curtis Langley in 1839. The present owners of 25 are John Simpson, A. A. Manning, Enos Hutson, D. W. Bowers, W. and C. Colson, J. Parker and John Miller. The plat of the village of Gilman covers some 110 acres in the south part of the section, and school No. 12 is located in the southeast quarter.

The first entry of land in section 36 was made by Isaac Adamson on October 18, 1832, and this was the first purchase of public land ever made in Harrison township. The tract was the southeast quarter of the section, 160 acres, now owned by Eliza and O. P. Jones, Jr. Other entries were made in the section by Archibald Parker, in 1833 and '35, by John Parker, John Fenny, and John Crawson in 1835, Stephen Crawson and Samuel Langley in 1836, and Miles Marshall and Nathan Hodgson in 1837. The present land owners in section 36 are William and S. Lee, Gas Center Land Company, O. P. Jones, E. Jones, J. Curtz, S. M. Miller, and T. G. Neely. Big Killbuck creek crosses the east half of the section, and a large portion of the village of Gilman is located in the north part of the section. The only drawback to that portion of the village that lies on the east side of the county line is the lack of improvements and inhabitants, for all must admit that it is a very pretty place to build a town.

Section 1 in range 9 east in Harrison is in the northeast corner of the township. The first purchase of government land in this section was the soutewest quarter, now owned by Francis Bilby, 160 acres. This purchase was made by Jonathan Johns on August 13, 1836, after which time purchases follow in rapid succession by Bernard F. Hook, John Sutton, John Conner, James Ashcraft and David Enry in 1836, William Gard and Samuel P. Anthony in 1837, and the last 40 acre tract by James Ashcraft in 1841. The present owners of this section are J. N. Cox, E. L. Miller, W. H. Young, S. Kinnett, M. Crampton, I. E. Crampton, H. Bowen, E. M. Carter, and Francis Bilby. The section has something more than 2½ miles of public highway which includes the Muncie and Wheeling free gravel pike which angles across the east half of the section and Kill Buck creek crosses the southeast corner.

Jonathan Johns was also the first to purchase land in section 2, entering the southeast quarter, 160 acres, on the same day as he did his purchase in section 1, (Aug. 13, 1836,) which gave him 320 acres all lying in a body, the same year (1836) on Nov. 15 Jonathan Stewart entered the southwest quarter, Dec. 7, 1836 Job Garner entered the south half of the northwest quarter, 80 acres, Jan. 21, 1837 John D. Jones entered the north half of the northwest quarter 98 84-100 acres, and in 1839 Samuel P. Anthony purchased the north half and David Hays the south half of the north east quarter. Section 2, is owned at present by M. Driscoll, P. Dunn, W. T. Janney, J. Cheesman, W. Stanley, Francis Bilby, C. Steel, A. Rector, W. Rector and G. Wilson. The section has two miles of public road.

There was but one-quarter of section 3 taken up in 1836, that being by Gideon McKibban on May 30 of that year and was the southeast quarter of the section now owned by S. J McCreery, T. Beamer and S. Muller. The other lands of this section were purchased by John Tomlinson and John Collins in 1837 and Samuel McCreery in 1838. We find the present owners of section 3 to be W. B. Woodring, Thomas McCreery, J. W. McCreery, William McCreery, S. J. McCreery. S. Muller and T. Beamer. The section has 3½ miles of public road, 2¼ of which is free gravel pike.

There were no entries of the public domain in section 4 until 1836 in which year there was one 80 and two 40 acre tracts taken up by Joseph Gobie and John Gilliland. Samuel Richerson made the only entry in the section the north half of the northeast quarter, 100-14 acres, in 1837. During the year of 1838 entries were made by Henry W. Smith, and Samuel McCreery and in 1839 by Andrew Welch and William Bentley. The present land owners in section 4 are J. H. Gruver, R. M. Miller, S. McCreery, S. D. Ferguson, R. Miller, Josiah Ferguson, J. W. McCreery and A. Oxley. The section has 4 miles of public highway, that along the east line being the free gravel pike running south from the village of Gaston which is one half mile north of the northeast corner of this section.

The first purchaser of public land in section 5 was Samuel Brady, who entered two 40 and one 80 acre tract on October 20, 1836. Joseph McGilliland and George W. and Jefferson N. Horine made purchases during the same year (1836). In 1837 two purchases were made, one by Reason Davis and the other by Jacob C. Palsley. There were no purchases made

## HARRISON TOWNSHIP. 171

in 1838, but the remaining lands were entered in 1839 by Elisha Galemon and Harrison Dean. Section 5 is owned at present by A. and L. Stephenson, H. B. Trout, J. Burgess, L. Stephenson, W. Duncan, F. Sharp, J. E. Sharp, J. W. McCreery, A. Oxley, A. C. Brady, F. R. Langsdon, S. Ferguson and L. and A. Bond. This section has four miles of public road and is divided into small farms.

Section 6 was late in coming into market as there was no purchases of public land within the section until February, 1837, however all the section except the north half of the northeast quarter was entered during this year (1837) by Reason Somers, Jacob Beals, Zachariah Cook, Jesse Mellett and John Perdue. The tract excepted was entered in 1839 by Harrison Dean. At present section six is owned in small farms by J. Newberger, F. Sharp, J E. Sharp, W. P. Brimhall, S. F. McNett, L. Jackson, J. Underwood, R. Ady, Benjamin Barclay, H. L. Miller and W. F. Carpenter. Six has four miles of public road and school No. 4 is located in the southwest corner of the section.

It was almost fifteen years from the time of the first purchase of public land in section 7 by Amos Ratcliff on December 7, 1836, until the last entry in the section by James H. Swoor on June 18, 1851. The first being the southwest quarter and the last the east half of the northeast quarter. Between these, purchases were those of Vincent Garner 1836, John Perdue and Robert Robe in 1837, Henry Garner and Giddeon McKibben in 1838, and Jacob French in 1839. Section 7 is now owned by A. E. Vanlandingham, M. L. Thurston, J. Ocker, A. Morris, J. and M. Findley, W. S. Findley, W. Walling, J. M. Love and C. S. Thomas. This section has but two miles of public highway, consisting of a road on the north and one on the south line of the section.

Section 8 was all purchased by three persons as follows: Josiah Robe entered the northwest and southeast quarters (320 acres) on December 7, 1836. Thomas Dean entered the northeast quarter (160 acres) on November 15, 1836, and Robert Robe entered the soutewest quarter May 1, 1837. From the original three owners the section has been subdivided until we now find the unlucky number of thirteen representing the ownership of section 8. They are M. Gronnendyke, W. Robe, M. J. Robe, L. and A. Pond, S. Barclay, M. Parker's heirs, T. M. Oxley, M. Beuoy, R. Thomas, J. F. Sollars and H. Heath. The section has 3 miles of public road, they being on the north and south lines and also crossing the west half, north and south.

The first entry of public land in section 9 was an 80-acre tract in the northwest quarter of the section, by Anderson Miller, on the 28th day of October, 1836, another So was entered in the southwest quarter by Aaron Adamson the following December 17th. In 1837 but one entry was made and that by William Gard. In 1838 all the remaining public land of the section was entered by Job Garner and Michael Null. The present land owners of this section are Thomas McCreery, R. M. Miller, T. McCreery, O. L. and S. Stokes, L. B. Wiggins, J. and M. Gray, John VanBuskirk, G. W. Boxell and R. J. and F. Woodring. Section 9 has four miles of public road, that on the east line being free gravel pike. School No. 3 is located in this section near the northwest corner.

Section 10 was purchased of the government in 1836 and '37, in four 80 and two 160-acre tracts. The purchasers in 1836 were Samuel McCune and Prior Rigdon. In 1837 they were Samuel McCune, Mathew Burrows and John Woods, Samuel McCune and Mathew Burrows securing each 240 acres.

We find the present land owners in this section to be M. E Johnson, J. W. McCreery, S. J. McCreery, C. M. Rector, C. W. Rector, Emerson McColm, L. M. Chalfant, T. J. Freeman and Ella McColm. The section has four miles of public road, more than one-half of which is free pike, and school No. 2 is located on the north line one-quarter of a mile east of the northwest corner.

Section 11 was also entered in the years 1836 and '37. October 12, 1836, Lewis M. Wilson entered the northeast quarter, and on December 3 of the same year Anderson Merritt entered the southeast quarter. The two remaining quarters were entered the following year (1837) by John Tomlinson, Thomas Brumfield, Thomas Collins, James Washington Cload and John Collins.

The lands of section 11 are now owned by Arthur Rector, James Rector, Allen Benadum estate, E. O. Drake, F. Benadum and W. Benadum. The section has some 2½ miles public road, one mile along south line of which is free pike. The U. B. Church is located at the south center of this section.

Section 12 joins Hamilton township on the east. The first land owner in this section was Oliver H. Cogshill, who entered the east half of the northeast quarter August 13, 1836. During the same year entries were made in the section by Owen Morris, Asher Storer, Watson W. Fitzpatrick and Jonas Sutton and in 1837 by Jane Stafford and Abraham McConnell. None of the names of the original owners of land is now found in this section, but instead we have the names of W. and J. Langsdon, C. Murphy, C. C. Crampton, M. Langsdon, W. H. Brown, J. S. Brown, and W. and E. E. Bell as the parties holding the land titles in section 12. The section has something more than 2½ miles of public road,

### PRESIDENT FRANKLIN A. R. KUMLER, A. M., Ph. D.

Was born near Hamilton, Ohio, 1854. His early education was acquired in the common schools of Butler county, Ohio. After reaching his majority he entered the Normal University at Lebanon, Ohio, and remained there two years. He then entered Otterbein University at Westerville, Ohio, and continued his studies six years, graduating in the classical course. Two years were then spent in the study of medicine in the Cincinnati Medical College. To complete his education more fully, especially in the classics, Mr. Kumler spent ond year in Berlin, Germany. He has attained the degrees A. M., Ph. D. Prof. Kumler servee as President of Avalon College, Trenton, Mo., for ten years, ending in June, 1897. Since then he has spent a large portion of his time in Muncie in the organization of the University.

## HARRISON TOWNSHIP. 173

that on the south line being free pike, and the Muncie and Wheeling pike crosses the northeast corner. School No. 1 is located on the southeast part of the northwest quarter of the section.

In section 13, Harrison township, there were two 80 acre tracts entered in 1836, Samuel Moore securing the east half of the southeast quarter and Samuel Snider the west half of the same quarter, the first, dated Oct. 4, and the latter and day thereafter (Oct. 5). In 1837, entries were made by Daniel Jarrett, Hiram Adams, William Beaty and a second entry by Samuel Snider. The last entry of the section was made by Jacob Miller on June 15, 1839, the tract so entered by Mr. Miller was the northwest quarter of the northwest quarter (40 acres) now owned by J. A. Rector. The present land owners of section 13 are C. and A. Kiracof, A. and J. Mulreed, L. Rees, J. A. Rector, H. Clements, George Phibbs, C. Delaney and L. M. Hawkins. The section has three miles of public road, that along the north line being free pike. Scotts ditch, one of the tributaries of Kill Buck creek, drains the south part of the section.

Section 14, lying west of 13, was entered by Geogre Griffin. Thomas Anthony and Thomas B. Jenett in 1836, Isaac Barnes ann Benjamin Wallingsford in 1837 and Jacob Miller in 1839. Mr. Miller's entry was dated June 15, on which day he made numerous entries in different parts of the township. Section 14 is now owned by M. E. Cary, J. and L. Richardson, W. T. Downing, J. Brown, C. W. Porter, J. H. Moore, E. Kitzmiller, Samuel Gray and W. H. Brown. This section is well supplied with public roads having one on each section line and another north and south thongh the center. The south half of this section is also drained by the Scott ditch.

Section 15, was all purchased of the government in 1836 by four pearsons, each entering a quarter section as follows: James Newhouse entered the southwest quarter May 30, 1836, Thomas Haworth, the northwest quarter June 3, 1836, Joseph Lafavor the southeast quarter August 12, 1836 Geo. Griffin the northeast quarter and October 18, 1836. These pioneer names have all disappeared from the records of land titles so far as concerns section 15, in Harrison township and we find in their stead as land owners, the names of A. S. Cecil, Mathew Gray's heirs, A. Trobridge, J. and L. Richardson and J. H. Null. The section has public roads on each of its borders, that on the west and one fourth of a mile on the north line being free gravel pike. School No. 7 is located in the southwest corner and the north part of the section is drained by Big Kill Buck creek.

Next in this tier of sections, going west, is school section No. 16, which was sold on November 11, 1836, to the following named persons at the prices named: South half of the northeast quarter (80 acres) to Bigger and Kennedy for $140.50; northeast quarter of the northeast quarter (40 acres) to John Coon for $76.00; northwest quarter of the northeast quarter (40 acres) to Eleazer Coffeen for $70.00; to William Martendale, the west quarter of the northwest quarter (80 acres) for $230.00; the east half of same quarter (80 acres) for $160.00; the east half of the southeast quarter (80 acres) for $160.00; and the west half of the same quarter (80 acres) for $160.00, Mr. Martendale thus securing one-half of the section; to A. Adamson, the southwest quarter (160 acres) for $300.00, the entire section bringing the aggregate sum of $1,296.50.

We find none of the original owners' names now in this section as landlords, the titles having passed to T. McCreery, J. W. McCreery, J. and M. Gray, J. and M. Whistler, E. M. McClelland, P. N. Stout, T. J. Bowles, et al., L. E. Archer, E. Gumm, and V. Stout. The section has three and a quarter miles of public roads, one mile of which is free pike. Killbuck creek crosses the southeast and the McClelland ditch the northwest corners of the section.

The southwest quarter of section 17 was entered on October 15, 1836, by Thomas I. Collins taking the east and Jonathan West the west half. The east half of the section (320 acres) was entered by George Rouse on October 18, 1836; the west half of the northwest quarter (80 acres) by Stephen C. Collins April 3, 1837, and the east half of the northwest quarter by Michael Null, December 17, 1838.

The present land owners in section 17 are D. Gunning, E. M. McClelland, John Howell, W. A. Jackson, G. Besser, E. Gumm, J. and M. Gray, J. and M. Fuller, J. J. Lake and W. Lake. The section has three miles of public road. The McClelland ditch crosses the southeast and the Jones ditch the northwest corners of the section.

Section 18 was first entered by John Starr, who secured the southeast quarter and the east half of the sothwest quarter on March 17, 1836. The next was Benajah French, October 24, 1836. There was but one entry made in 1837, that of David Whitson Cook. February 21, 1839, Wiliam Brady entered a 40-acre tract. This left three tracts, containing in the aggregate 188 16-100 acres, which found no purchaser until finally entered by James H. Sworr on January 18, 1852.

The land in 18 is now owned by G. W. Maynard, Joseph A. Quick, C. S. Thomas, W. Wilson, W. Walling, W. Zimmerman, M. L. Brunton, L. A. Johnson, J. W. Christie, C. and S. Swindell and V. E. Garner's heirs. This

## HARRISON TOWNSHIP. 175

section has two miles of public road, and the southeast corner is drained by the Johns ditch.

The pioneeer entries in section 19 were made in 1836 by John Starr, Henry W. Smith, John Smith, and William Campbell. In 1838 all the land unentered by the settlers of 1836 consisted of an 80-acre tract in the southeast quarter, which was entered by Job Garner on October 17.

At present 19 is owned by I. N. Poole, M. Smith, L. Beall, H. Simpson, C. V. Parker, A. C. Ellmore, S. H. Jackson, C. Pierce, T. C. Pierce, B. Simpson, E. Stafford, J. E. Fuson and W. Hayhow. The section has some three miles of public highway, more than a mile of which is free pike, which crosses the section in a northwest to southeast direction. School No 5 is located on the west line of this section.

Land in section 20 was entered as early as 1834, when Job Garner purchased the east half of the southeast quarter (80 acres) on the 17th day of January of that year. (Prior to this time there had been but two entries in the township, and they were both in section 36, range 8.) This was the land afterwards owned by Jacob Miller, and where he established the first merchandizing enterprise of the township. After Mr. Garner's entry others were made in the section by Isaac Ridout, William Ridout, Tobias Renner, James Stout, Isaac Stout, Joel Biggs and Levi Lynn in 1836, and the last entry by Isaac Stout January 21, 1837.

The present owners of this section are E. Duckett, N. V. Markle, S. Sites, Joseph A. Quick, H. Miller, L. A. Johnson H. Vennemen, and William Wilson. The section has nearly four miles of public road, one mile of which is pike. Killbuck creek crosses the section in a southwest course, and the village of Bethel is situated in the southern part.

In section 21 the first land entry was also made on the same day as that of Mr. Garner in section 20, January 7, 1834, and joined that tract, being in the southwest corner of section 21, both tracts now owned by H. Miller. This entry was made in the name of William Barton Wilson. Other entries were made in this section by William Newhouse and James Newhouse in 1836, and the last of the public land of the section was taken up by James Newhouse, February 27, 1837. Section 21 is now owned by T. J. Bowles et al., J. Black, J. M. Conner, M. V. Markle, M. J. Richey, E. J. Stinson, F. B. Miller, C. F. Miller and H. Miller. The section has three miles of public road, one of which is free pike. Killbuck Creek crosses the northwest corner of the section. The lands in section 22 were entered by Isaac Ridout, John McCarty, James Newhouse, Thomas Brumfield, Solomon Williams and Elijah Newhouse in 1836, John H. Garner and

Mary Jones in 1837, and Vincent Garner in 1838. The present land owners in this section are J. W. Gray, I. Coffin, P. Schwinn, S. B. Childs, W. Bailey, J. and R. Miller, A. J. Miller, W. A. Branson, P. M. Ruddy and S. Lee. The section is well supplied with public roads, having one on either section line, that on the west line being a free graveled pike from the village of Cammack in Mt. Pleasant to Gaston in Washington township.

All of section 23 with the exception of one 80-acre tract was entered in 1836 by Joseph Lefavor, Jacob Calvert and Oliver H. Smith. The exception above mentioned was the east half of the southwest quarter, which was entered by James Marshall, January 31, 1839. This 80 is now owned by J. C. Smith and was the last entry made in the section. The present land owners in the section are A. Gough, M. Gough, D. L. Williams, A. P. Gray, D. and G. Smith, S. A. Smith and M. A. Modlin. The section has a public road on each section line, and School No. 8 is located in the northeast corner. All the land in section 24 was entered in the year of 1836, from July 21 to November 17. The first of these entries was made by John Applegate on July 21 and was the west half of the southwest quarter of the section, and now the west half of the farm is owned and occupied by Enoch Drumm. The next entry was made by William Cavitt, August 21, which was the east half the southwest quarter, and the whole of the southwest quarter was entered by Charles Thatcher, October 4, and the northwest quarter by Jacob Haynes, November 17. The landlords of 24 are now A. Watson, O. H. Scott, R. E. Needler, D. Stewart, S. J. Newman, F. Rhoades and Enoch Drumm. Twenty-four is well supplied with highways, having a road on each section line.

Section 25, in Harrison, is the east section of the second tier north of Mt. Pleasant township. The land of this section was all purchased of the government in 1836, from March 9 to October 28, by William Cantwell, John Applegate, William Moore, Josiah Williams and James Freeman. The land in 25 is now owned as follows: that entered by Wm. Cantwell by J. Newman, R. W. and P. T. Moore. The entry of Wm. Moore by S. H. Hartley. The entries of John Applegate by Wm. Bennett, L. Fulhart, M. Deviney, C. Deviney, J. R. Fimple and L. Bennett. The entry of Josiah Williams by H. E. Hartley and that of James Freeman by D. Scott. The section has 4 miles of public road and is drained by two branches of Jakes creek.

In section 26, James Smith entered two 40-acre tracts (one being the southwest quarter of the northeast quarter and the other the southeast quarter of the northwest quarter and consequently adjoining each other making him 80 acres in a

## HARRISON TOWNSHIP.

body) on September 3, 1834. George Shafer entered the west half of the northwent quarter October 30, 1835. Nicholas Maceltree entered a 40 acre thract in the southwest quarter November 7, 1835 and the remaining public land of this section was all entered in 1836 by John Applegate, Thomas Applegate, Daniel Jarrett, Thomas Nottingham, Peter Simmons and John Nottingham. Twenty-six is owned at present by L. Fullhart, J. M. Hartley. J. O. Hartley, J. C. Smith, W. Richey, G. McWilliams, S. Branson. M. J. Hartley, I. F. Brimhall, S. C. Tuttle, E. Nottingham and D. G. Root. The The section has 4 miles of public road, the Bethel free gravel pike crosses the northwest corner and School No. 9 is located in the southeast corner. Jakes creek crosses the central part of this section in a westerly course. The settlement of section 27 might be considered early when compared with other sections of Harrison township. The first land entry in this section being on December 26, 1833, when Isaac Tildon entered two 40 acre tracts in the eastern part of the section. The remaining entries were all made in 1835 by George Shafer, James Garner, Christopher Wilson and William Patten. The present land owners in this section are G. McWilliams, Samuel Gayman, M. E. Daugherty, S. M. Lee, L. Kendall, G. A. Lee, E. Hawkins and J. J. Snodgrass. The section has nearly five miles of public road, more than two miles of the same being free pike, Jakes creek passes westerly through the central part of the section.

The public land in section 28, was purchased by Jacob Meek Holloway in 1834, William Patten and John Coon in 1835 and John Woods, John Coon, Elias Wilson, Caviner Conner, Job Garner, Thomas Haworth and Jacob Cline in 1836. Section 28 is now owned in small farms by C. A. Taylor, H. Taylor, S. Lee, E. Wallace, O. F. Miller, C. B. Miller, H. Miller, J. W. Smith, M. Martin, S. Gayman, E. Grice, R. Conner, O. P. Snodgrass, E. Rutledge, E. E. Reynolds and W. W. Hensley. The section has some 4 miles of public road 2¼ of which is free pike, Jakes creek drnins the north half of this section.

The public lands in section 29 were entered in the years of 1834-35 and '36, by Job Garner in 1834, Joel Briggs and Charles Stout in 1835, and John Woods, Jacob Cline, Jonathan Eddy and Jesse Stout 1836. It was in the southwest part of the section where Jesse Stout erected his distillery before mentioned in these pages.

The owners of the real estate in section 29 at present are H. Miller, J W. Smith, J. Null E. J. Hayden, J. McKinley, J. R. Antrim, S. and J. Hiser, O. F. Miller, J. Icley, S. A. Gwaltney, M. F. Harris, J. and S. Tuttle, G. Benner and M. L. Smith. The section has 3½ miles of public road.

The northwest part of the section is drained by Kill Buck and the northeast by Jakes creek, they forming their junction in the northeast part of the northwest quarter.

Hugh Finley was the first to enter land in section 30; his entry is dated November 9, 1835, and the land described in this entry is the east half of the southwest quarter, 80 acres, and now owned by J. J. Baker. The next entry in the section was made on the 30th of the same month by Abraham Smith and was the east half of the northeast quarter, 80 acres, now owned by T. C. Pierce and M. J. Hall. After this, entries were made in 1836 by Abraham Smith, Nicholas Reel, Luke Wright, Jonathan Langley, James Wright and John Langley. The present owners of land in this section are T. C. Pierce, M. J. Hall, O. L. McLaughlin, J. and C. Jester, J. E. Fuson, O. Wasson, J. W. Jones, Joseph Stradling, J. J. Baker and William and S. Lee. The section has three and thrre-quarter miles of public highways. The southeast part is drained by Kill Buck creek and the northwest by Johns ditch.

Section 31, one mile east of Madison county line, and bordering on Mt. Pleasant township, was first entered by Oliver Perry Jones, October 12, 1833; then by Wm. Miller in 1834, James Fortner, William Miller and John P. Jones in 1835, and William Palmer, William Miller, Jacob Crouson and Samuel Adamson in 1836. The present land owners of section 31 are D. Mahoney, Joseph Stradling, H. Miller, C. M. Riggin, William and S. Lee, M. Antrim, James Reed, J. A. Wright, I. Wright and O. P. Jones et al. The section has 3¼ miles of public road, three-quarters of which (along the south line) is the Jackson street free pike

Section 32 was entered in 1836-37 by Jacob Miller, Moses Shepherd, William Palmer, Solomon McLaughlin and James McLaughlin in 1836, and by James Williams in 1837. The section is at present generally divided into small, well improved farms, and is owned by C. Nauman, A. S Gwaltney, S. Icley, A. L. Snodgrass, J. Antrim, W. J. Antrim, W. and A. Antrim, D. Mahoney, M A. Folkner, A. E. Stevenson, F. W. Heath, M. Heath, M. Reed, M. Hawkins and J. H. Snodgrass. The section has three miles of public road, and the southeast corner joins the village and railroad station of Reed in Mt. Pleasant township.

In section 33 the first entry of public land was made by James McLauglin in the southwest quarter on April 5, 1836. The other entries made in this section during this year were Thomas Patton, Dickson Thomas, Jacob Cline, Daniel Vanbuskirk and William Reed. Elias Humbert entered a 40 acre tract in 1837 and Amos Jenna the last 40 acres on November 23, 1838. Section 33 is now owned by F. M. Lee, J. F. Rees, A. L. Snodgrass, S. R. Snodgrass, O. Snodgrass,

## HARRISON TOWNSHIP. 179

J. O. Snodgrass, S. and I. Stephenson, A. E. Stephenson and F. W. Heath. The section has 3 miles of public highway, one mile, (that on the east line) being free pike. School No. 10 is located in the northeast corner of the section.

Section 34 was purchased originally of the government in 1836 by Samuel C. Bradford, Oliver H. Smith and Christopher Wilson. In 1837 by Jane Williamson, Philander Cassman and Samuel P. Anthony. The section is now owned by John W. Taylor, Samuel Gayman, M. Carter, R. Williams I. Branson, R. B. Bradbury, M. Fallis and J. H. Hayden. The section has 2½ miles of public road, one mile of which is free pike.

In section 35, there were originally eight entries of public land and all of these were recorded in the year 1836, the first by John McBride on March 8 and the last by William H. Brumfield November 8. The parties making purchases between those dates were Daniel Jarrett, James Williamson and John Vanbuskirk.

Section 35 is owned at present by W. Stephenson, J. Brown, William Bennett, E. Baker, G. L. Nottingham, D. P. Root, T. H. Fimple and S. B. Bradbury. The section has 2 miles of public road beside one mile of the Bethel free pike, which crosses the northeast part of the section.

Section 36 is the southeast corner section of Harrison township and its lands were all entered in 1836 by Daniel Jarrett March 10 and April 14. John Hayhurst and Thomas Williamson Sept. 24 and Thomas Brumfield November 9. The lands in this section are now owned by T. H. Fimple, J. F. Drumm, L. Bennett, M. J. Armintrout, S. A. Smith, C. and M. Galliher, S. E. Crumm, M. Mann, J. Wiers heirs and J. R. Fimple. The section has about 4 miles of public road, including the Bether pike, which angles through the center part of the section in a northwest to southeast course.

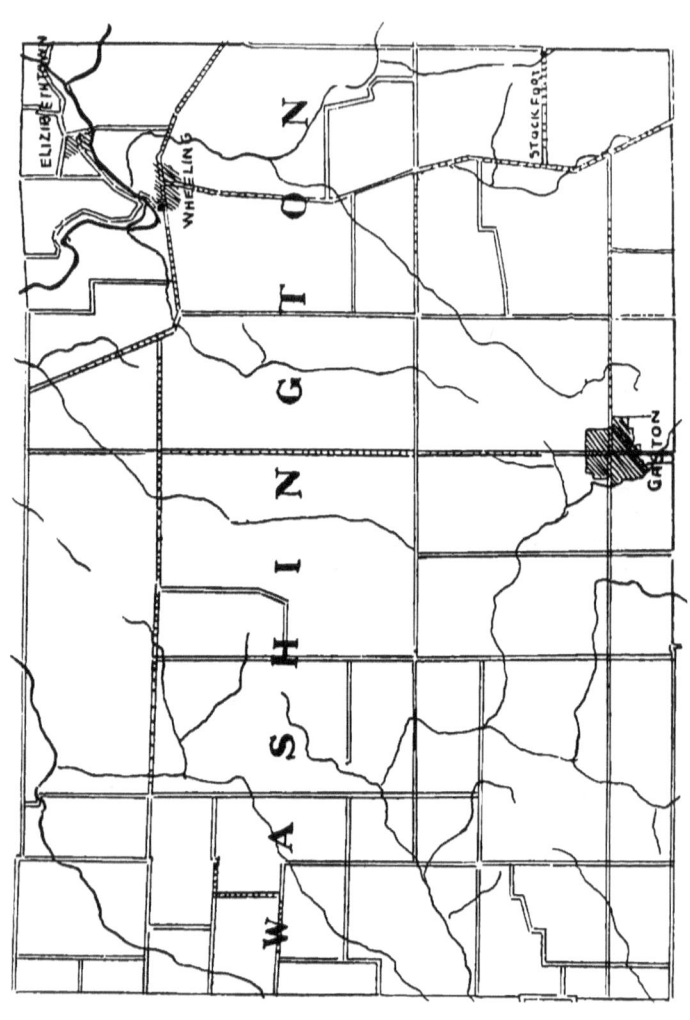

### WASHINGTON.

Washington township, thy name we revere,
A name to every American dear,
The pride of a nation, with never a peer,
A name you may mention wherever you will.
When coupled with Trenton or old Bunker Hill,
Will cause the American heart to thrill.
A name that caused our fathers to start
From the field or forum or busy mart,
And shouldering their guns, with manly tread
They followed where the peerless Washington led,
A name our mothers learned us to say
When at her knees she taught us to pray,
Thanking our God for the gift of His son,
For our beloved country and Washington.
Now, as in days of old the same,
The little ones learn to lisp that name,
For each little "tot" can tell you when
George Washington's birthday comes again,
So, Washington township, we confess
That thou hast made a great success,
But how couldst thou have done any less,
Directed by thy sons of toil,
To fell the forests and till the soil,
Where teachers taught in church and school,
That he was either knave or fool
Who lived not by the Golden Rule.
With these, I say, 'twould be a shame
For you to fail with such a name,

## Washington Township.

Washington is the northwest township of Delaware county. A portion of Grant county bounds it on the north, Union township on the east, Harrison township on the south and a portion of Madison county on the west. The township is seven miles long east and west, by five miles wide north and south.

Washington lies wholly in Congressional township 22 north. The west tier of sections are in range 8 east, and the balance of the township in range 9. The general nature of the surface of the land in Washington is level, except in the vicinity of the streams, the principal one of which is the Mississinewa river in the northeast part of the township. In the neighborhood of the river the surface is generally rolling, and in many cases terminates in high hills and precipitous bluffs. These bluffs we generally find on but one side of the river (as seems the case with streams in all instances), while on the opposite side of the stream are wide stretches of fertile bottom lands, stretching back to sloping second bottoms. Passing along the stream the scene changes, the rich bottoms narrowing down until they run to a point and the bluff banks and hills come close to the stream, but as the valleys cease on the one side they commence on the other, as if nature desired to treat the inhabitants equally fair on both sides of the stream.

Washington township has a marked diversity of soil—black loam, underlaid with clay, and clay soil with a substratum of sand or gravel being often found in the same neighborhood. The admixture of sand and gravel becomes a more prominent feature as we approach the Mississinewa river.

There is much fertile land in Washington, but perhaps more original swamp land than in any other of the townships of the county, which accounts for the lateness of the purchase of some of the public lands in this part of the county. These swamp lands, however, have been drained, and in the majority of cases have become very valuable to their owners.

From the fact that Pipe Creek, in the southwest part of the township, flows to the southwest, seeking its outlet into White river, and that Hoosier creek, in the northwest part, flows northeast to the Mississinewa, we must conclude that the dividing ridge or elevation is between the sources of those tributaries, and that the land is well elevated, although flat. The township was orignally well timbered with all the varieties of this section of country, with the exception of the swamp land, which is believed at no distant day in the past to have been a lake or inland sea, and was barren of timber.

The first public land in the township purchased of the government was by David Conner, on December 23, 1823. This was the east half of the northeast quarter of section 15. The north half of this 80-acre tract is a portion of the McCormick farm, lying one mile west of the village of Wheeling. The traveler will know this oldest of Washington township settlements when we inform him that in passing west from Wheeling along the old state road, that where the road makes its first divergence or angle to the north, is the east line of the Conner purchase, and where the gravel pike running west leaves the state road, just north of the McCormick residence, is the north line of this purchase. So, while passing between these two points (some fourth of a mile), we are not only on the first land entered in the township, but we pass in that short distance a place of much historical interest.

It was here that a Mr. Broderick, early in 1824, established a trading station and tavern, the first for the traffic with the tribes of Miami, Delawate and Pottawatomy Indians still remaining in the vicinity, and the second for the patronage of emigrants moving further west, as well as the trade he had with the wandering white hunters and trappers who chanced to come his way. It is said his stock consisted chiefly of a few articles of merchandise, ammunition, and an unlimited supply of wiskey, and for some three years he was the only white resident of the township, one of his nearest neighbors being John Boyles (or Jacky Boyles) in Delaware township— Black's Mills—some twelve miles up the Mississinewa. At the expiration of Mr. Broderick's lease he was superseded by Robert Sanders, who carried on the business of "tavern keeping" and general trader or merchant for a number of years, but finally changed his business, and gave his attention more exclusively to that of farming, having cleared a tract of land and made various improvements.

In 1829 Robert Sanders sold his home to William McCormich, and on November 13, 1830, he entered an 80-acre tract in Section 14, it being the west half of the northwest quarter, adjoining his former home on the east, and is a part of the farm now owned by Samuel M. Gregory. Mr. McCormick afterwards entered three 80-acre tracts in Section 15, besides which numerous purchases were made by him at different times in other sections of the township.

During the year 1829 William Heal, of Muskingum county, Ohio, left his home, traveling on foot, prospecting. He came on west until he finally decided that he had found the place to build his future home, and going to the land office at Fort Wayne he purchased three 80-acre tracts in section 11, Washington township, his purchase being on both sides of the Mississinewa river. After securing his land Mr. Heal returned to his Ohio home. William Heal's entries are dated September 12, 1829. Upon his return, Mr. Heal at once set to work getting ready to bring his family to his western home, and, starting with three wagons, they came on to Columbus, Ohio, where they fell in with the family of Thomas Littler, who were also seeking a western home. Acquaintances were soon formed in these early days, and these families, cutting their road through the woods by day and surrounding the same campfire by night, soon formed a friendship that could not be easily severed, and when Mr. Heal reached his destination it did not take much persuasion to induce Mr. Littler and his family to remain, and so on November 17 of the same year (1829) we find Mr. Littler entered the tract of land adjoining that of Mr. Heal on the west. And here these families lived side by side for more than thirty-five years, neither having cause to regret the formation of their friendships, nor the choice of location of their western homes. These families can safely be called the pioneer families of Washington township. Other early settlers in Washington were the families of John Graham in section 11, 1830; John Cephus and Silas Dille, in section 12, 1830; Joseph Wilson, Robert Wharton, John Ginn and James Watson, in section 12, and Eli Lansing, in section 11, were also settlers of the year 1830. The interior of the township did not settle up so early as that portion along the Mississinewa by a few years, for we find but little, if any, lands entered in the interior until the choice lands were all taken in the vicinity of the river.

The first white male child born in Washington township was John W. Heal, February 12, 1831, and the first white girl baby was Mary Graham. This happened about the same time.

The first marriage was solemnized at the residence of Robert Sanders, in 1834, the high contracting parties being Nancy Sanders and Nathaniel McGuire.

The first cemetery in the township was Olive Branch cemetery, at the north center of section 11, and near the Grant county line It consisted of one acre of land, and was donated by William Heal, in 1836, to the township. The first person buried in this cemetery was the remains of John Watson, who died in 1837.

The first school in the township was taught in the winter of 1833 and 1834, by Mrs. Olive Heal, wife of William Heal, in a room of their home, at $1.25 per scholar. However, the first school house was built in 1839, and Ezra Maynard engaged as teacher. Mr. Maynard afterward became a minister in the M. E. church, and still later a successful merchant in the village of Albany.

Elizabethtown, the oldest village of the township, it is said, once aspired to the honor of becoming a county seat. But as fate would have it, the county lines were drawn in the wrong place, and the court house and other public buildings seen in the day dreams of the people of the northeast corner of Washington township proved to be but "castles in the air," and so the mayor's scepter of the great city was turned into plowshares and pruning hooks, and Elizabethtown is no more, and the only towns or villages of Washington township are Wheeling and Gaston. The latter has passed through the ordeal of undergoing some two or three changes of name, such as "Snagtown," then "New Corner," and now Gaston. However, the little city has stood all this nobly, and is now threatening some older places in the way of becoming a rival for railroad honors.

To avoid confusing the reader in the study of the history of Washington township, we will first take up the west tier

WASHINGTON TOWNSHIP. 185

of sections, that tier bordering on Madison county. This we more especially do because each of these sections has its duplicate in other parts of the township. This is caused from the fact that Washington like each township in the west tier or district No. 1, lies in two different ranges east, that is, the west tier of sections are in range 8, while the balance of the township is in range 9. With this explanation we commence with section 12, which is the northwest section of both the township and county. The public lands of this sectoin were all purchased in the years 1836 and '37. The first of these purchases were made by Frederick Ice and Robert Burke on August 22, 1836. Mr. Ice taking the east half and Mr. Burke the west half of the southwest quarter of the section.

During the same year in October, Christopher Hudson entered the east half and Robert Hudson the west half of the northwest quarter. Joseph Farley purchased the northeast quarter in February and November, 1837, and Christopher Scott and John Ellison the southeast quarter on February 6, the same year (1837).

The parties now owning land in section 12 are Daniel Richards, H. W. Foster, K. T. Grave, J. V's McCune, D. Richards, C. H. Conkle, J. W. Foster, R. E. Glass and H. S. Rominger. The section has 4¼ miles of public road and Hoosier creek crosses the southeast part of the section in a northeast course.

Section 13, just south of 12, and therefore adjoining Madison county also, was entered as early as 1836, and as late as 1850 as follows: George Lewis, Ephriam Lewis and Isaac Foster in 1836, patrick O'Brien, Hiram Lee and Madison Broyles in 1837. James Paine and Francis Ice in 1838. Madison Broyles again in 1849 and Lewis Hull on January 18, 1850, entered the northwest quarter of the northeast quarter now owned by E. Musick et. al.

This section (13) was originally entered in eleven separate lots and is still held in small parcels as follows: J. Janney, Benjamin Ice, E. Musick et. al., M. Powers, H. Dunlap, E. Benbow, E. Caplinger, R. C. Howard, S. and M. Evans, S. Evans, O. C. Atkinson, G. R Thurston, C. A. Broyles and J. E. Broyles. This section has 4 miles of public road, 1½ miles of which is free gravel pike. A cemetery, M. E. church and school No. 5 are located in the southeast part of the section.

Going south we pass into section 24. This section was purchased of the government in six original parcels or lots as follows: By William and Henry Walker in 1835, Jediah Adams and Anderson H. Broyles in 1836. Thomas Broyles in 1837 and John Farley, Jr., in 1838.

Twenty-four is now owned by O. and C. Webster, J.

Quinn, O. A. Todd, S. Janney, M. Andrews (trustee), M. Harris, W. H. Broyles, H. Broyles' heirs, A. E. Broyles and J. W. Hamilton. The section has 3¼ miles of public road, and is well drained by Little Pipe creek crossing it diagonally through the center.

Section 25 was secured of the government in nine parcels as early as August 29, 1836 and as late as September 8, 1838. The purchasers of this section were Amos Ratcliff, Eli Hockett, and Solomon Fussell in 1836, Jesse Munden, Nathan Macy and Thomas Broyles and Wilson Burass in 1838, Eli Hockett having made two entries. The land owners of section 25 are now A. E. Broyles, J. A. Broyles, L. and S. Davis, James Thomas Broyles, J. W. Hamilton, J. Barrett, D. Spitzmesser, M. Millhollin and S. M. Roseboom.

Section 36 in range 8, is the southwest section of Washington township. The first entry of land in this section was made on October 29, 1836. At which time Samuel Brown entered an 80 scre tract in the northwest quarter and Isaac Marshall on the same day entered a 40 acre tract in the southwest quarter. In 1837 entries were made in this section by Jesse Munden, William Burass, Phineas Hall, John Hall and William Laurk. Then on November 12, 1838 Asa Davis purchased the southeast quarter of the southwest quarter (40 acres) it being the last of the publib lands in section 36. This 40 acre tract is now owned by James B. Barwick and M. B. Gill. The other owners of land in this section are James T. Broyles, William H. Broyles, J. W. Broyles, George Perdue, H. Brown, William Long, J. Barrett, E. Brady, M. Styers and R. Livingston, 36 has 4¾ miles of public roads and School No. 12 is located in the northeast corner of the section. Section 7 is in the north tier of sections of both the township and county. The section is ten acres short of the 640 acres, said shortage being taken out of the westside of the section. The first entry of public land in this section was made by John Beauy on January 9, 1834, and comprised two 40 acre tracts in the east center of the section, Other entries were made during the same year by James Hinton and William Knight. One entry was made in 1835 by David Hinton. In 1836 James Hinton and William Knight made each another purchase, during 1837 pnrchases were made by Elles Jones, Willinm Knight and David McCormick; leaving the west half of the southwest quarter 76 52-100 acres which was taken up by John Hanway and George Kramer on January 5, 1838.

We find the section now owned by W. Millspaugh, J. A. J. Brunt, R. C. Howard, Isiah Howard, Daniel Richards, James Knight, M. F. Carpenter, J. McShay and P. Creamer. The section has 4 miles of public road, one half mile of which

## WASHINGTON TOWNSHIP.

is free gravel pike, while Hoosier Creek drains the north, half and School No. 4 is situated in the center of the section.

On October 29, 1834, Sampson Brewer entered 40 acres of public land in the northwest qnarter of section 8 and the public land in this section was in the market for sixteen years thereafter, the purchases occurring as follows: Samuel Beouy in 1835. Gabriel Ginn, Sampson Brewer, Thomas Beouy, John Beouy and Richard Dickerson in 1836, Richard Dickerson and William Beouy in 1837 and Joshua Dickerson in 1850. These lands are now in the names of John W. Richards, W. W. Hoover, J. A. J. Brunt, B. and J. Newberger, R. C. Howard, J. N. Reynolds and J. S. Richards. The section has a public road on the north, which is also the county line, and a free gravel pike on the south line. The northwest corner of the section is crossed by Hoosier Creek.

The public lands in section 9 except one 80 acre tract was taken up in the year of 1836 by Willard Swain, John Wesley McCormick, John Hawkins, Gabriel Ginn, Amos Janney and Samuel Knight, leaving an 80 acre tract as before mentioned, which was purchased by Ira Swain on January 5, 1837, and was the east half of the southwest quarter of the sectron.

Section 9 is now owned by R. C. Nottingham, R. Beouy, M. Cory, L. Nottingham, B. W. Lewis, S. Lewis, and William I. Janney. The section has public roads on the north and east, with a free gravel pike on the south line.

In section 10 we find the first entry of public land made by William McCormick on May 16, 1831. This is the east half of the southeast quarter, and still remains in the McCormick family. After this purchases were made in section 10 by Samuel Moore and Thomas Beouy in 1832; by John Dunn in 1833; William Wharton in 1834; Thomas Dunn in 1835; William McCormick again in 1836, and the last by John Wesley McCormick in 1837.

The land owners in 10 are now John Dunn, Jr., R. Beouy, William McCormick, A. H. Benbow, E. Beouy, and Benoni Beouy. Section 10 has four and one-half miles of public road, two and one-half of which is free pike.

The first public land in section 11 was purchased by William Heal on September 12, 1829, and the next by his old friend and neighbor, Thomas Littler, on November 17 in the same year. In 1830 purchases were made by Eli Lansing and Thomas Wharton; in 1831 by William McCormick; in 1832 by Thomas Wharton, and in 1834 the second purchase of Thomas Littler was the last of the public domain in section 11.

The present owners of the section are G. E. Heal, D. Heal, Ed Beouy, W. R. Moore, S. A. Milhollin, B. and J. Newberger, J. Newberger, Samuel M. Gregory and William

McCormick. Section 11 has more miles of river than any section in the township. It has about three miles of public road, some of which is rather crooked in its efforts to follow the windings of the Mississinewa river along its northern banks.

Section 12 is the northeast corner of Washington township. The southwest quarter of this section was entered by John Dillie on March 3, 1829, and all the remaining public land of the section was purchased the following year (1830) by Robert Wharton, Joseph Wilson, James Watson, and John Ginn.

We find the present owners of realty in section 12 to be L. Watson, M. Butcher, G. E. Heal, E. Beony, Liberty Ginn, A. Shafer, and Sarah F. Ginn.

It was in this section that the old town of Elizabethtown was laid out, on the north side of the Mississinewa, but was never destined to reach the prominence and importance anticipated for her by the founders. The section has something more than three miles of public road, but much of it is so angling and ill-shaped that we will not undertake to give its exact length, as we are a little rusty in our geometry.

Section 13, Washington township, lies one mile south of the Grant county line, and joins Union township on the east. The Albany and Jonesboro pike passes through the north half of the section, which is the only highway the section can lay claim to except a fourth of a mile on east line at the southeast corner. The first entry of land ever recorded for this section was that made by Joseph Wilson, May 27, 1830. The second entry was made November 13 of the same year by Thomas Reynolds, after which there were no further entries made until 1833, when John Ginn entered 80 acres. In 1834 William Richeson entered 160 acres. In 1835 entries were made by John Sanders and Margaret Watson. In 1836 one entry was made, by Jacob Holland Bowers, and the last 40 acre tract was entered by Jesse W. Thompson on January 5, 1837. The owners of section 13 at this time are Liberty Ginn, O. and S. Baldwin, R. Trout, M. M. Henley, Sarah Ginn, James S. Rigdon, S. J. Ginn, Caleb Johnson, H. and S. Brown and N. and C. Mahoney.

Pipe creek crosses the west half of the section and the east part of the village of Wheeling, with School No. 2 in the northwest corner.

In section 14, the first entry of government land, was made by Robt. Sanders, before mentioned in these pages. The time of this entry was November 13, 1830, and the tract entered was the west half of the northwest quarter. After Mr. Sanders' purchase there were no others until November 4, 1833, when William McCormick purchased the east half of

INTERIOR OF THE MERCHANT'S NATIONAL BANK,
Corner Main and Mulberry Streets, Muncie, Ind.

Capital, $100,000.00
Surplus and Profits, $28,000.00.

OFFICERS, { HARDIN ROADS, Pres.
{ FRANK A. BROWN, Cash.

INTERIOR VIEW OF THE MUTUAL HOME AND SAVINGS ASSOCIATION.
Incorporated 1889. Authorized capital, $1,000,000.

Officers: D. A. McLain, Pres.
S. M. Reid, Treas.
Geo. N. Higman, Sec.
Edward M. White, Atty.
109 East Adams Street, Muncie, Ind.

Board of Directors: D. A. McLain,
E. P. Smith,
H. C. Haymond,
S. M. Reid,
Carl P. Franklin.

the northeast quarter, containing 79 88-100 acres. John Wharton made three purchases in this section in 1835, and John Crow the last 80 acres, September 28, 1836. The land owners in section 14 are now James S. Rigdon, Samuel S. Gregory, William McCormick, N. and C. Mahoney, Nathan Millhollin and Michael Crow. The Albany and Jonesboro pike crosses the north, and the Muncie and Wheeling pike the east part of the section. There is also a public road on the west line, except some fifty rods of the north end of this line. The greater part of the village of Wheeling is in the northeast quarter of this sdction.

As heretofore stated, the first land ever purchased of the government in Washington township was that purchased by David Conner, being the east half of the northeast quarter of section 15, on December 23, 1823, after which time there were no other entries in this section for almost eight years, which must have seemed a long time to persons so isolated. The next to purchase in the section after Mr. Conner was William McCormick, in 1831; then David Beouy and John Dunn, in 1832; William McCormick, two tracts in 1833; William McCormick, another 40-acre tract in 1835; Thomas Beouy, in 1836, and David Beouy, the last 40 acres, in 1837.

Section 15 is now in the names of William McCormick, A. Beouy, N. Beouy, G. W. Beouy, Benoni Beouy, Michael Crow, John Dunn, Jr., J. Dorton and R. Dorton. This section has some three miles of public highway, two miles of which is free pike.

School section No. 16 was sold on April 14, 1855, in lots as follows: Lot 1, northeast quarter of the northeast quarter (40 acres), to Levi Adison at $7.03 per acre; lot 2, northwest quarter of the northeast quarter (40 acres), to John Dickeson at $7.50 per acre; lot 3, northeast quarter of the northwest quarter (40 acres) to Thompson Gherton at $7.00 per acre; lot 4, northwest quarter of the northwest quarter (40 acres) to Thompson Gherton at $7.00 per acre; lot 5, southwest quarter of the northwest quarter (40 acres) to William McCormick at $7.10 per acre; lot 6, southeast quarter of the northwest quarter (40 acres) to David Beouy at $7.00 per acre; lot 7, southwest quarter of the northeast quarter (40 acres) to David Beouy at $7.12 per acre; lot 8, southeast quarter of the northeast quarter (40 acres) to Streeter & Ginn at $7.00 per acre; lot 9, southeast quarter (160 acres) to Streeter & Ginn at $4.01 per acre, and lot 10, southwest quarter (160 acres) to Robert Winton at $4.00 per acre. Thus the section (640 rcres) brought the total sum of $3,552 40. The present owners, as near as possible to ascertain, are Benoni Beouy, B. W. Lewis, Nathan Millhollin, H. Dorton (heirs),

M. Dorton, B. and J. Newburger, I. B. Miller and John Dorton.

Section 16, like 15, has three miles of public road, two miles of which is free gravel pike, and school No. 3 is situated in the northeast corner of this section.

Amos Janney entered the east half of section 17 (320 acres), on October 27, 1836. On February 2, 1837, Isaac Whiteley entered the northwest quarter (160 acres) and on the same day Wright Anderson entered the west half of the southwest quarter (80 acres) and then on the 6th day of December of the same year (1837) William Miller obtained the remaining 80 acre tract, the east half of the northeast quarter.

Section 17 is now owned by D. Miller, S. Hayden, A. F. Janney, H. Hyer, C. B. Hyer, J. S. Richards, W. T. Janney, Harriett Janney, M. A. Brown and M. S. Thorn. Section 17 has one mile of free pike and two miles of other public road.

The entries of the public domain in Section 18 were as follows: Isaac Farmer, in 1836; Joseph Jones in 1838, and Jacob Miller and Robert Dunlap, in 1839. Section 18 is now owned by J. J. Corn, W. Foster, H. B. Dawson, Amanda Carter, S. Hinton, M. Ice, Hinton & Hyer, M. & M. Sitze, M. & G. Hayden, M. M. Gwinnup and D. L. Richards. Section 18 has two miles of public highway, three-fourths of which is pike.

The first land owners in Section 19 were Samuel Sweaney, Robert Dickey, Nathan Henderson, Griffin Tira and William Drennen, 1837; John C. Gustin, in 1838, and Michael Messenger, in 1839. After a lapse of some sixty years and numerous transfers we find the present owners of land in Section 19 to be H. Sweaney, M. M. Gwinnup, J. W. Sweaney, J. M. Harris, M. E. Hazelbaker, J. M. Robertson, W. W. Orr, A. L. Broyles, J. T. Broyles, L. H. Broyles and W. H. Broyles. Section 19 has four miles of public roads, and the south half of the section is crossed by Big Pipe creek.

Sectiod 20 was in the market for seventeen years, it being that length of time between the first and last entries of its lands. The first entries were in 1836 and were made by Amos Janney and John Johnson. In 1837 Hugh Hazelbaker, William Carmin and Simeon Dickenson; in 1838, Nathan Maynard, and on July, 16, 1853, Dr. Robert Winton entered the northwest quarter of the northeast quarter of the section, it being marked "swamp land." This is one of the latest entries of the county there being some four or five entries made on the same day.

The present owners of section 20 are Harriett Janney, Jeff Janney, W. T. Janney, W. R. Janney, A. G. Kennard, H. Munk, D. Miller, G. A. Schlenker and J. B. Vannater.

DR. GEO. R. GREEN,
Born and raised in Hamilton Township, now a resident of Muncie.

## WASHINGTON TOWNSHIP.

Section 20 has four miles of public roads, and School No. 6 is situated in the east center of the section.

Government land sales commenced in section 21 in 1835. The purchaser in that year was Jonathan McCarty. In 1836, John Dunn and John Johnson; in 1837, Joseph Grimes, and in 1839 Samuel P. Anthony and William Vannater. The present landlords of section 21 are H. Barrett, James A. J. Brunt, M. P. Dunn, T. W. Petty, S. A. Dunn, and B. F. Beouy. Section 21 has a public road on the south and free gravel pike on the east line.

Section 22 was entered in the years of 1832 to 1853, by Samuel Carmin, in 1832, 1833 and 1835; John Knight in 1834 and 1836; Peter Thorn in 1837, and Robert Winton in 1853, which last entry was also recorded "swamp land." The present land owners in section 22 are William McCormick, C. Carmin, O. L. Hall, N. Millhollin, M. A. Skillman, J. Brock, S. L. Miller, S. Vannater N. Lawson and W. C. Huffman. The section has three miles of highway, one mile of which is pike, and School No. 7 is in the west center.

Section 23 was entered in five tracts by John Kain, Samuel Knotts and John Johnson in 1834; Mowerry H. Thompson in 1835, and John S. Thompson in 1836. The present owners of these lands are Nathan Millhollin, G. Powers, M. C. Braddock, I. Parkison, A. Parkison, W. Crow, I. Keller, M. Powers and J. Y. Rowzie. This section has four miles of public road, nearly one-half of which is free gravel pike.

Section 24 was purchased originally in five tracts, by four persons, as follows: William Carman (1), Mowerry H. Thompson (2), and Stephen Swain (1) in 1835, and Moses Hinton (1) in 1837. After many changes and transfers, section 24 is now owned by A. M. Shafer, Nathan Millhollin, Joseph Hinton, John R. Cox, J. Swain and W. A. Swain. Section 24 has about three and one-half miles of public highway, and the section is drained by Pike creek.

South of section 24, in Washington township, and also joining Union township, is section 25. The first purchase of land of the government in this section was made by James Ashcraft on October 14, 1833, when he entered two tracts, they being the west half of both the northwest and southwest quarters of the section, making him a strip of land 80 rods wide by 1 mile long, north and south. At present the Muncie and Wheeling pike runs through this strip of land, very near the center. We are crossing this first entry (in traveling north on this pike) for the distance of one mile immediately after passing the postoffice of Stockport. After Mr. Ashcraft the next to secure public land in section 25 was Mowery H. Thompson, in 1835, and the remainder of the public domain was purchased in 1837 by Absolam Williams, John Kain, David Williams and James Hamilton.

At present the section is owned by Joseph Hinton, John W. Mills, H. H. Williams, D. M. Williams, and Jesse Nixon. The section has public roads on the north and east lines; also free pikes on the south line and across the west half as before mentioned. School No. 8 and a Baptist church are situated in the southwest corner of the section, one on either side of the Muncie and Wheeling pike.

The public lands in section 26 were purchased of the government as follows: By John S. Thompson, James Aschcraft, Jonathan Barton, and William Conner in 1836; by Henry Smith, Amos Grubb, and George Tippin in 1837, and the last tract by Margaret Taylor December 15, 1838.

At the present time we find the land in section 26 in the names of J. A. Bryan, G. K Lewis, A. Campbell, William McCormick, Jesse Nixon, N. Shinn, R. Strohm, A. Sailors, J. Pittenger, M. E. Templin, M. Beouy, J. F Bryan, S. Gruver, and E. M. Carter. The section has three miles of highway, three-fourths of a mile being free pike.

In section 27 the first entry of land was made by John Johnson, on September 28, 1836, it being the northeast quarter, and now held as trustee by John Swisher. After this entries were made by Philip Woodring and Isaac Coe in 1837; by James Burgess, John Burgess, and Christopher Grimes in 1838, and the last tract by Jacob Miller in 1839.

The section is now owned by John Swisher (trustee), R Woodring, William F. Burgess, George N. Shaw, M. Beouy, J. Kirklin, M. E. Hedgland and John Burgess. The section has public roads on the east, west and north, and that on the west line is free gravel pike.

Section 28 was originally purchased and owned in six tracts by that many persons, the purchases being made as follows: By John Johnson, in 1836; Thomas Beouy, in 1837; Elizabeth Umphreys and Ann Umphreys, in 1838, and Michael Messenger and John Black, in 1839. Section 28 is now owned by numerous small farmers as follows: B. F. Beouy, Emily Grimes, E. E. Grimes, William B. Carmin, J. Brock, W. Minton, Jr., I. H. Gray, George Boyles and A. H. Miller. Section 28 has four miles of public highway, one mile (that on the east line) being free gravel pike.

In section 29 the original purchases were all made in small tracts, there being but two 80 acre tracts entered, all the balance having been taken up in 40 acre lots, making fourteen entries in all, although several parties made two entries. The original owners were John Johnson, in 1836; James Porter and David Hatfield, in 1837; Orin Chapin, John Summers and Levi Miller, in 1838; John Summers, Levi Miller, Hiram

## WASHINGTON TOWNSHIP. 193

Hendricks, Hugh Sharp and Thomas Morley, in 1839. Then on July 16, 1853, Jeremiah Wilson and John McCulloch each entered a 40 acre tract of registered swamp land.

Section 29 is now owned by William H. Carmin, B. F. Beouy, J. W. Gilmore, I. Gilmore, A. G. Gilmore, W. H. Gilmore, C. C. Boyle, F. Huber, A. H. Miller, C. and F. Guinnup, Wash Maynard and W. M. Grimes. This section has three miles of public road. School No. 11 is located on the south line of the section, one-fourth mile west of the southeast corner.

In section 30, the first land owner was Michael Messenger, who entered two 80 acre and one 40 acre tract on May 4, 1831, after which time entries were made in the section by Samuel Richardson, Felix E. Oliphant and John Rains, in 1837; John Farley, Jr., in 1838, and Thomas Morely, in 1839. We find the lands of section 30 now owned by E. H. Stradling, G. Newberger, J. H. Schlenker, J. Johnson, Joseph A. Broyles, A. F. Patterson, C. L. Pence, W. H. Howe and James T. Broyles. The section has 3½ miles of public road, and is drained by Pipe creek and its tributaries.

Section 31 is one mile east of the Madison county line and joins Harrison township. The land in this section was somewhat late in coming into the market, as there were no purchases made within its boundary until March 1, 1837, when Purnell F. Peters purchased the east half of the southeast quarter, a portion of which is now owned by R. S. Gregory. Following the purchase of Mr. Peters were the entries of John Barkaloo and Stephen Thorn during the same year (1837), John Hanway and George Kramer in 1838, and John Goarle in 1839. Since this time, through many transfers, we now find the lands in section 31 in the names of J. F. Nickey's heirs, James T. Broyes, S. Culbertson, M. Conk, O. Spears, William H. Broyles, R. S. Gregory, P. Mast & Co. and J. Thompson, W. A. Meeks, I. N. Miller and J. W. Broyles. This section has three miles of public road.

Section 32 was also late in being settled up, as there were no lands purchased of the government until 1838, when entries were made by Woodson Cummins, Levi Miller and Purnell F. Peters. The remaining public land in the section was all secured during the following year (1838) by John R. Williams, Samuel Clevenger, Levi Miller and John Hanway and George Kramer. The section is now owned in small tracts by H. W. Larue, J. O. Needher, J. A. McLaughlin, Wash Maynard, V. Nickey, J. F. Nickey's estate, V. and J. Nickey et al., M. V. Rhoads and P. P. Mast & Co. and J. Thompson. The section has 3½ miles of public road.

Section 33 was all entered in 1837 and 1839. Those purchasing in 1837 were William O. Bryant, Thomas Bartlett and Benjamin Bartlett. In 1839, January 18, William Vannata entered the two remaining 80-acre tracts. The present land owners of section 33 are John Burgesr, W. Minton, J., D. Rowlet, L. Miller, George Boyle, Thompson Sharp, N. S. Sharp and J Ferguson. The section has four miles of public highway, one mile (that on the east line) being free gravel pike. The village of Gaston lies on the east side and about one-half of the town within this section.

The firsty entry of land in Section 34 was the northeast quarter, 160 acres, by Thomas Veach, December 9, 1836. The nexty entry in the section was made by Sarah Wharton, Jr., in February, 1838, then by Jefferson N. Horine in the same year, after which the remainder of the section was taken up by John G. Collins, Thomas Covalt, John Burgess, Thomas Dillon and James Hamilton, in 1838.

Section 34 is now owned by G. W. Bryan, S. L. Bryan, W. R. Bryan, S. Bryan, M. E. Hedgland, John Burgess, M. J. Clemons, A. Boyle, J. Kirklin, G. R. Hedgland, J. Munsey, H. A. Jones and L. H. Larue. This section has three miles of public road, two of which are free pike. The east half of Gaston is in this section, and School No. 10 is situated in the section, being in the northeast part of the village.

Section 35 was also all purchased of the government during the years of 1836 and 1838. The purchases in 1836 were those of Lewis and William H. Veach. In 1837 the entries were made by Joseph Tippin, John Tippin and Samuel Nickson. This section is now owned by L. J. Hooke, S. Moomaw, R. J. Bryan, S. Needler, C. Needler et al., E. M. Carter et al., D. O. Munsey, Lewis Bond, M. Driscoll and Sol Mier. The section has a public road on the west line and "Two Mile" pike east and west through the center. School No. 9 is located in the east center of this section.

Section 36 is the southeast corner of the township. Its lands were purchased of the government by James Ashcraft in 1833; Mathew Xorner in 1834; William Daily in 1835; Hannah Corner in 1837, and James Ashcraft in 1841.

We find the present land owners of 36 to be C. Lecington, John Clark. P. Hayden, A. Campbell, L. A. Moomaw, Joseph Hinton, S. Markle, and W. A. Allison. The Muncie and Wheeling pike crosses the west half of the section and a free pike runs along the greater part of the north line. The postoffice of Stockport is situated in this section in the northwest part.

THE END.

www.ingramcontent.com/pod-product-compliance
Lightning Source LLC
Chambersburg PA
CBHW032145230426
43672CB00011B/2458